Focus on Grammar

An **INTERMEDIATE** Course for Reference and Practice

Marjorie Fuchs

Miriam Westheimer

with Margaret Bonner

Sharon Hilles, grammar consultant

Longman

To the memory of my parents,
Edith and Joseph Fuchs—MF

To my parents, Ruth and Fred Westheimer,
and to my brother, Joel Westheimer—MW

**Focus on Grammar: An Intermediate Course for
Reference and Practice**

Editorial Director: Joanne Dresner
Development Editors: Penny Laporte, Louisa Hellegers, Joan Saslow
Production Editorial: Helen B. Ambrosio, Lisa A. Hutchins
Text Design: Six West Design
Cover Design: A Good Thing, Inc.
Book Production: Circa 86, Inc.
Text Art: Burmar Technical Corporation, Marie DeJohn, Marcy Ramsey,
        Jill Wood

Library of Congress Cataloging-in-Publication Data
Fuchs, Marjorie, 1949–
    Focus on grammar : an intermediate course for reference and
practice / Marjorie Fuchs, Miriam Westheimer, with Margaret Bonner.
        p.   cm. —
    ISBN 0-201-65685-X
    1. English language—Textbooks for foreign speakers.   2. English
language—Grammar.   I. Westheimer, Miriam.   II. Bonner, Margaret.
III. Title.   IV. Series.
PE1128.F794 1994
428.2'4—dc20   93-20976
                                                                    CIP

        4 5 6 7 8 9 10-KE-98979695

Contents

Focus on Grammar: An Intermediate Course for Reference and Practice

Appendices

About the Authors

Marjorie Fuchs taught ESL for eight years at New York City Technical College and LaGuardia Community College of the City University of New York and EFL at the Sprach Studio Lingua Nova in Munich, Germany. She has authored or co-authored many widely used ESL textbooks, notably *On Your Way, Crossroads, Top Twenty ESL Word Games, Around the World: Pictures for Practice, Families: Ten Card Games for Language Learners,* and the *Workbooks* to the *Longman Dictionary of American English, The Longman Photo Dictionary,* and the *Vistas* series.

Miriam Westheimer taught EFL at all levels of instruction in Haifa, Israel, for a period of six years. She has also taught ESL at Queens College, at LaGuardia Community College, and in the American Language Program of Columbia University. She holds a doctorate in Curriculum and Teaching from Teacher's College of Columbia University. She is the co-author of a communicative grammar program developed and widely used in Israel and currently teaches curriculum development.

Margaret Bonner has been teaching and writing since 1978. She has taught at Hunter College, the Borough of Manhattan Community College, and the National Taiwan University. Currently she is teaching in the Center for International Programs at Virginia Commonwealth University. She worked for three years as a textbook author for the school system of the Sultanate of Oman, and she has contributed to the *On Your Way* series. Her most recent text is *Step into Writing.*

Introduction

Focus on Grammar: An Intermediate Course for Reference and Practice is the second text in the four-level *Focus on Grammar* series. Written by practicing ESL professionals, the series focuses on English grammar through lively listening, speaking, reading, and writing activities. Each of the four Student's Books is accompanied by a Workbook, Cassettes, and a Teacher's Manual. Each Student's Book stands alone as a complete text in itself or can be used as part of the *Focus on Grammar* series.

Both Controlled and Communicative Practice

Research in applied linguistics suggests that students expect and need to learn the formal rules of a language. However, students need to practice new structures in a variety of contexts to help them internalize and master them. To this end, *Focus on Grammar* provides an abundance of both controlled and communicative exercises so that students can bridge the gap between knowing grammatical structures and using them. The many communicative activities in each unit enable students to personalize what they have learned in order to talk to each other with ease about hundreds of everyday issues.

A Unique Four-Step Approach

The series follows a unique four-step approach. The first step is **contextualization.** New structures are shown in the natural context of passages, articles, and dialogues. This is followed by **presentation** of structures in clear and accessible grammar charts and explanations. The third step is **focused practice** of both form and meaning in numerous and varied controlled exercises. In the fourth step, students engage in **communication practice,** using the new structures freely and creatively in motivating, open-ended activities.

A Complete Classroom Text and Reference Guide

A major goal in the development of *Focus on Grammar* has been to provide a Student Book that serves not only as a vehicle for classroom instruction but also as a resource for self-study. The combination of grammar charts, grammar notes, and expansive appendices provides a complete and invaluable reference guide for the student at the intermediate level. Exercises in the Focused Practice sections of each unit are ideal for individual study, and students can check their work, using the complete answer key at the back of the book.

Thorough Recycling

Underpinning the scope and sequence of the series as a whole is the belief that students need to use target structures many times in many contexts at increasing levels of difficulty. For this reason new grammar is constantly recycled so that students will feel thoroughly comfortable with it.

Comprehensive Testing Program

SelfTests at the end of each of the eight parts of the Student Book allow for continual assessment of progress. In addition, diagnostic and final tests in the Teacher's Manual provide a ready-made, ongoing evaluation component for each student.

PART AND UNIT FORMAT

Focus on Grammar: An Intermediate Course for Reference and Practice is divided into eight parts comprising thirty-eight units. Each part contains grammatically related units with each unit focusing on a specific grammatical structure. Where appropriate, contrast units present two contrasting forms (for example, the simple present tense and the present progressive). Each unit has one or more major themes relating the exercises to one another. All units have the same clear, easy-to-follow format:

Introduction

The Introduction presents the grammar focus of the unit in a natural context. The Introduction texts, all of which are recorded on cassette, present language in various formats. These include newspaper and magazine excerpts, advertisements, instructions, questionnaires, and other formats that students encounter in their day-to-day lives. In addition to presenting grammar in context, the Introduction serves to raise student motivation and to provide an opportunity for incidental learning and lively classroom discussions. Topics are varied, ranging from employment, the weather, and marriage to homelessness, the environment, and future technology.

Grammar Charts

Grammar Charts follow each Introduction. These focus on the form of the unit's target structure. The clear and easy-to-understand boxes present each grammatical form in all its combinations. Affirmative and negative statements, *yes/no* and *wh-* questions, short answers, and contractions are presented for all tenses and modals covered. These charts provide students with a clear visual reference for each new structure.

Grammar Notes

The Grammar Notes that follow the charts focus on the meaning and use of the structure. Each note gives a clear explanation of the grammar point, and is always followed by one or more examples. Where appropriate, timelines help illustrate the meaning of verb tenses and their relationship to one another. *Be careful!* notes alert students to common ESL/EFL errors. Pronunciation Notes are provided when appropriate, and cross-references to other related units and the Appendices make the book easy to use.

Focused Practice Exercises

These exercises follow the Grammar Notes. This section provides practice for all uses of the structure presented in the notes. Each Focused Practice section begins with a "for recognition only" exercise called Discover the Grammar. Here, the students are expected to recognize either the form of the structure or its meaning without having to produce any language. This activity raises consciousness as it builds confidence.

Following the Discover the Grammar activity are exercises that practice the grammar in a controlled, but still contextualized, environment. The exercises proceed from simpler to more complex. There is a large variety of exercise types including fill-in-the-blanks, matching, multiple choice, question and sentence formation, and error analysis. As with the Introduction, students are exposed to many different written formats, including letters, postcards, journal entries, resumes, charts, schedules, menus, and news articles. Many exercises are art-based, providing a rich and interesting context for meaningful practice. All Focused Practice exercises are suitable for self-study or homework. A complete answer key is provided at the end of this book.

Communication Practice Exercises

These exercises are intended for in-class use. The first exercise is called Practice Listening. After having had exposure to and practice with the grammar in its written form, students now have the opportunity to check their aural comprehension. Students hear a variety of listening formats, including conversations, radio announcements, weather forecasts, interviews, and phone recordings. After listening to the tape (or hearing the teacher read the tapescript, which can be found in the Teacher's Manual), students complete a task that focuses on either the form or the meaning of the structure. It is suggested that students be allowed to hear the text as many times as they wish to complete the task successfully.

Practice Listening is followed by a variety of activities that provide students with the opportunity to use the grammar in open-ended, interactive activities. Students work in pairs or small groups in interviews, surveys, opinion polls, information gaps, discussions, role plays, games, and problem-solving activities. The activities are fun and engaging and offer ample opportunity for self-expression and cross-cultural comparison.

Review or SelfTest

At the conclusion of each part there is a review feature that can be used as a self-test. The exercises in this section test the form and use of the grammar content of the units in the part just concluded.

Appendices

The Appendices provide useful information, such as lists of common irregular verbs, common adjective-plus-preposition combinations, and spelling and pronunciation rules. The Appendices can help students do the unit exercises, act as a springboard for further classroom work, and serve as a reference source.

SUPPLEMENTARY COMPONENTS

All supplementary components of *Focus on Grammar,* the Workbook, the Cassettes, and the Teacher's Manual, are tightly keyed to the Student Book, ensuring a wealth of practice and an opportunity to tailor the series to the needs of each individual classroom.

Cassettes

All of the Practice Listening exercises and Introductory texts as well as other appropriate exercises are recorded on cassette.The symbol ●● appears next to these activities. Listening scripts appear in the Teacher's Manual and may be used as an alternative way of presenting the listening activities.

Workbook

The Workbook accompanying *Focus on Grammar: An Intermediate Course for Reference and Practice* provides a wealth of additional exercises appropriate for self-study of the target grammar of each unit in the Student Book. Most of the exercises are fully contextualized. Themes of the Workbook exercises are either a continuation or a spin-off of the corresponding Student Book unit themes. There are also eight tests, one for each of the eight Student Book parts. These tests have questions in the format of the Structure and Written Expression section of the TOEFL®. Besides reviewing the material in the Student Book, these questions provide invaluable practice to those who are interested in taking this widely administered test.

Teacher's Manual

The Teacher's Manual, divided into three parts, contains a variety of suggestions and information to enrich the material in the Student Book. The first part gives general suggestions for each section of a typical unit. The next part offers practical teaching suggestions and cultural information to accompany specific material in each unit. The Teacher's Manual also provides ready-to-use diagnostic and final tests for each of the eight parts of the Student Book. In addition, a complete script of the Practice Listening exercises is provided as is an answer key for the diagnostic and final tests.

Acknowledgments

Writing a grammar book is a long, difficult, and humbling process. We couldn't have done it without the help of many people.

We are grateful to:

Joanne Dresner, who initiated and oversaw the entire project. She helped conceptualize our general approach and always managed to keep high spirits and a positive outlook, even when we could see no end in sight.

Nancy Perry, who helped us through the initial stages, during which the concept of the book was developed. She worked tirelessly and meticulously on the early units.

Penny Laporte, who enthusiastically inherited the project midstream. She was always committed to the highest of standards.

Sharon Hilles, who was able to take complicated concepts and make them understandable. We appreciate her insight, candor, and humor.

Louisa Hellegers, who provided feedback with grace and good sense. She was a pleasure to work with.

Margaret Bonner, who joined the author team toward the end with a great amount of creative energy. She made a significant contribution to the book, both qualitatively and quantitatively.

Joan Saslow, who worked with enthusiasm, diligence, and speed as our final editor. She was a welcome addition to the project.

Helen Ambrosio and Lisa Hutchins, who expertly guided the book through all stages of production. They kept tight control of details while never losing sight of the project as a whole.

Sandra Bergman, Laura T. LeDrean, Sarah Lynn, Alice Lyons-Quinn, Ellen Rosenfield, Jacqueline Schachter, Grace Tanaka, and Cynthia Wiseman, who reviewed numerous drafts and provided intelligent and constructive criticism.

Joel Einleger, who helped initiate our involvement in the project. His genuine understanding of the meaning of partnership made it possible for Miriam to work late nights, early mornings, and weekends.

Ari Einleger, who was born during the writing of this book. He unknowingly contributed endless hours of "quality time" with his mother.

Rick Smith, for keeping us mindful of goals, time frames, and the bottom line. He was a great source of support and encouragement for Marjorie.

To all these people and to the many students and teachers we have had, we say thank you!

Marjorie Fuchs

Miriam Westheimer

Present

INTRODUCTION

Read and listen to this news item from a TV news broadcast.

Newscaster: And now some local news. Jane Hill is at Arkansas Children's Hospital with an interesting story. Jane, what**'s happening**?

Jane: Well, as you can see, I**'m standing** here outside Children's Hospital where quintuplets were just born to Mary and John Quincy of North Little Rock. We don't know much about the proud parents except that John is an engineer, and Mary **is studying** computer programming. The doctors **are getting ready** for a press conference, but they tell us the mother and all five babies **are doing** fine. I'll give a complete report on the ten o'clock news tonight. Now, back to you in the studio.

PRESENT PROGRESSIVE

STATEMENTS

SUBJECT	BE	(NOT) + BASE FORM OF VERB + -ING
I	am	
You	are	
He She It	is	(not) standing.
We You They	are	

YES / NO QUESTIONS

BE	SUBJECT	BASE FORM OF VERB + -ING
Am	I	
Are	you	
Is	he she it	standing close enough?
Are	we you they	

SHORT ANSWERS — AFFIRMATIVE

	you	are.
	I	am.
Yes,	he she it	is.
	you we they	are.

SHORT ANSWERS — NEGATIVE

	you're not. OR you aren't.			
	I'm not.			
No,	he's she's it's	not. OR	he she it	isn't.
	you're we're they're	not. OR	you we they	aren't.

WH- QUESTIONS

WH- WORD	BE	SUBJECT	BASE FORM OF VERB + -ING
How What	am	I	
	are	you	
	is	he she it	doing?
	are	we you they	

CONTRACTIONS

I am	=	I'm
you are	=	you're
we are	=	we're
they are	=	they're
he is	=	he's
she is	=	she's
it is	=	it's

I am not	=	I'm not		
you are not	=	you're not	OR	you aren't
we are not	=	we're not	OR	we aren't
they are not	=	they're not	OR	they aren't
he is not	=	he's not	OR	he isn't
she is not	=	she's not	OR	she isn't
it is not	=	it's not	OR	it isn't

Grammar Notes

1. Use the present progressive (also called the present continuous) to describe something that is happening right now—at the moment of speaking.

> I **'m standing** outside Children's Hospital right now.

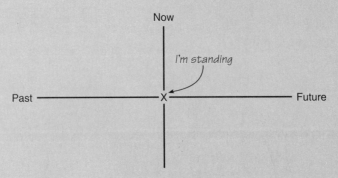

2. Use the present progressive to describe something that is happening in the extended present time (for example, *nowadays*, *this month*, *these days*, *this year*), even if it's not happening at the moment of speaking.

> Mary Quincy **is studying** computer programming this semester.

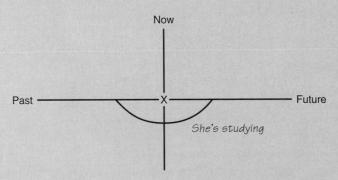

3. The present progressive is often used to show that the action is temporary.

> She **is studying** computer programming.
> (She is studying now, but she won't be studying forever. At some point, she will probably finish studying and get a job.)

4. You can also use the present progressive to talk about the future. (See page 76 in Unit 9.)

5. The contracted form is almost always used in speech and is often used in informal writing. See Appendix 12 on page A7 for spelling rules on forming the present progressive.

FOCUSED PRACTICE

1. Discover the Grammar

Read the letter. Underline the present progressive verbs that describe something happening at the moment. Circle the present progressive verbs that describe things that are happening in the extended present.

Dear Andrea,

I'm sorry this letter is so late. I'm just so busy. I(m working) very hard at the office these days, and I'm still looking for a new apartment.

I have a new friend named Diana. Diana's terrific. She's really helping me a lot. She says I can live with her until I find my own place. We're good roommates. Right now Diana is in her room, and she's <u>studying</u> for a test. I'm sitting in the kitchen and writing to you.

I really miss you. How are you doing? Are you still working at the same place? Are you going to night school this year? Please write soon.

                                             Stephanie

---

2. Find the Errors

Read this student's postcard to a friend. It has five present-progressive mistakes. Find and correct them.

Dear Jerry,

       I'm sitting
Right now ~~I sit~~ in a park near my hotel. The sun *is* setting,
and it ~~get~~ *getting* a little cooler now. The view is beautiful. I'm glad
I have my camera with me. I *am* taking lots of pictures to
show you. How are you? Do you still working hard?
I'll write again soon. Wish you were here.

                    Your friend,
                    Elizabeth

3. Ice Cream or Exercise?

Complete the conversation. Use the present progressive. Use contractions.

Cynthia: Bye, Howard, I __'m leaving__ now.
1. (leave)

Howard: Where __are__ you __going__?
2. (go)

Cynthia: Running. It's the first day of our exercise program. Nancy __is waiting__ downstairs.
3. (wait)

Howard: Great! Why don't you take the dog out with you?

Cynthia: No, today's your day to walk him. Why don't *you* take the dog out?

Howard: I can't. I __am working__ at home today.
4. (work)

Cynthia: But you __are not doing__ anything right now. You __are__ just __sitting__ there.
5. (not do)   6. (sit)

Howard: That's not true. I __am sitting__ here, but I __am__ also __thinking__ about my
7. (sit)   8. (think)
work. Can't the dog run with you?

Cynthia: Well, not exactly.

Howard: What does that mean?

Cynthia: Well, after we run, Nancy and I want to get some ice cream at the Sweet Shop. And they don't allow dogs.

4. Press Conference

The Quincy's and the doctors are holding a press conference. Jane Hill, the reporter, is asking them questions. Read the answers to the questions. Then write the questions. Use the words in parentheses.

1. **Jane:** Hello. I'm sure you know everyone is waiting to hear about the quintuplets.

   __How is everyone doing?__
   (How/everyone/do?)

   Doctor: Everyone is doing very well. We are very pleased with the health of all five babies and with Mary Quincy's recovery.

2. **Jane:** It's very quiet. __Are the babies sleeping.__
   (babies/sleep?)

   Mary: Yes, the babies are all sleeping. And the nurses and I are resting, too.

3. **Jane:** __How many nurses are helping you with the babies.__
   (How many nurses/help you with the babies?)

   John: Right now, two. And, believe me, we need all the help we can get!

4. **Jane:** __How are you preparing for your return home.__
   (How/prepare for your return home?)

   Mary: We're learning all we can from the nurses, and we're asking all our friends and family to help.

5. **Jane:** __Are you planning to move?__
   (plan/to move?)

   John: We aren't planning to move right away. We need more space, but it's too expensive right now.

6. **Jane:** __Where are you living now?__
   (Where/live/now?)

   Mary: We're living in a two-bedroom apartment. Uh-oh, two of the babies are crying, and the others will probably start soon.

   Jane: We should stop the interview, then. Thanks for your time.

5. Child Development

Look at the child-development chart. Write about each baby. Describe what he or she is and isn't doing.

Three months old	Baby 1 (boy)	Baby 2 (boy)	Baby 3 (girl)	Baby 4 (girl)	Baby 5 (girl)
hold head up	yes	no	no	yes	yes
roll over	no	no	yes	yes	yes
reach for objects	no	yes	yes	no	no

1. Baby 1 <u>is holding his head up. He isn't rolling over, and he isn't reaching for objects.</u>

2. Baby 2 <u>is not holding his head up, He isn't rolling over, he is reaching for objects</u>

3. Baby 3 <u>isn't her head up, she is rolling over, she isn't reaching for object</u>

4. Babies 4 and 5 <u>are holding their heads up, They are rolling over. They aren't reaching for objects</u>

COMMUNICATION PRACTICE

6. Listening Practice

Rachel Griffin is a nurse. Listen to her phone conversation. Then listen again and check the things that are happening at the moment.

1. Rachel is talking on the phone. ✔
2. She's trying to go to sleep. ✔
3. She's working at the hospital. ✗
4. The boy across the hall is playing the drums. ✗
5. The boy is keeping her awake. ✔
6. She's talking to the boy's parents about the noise. ✗
7. She's ignoring the noise. ✗

7. Five Babies

Work with a partner. Look at the pictures of the Quincy quintuplets on their first birthday. Make a list of all the differences you see. Compare your list with your classmate's.

Baby 1   Baby 2   Baby 3   Baby 4   Baby 5

Example: Baby 1 is crying. The other babies aren't crying.

8. Where Am I?

Work in small groups. Think of a place you would like to be. What is happening in that place? Describe the activities to your group. The group will guess where you are.

Example:
A: There are many people here. Some people are swimming. Others are sitting in the sun. One little girl is building a sand castle. Where am I?
B: You're at the beach.

9. Charades

Work in small groups. Take turns. Act out a situation in front of your group.
The group asks questions to guess what you are doing.

Example:
(Student A pretends to swim.)
> **B:** Are you waving?
> **A:** No, I'm not.

> **C:** Are you calling for help?
> **A:** No.

> **D:** Are you swimming?
> **A:** Yes, I am.

10. Role Play

Work in pairs. Pretend you are walking down the street. You meet an old
friend. Tell your partner what you are doing these days, this year, and/or
this month.

Example:
> **A:** Hey, how are you doing?
> **B:** Great! I'm working hard, but life is good. And you?
>   What are you doing these days?
> **A:** Oh, the same old thing. I'm . . .

INTRODUCTION

Read and listen to this excerpt from a popular psychology magazine.

Psychologists **describe** two major personality types—Type A and Type B. People with Type A personalities **work** very hard. They never **relax**. They usually **rush** through their daily activities. They **get** angry easily and often **have** high blood pressure. In contrast, Type B personalities usually **take** life easier. They **remain** calm even in stressful situations and rarely **lose** their tempers.

SIMPLE PRESENT TENSE

AFFIRMATIVE STATEMENTS	
SUBJECT	**VERB**
I You* We They	always **work**.
He She It	always **works**.

NEGATIVE STATEMENTS	
SUBJECT	***DO NOT/DOES NOT*** **+ BASE FORM OF VERB**
I You* We They	**do not work**.
He She It	**does not work**.

CONTRACTIONS		
do not	=	don't
does not	=	doesn't

YES/NO QUESTIONS		
DO/DOES	**SUBJECT**	**BASE FORM OF VERB**
Do	I you* we they	**work?**
Does	he she it	

SHORT ANSWERS		
AFFIRMATIVE		
Yes,	you I/we you they	**do**.
	he she it	**does**.

SHORT ANSWERS		
NEGATIVE		
No,	you I/we you they	**don't**.
	he she it	**doesn't**.

WH-QUESTIONS			
***WH-* WORD**	***DO/DOES***	**SUBJECT**	**BASE FORM OF VERB**
Where When How long	**do**	I you* we they	**work?**
	does	he she it	

*You is both singular and plural.

Grammar Notes

1. Use the simple present tense to talk about what regularly happens, what usually happens, or what always happens.

> Type A personalities **rush** through life.
> Type B personalities **stay** calm.
> George **goes** to the office every day.

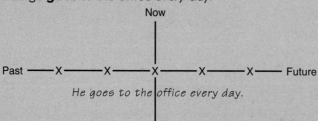

Now

Past ——X——X——X——X——X—— Future

He goes to the office every day.

2. Use the simple present tense to talk about situations that are not connected to time—for example, scientific facts and physical laws.

> Stress **causes** high blood pressure.
> Water **freezes** at 32° F.

3. Use adverbs of frequency with the simple present tense to express how often something happens.

100% *usually* *often* *sometimes* *rarely* 0%
always / . . . / . . . / . . . / never

> Type A personalities **never relax**.
> They **always seem** nervous.
> Type B personalities **usually take** life easier.

Be careful! Adverbs of frequency usually come before the main verb, but they go after the verb *be*.

> They **usually remain** calm.
> They **are usually** calm.

See Appendix 13 on page A8 for spelling rules for the simple present tense.
See Appendix 18 on page A12 for pronunciation rules for the simple present tense.

FOCUSED PRACTICE

1. Discover the Grammar

Here is part of a book review. Underline the simple present tense verbs. Circle the adverbs of frequency.

In today's fast-paced world, we (never) escape stress. It always affects us psychologically, but according to Dr. Roads, author of the new bestseller,

Calm Down!, stress also affects us physically. For example, stress causes high blood pressure. Most doctors agree with this view and often prescribe medication. Medicine usually lowers a patient's blood pressure. But, Dr. Roads claims, "You don't need pills. Relaxation exercises are always more effective and safer than pills. For example, breathing exercises both relax you and lower your blood pressure. It only takes a few minutes, several times a day." In *Calm Down!* Dr. Roads tells you how.

2.   TV Addicts

Two friends are talking about a problem. Complete their conversation. Use the simple present tense.

Jane: Every day my sister ____spends____ hours in front of the TV. She just ____sits____ there and
                        1. (spend)   2. (sit)
____watches____ one program after another.
      3. (watch)

Mary: I know what you mean. My husband ____does____ the same thing. He never ____reads____ a
                                             4. (do)   5. (read)
book anymore. And forget about exercise! After work, he ____hurries____ home. Then he just
                                                          6. (hurry)
____stays____ inside and ____switches____ channels with the remote control.
      7. (stay)   8. (switch)

Jane: It's awful. Sometimes my sister even ____cancels____ plans because a special show is on TV!
                                                9. (cancel)

3.   How Often?

Arlene is a Type A personality. Rewrite these sentences about her. Use the adverbs of frequency in the box instead of the words in italics.

always   usually   often   rarely   never

1. Arlene rushes to work *every morning*. Arlene always rushes to work.
2. She's in a hurry *all of the time*. She's always in a hurry
3. She *doesn't* have time for breakfast. She never has time for breakfast
4. She skips dinner *several times a week*. She often skips dinner
5. She goes on vacation *once every three years*. She rarely goes on vacation
6. She's nervous *most of the time*. She's usually nervous
7. She *doesn't* relax. She never relaxes
8. She sees her friends *once or twice a year*. She rarely sees her friends

4. Two Types

Complete this chart. Arlene is a typical Type A personality. Barbara is a typical Type B personality. They are completely different. Write about Barbara.

Type A: Arlene

1. Arlene doesn't relax.
2. Arlene rushes through the day.
3. Arlene speaks very fast.
4. Arlene finishes other people's sentences for them.
5. Arlene doesn't take time to enjoy the moment.
6. Arlene worries a lot.
7. Arlene doesn't have enough time to finish things.
8. Arlene has high blood pressure due to stress.
9. Arlene gets angry easily.
10. Arlene doesn't go on vacation every year.

Type B: Barbara

1. Barbara relaxes.
2. Barbara doesn't rush through the day.
3. *[handwritten] doesn't speak very fast*
4. *[handwritten] doesn't finish other people's sentences for them*
5. *[handwritten] Barbara takes time to enjoy the moment*
6. *[handwritten] Barbara doesn't worry much*
7. *[handwritten] has enough time to finish things*
8. *[handwritten] doesn't have high blood pressure due to stress*
9. *[handwritten] doesn't get angry easily*
10. *[handwritten] goes on vacation every year*

5. George's Schedule

George is an accountant. Look at his schedule. Ask and answer questions about his day on the next page.

6:00	get up
6:30–7:00	exercise
7:00	eat breakfast, read the newspaper
8:00–9:00	work on reports
9:00–12:00	see clients
12:00–12:30	lunch
12:30–5:00	return phone calls
5:30–7:00	attend night school
8:00–9:00	study

1. When/get up?

When does George get up?

He gets up at 6:00.

2. exercise in the morning?

Does he exercise in the morning?

Yes, he does.

3. How long/exercise?

How long does he exercise?

He exercises for half an hour.

4. work on reports in the afternoon?

Does he work on reports in the afternoon?

No, he doesn't

5. When/see clients?

When does he see clients?

He sees clients from 9 am to 12 noon.

6. take a long lunch break?

Does he take a long lunch break?

No, he doesn't

7. What/do/from 12:30 to 5:00?

What does he do from 12.30 to 5.00?

He return phone calls

8. Where/go/at 5:30?

Where does he go at 5.30?

He attends night school.

9. How long/his class last?

How long does his class last?

It lasts an hour and a half.

10. When/study?

When does he study?

He studies at night from 8 am to 9 am

COMMUNICATION PRACTICE

6. Practice Listening

A famous basketball player is giving a radio interview. Listen. Then listen again and check the correct column.

How often does he	Always	Sometimes	Never
1. get up early?	✔	☐	☐
2. exercise?	☐	☐	☐
3. go on vacation?	☐	☐	☐
4. go out with friends?	☐	☐	☐
5. go to the movies?	☐	☐	☐
6. attend sports events?	☐	☐	☐

7. Schedule Swap

Write your schedule for a typical day. (Use the schedule in exercise 5 as an example.) Then exchange schedules with a classmate. Write about your classmate's day.

Example:
George gets up at 6:00. He exercises for a half-hour. At 7:00 he . . .

_____

_____

8. Trivia Quiz

Work in small groups. Can you answer these questions? The correct answers are in the Answer Key.

1. How many times a day does the average human heart beat?
   a. 10,000
   b. 100,000
   c. 1,000,000

2. How long does it take the Concorde to fly from New York to Paris?
   a. three hours
   b. four hours
   c. five hours
3. How much caffeine does five ounces of decaffeinated coffee have?
   a. none
   b. 1 mg
   c. 3 mg

4. When does summer begin in the United States?
   a. June 1
   ✓ b. June 21
   c. July 4

5. Which animal doesn't eat meat?
   ✓ a. elephant
   b. dog
   c. lion

Write three more trivia questions to ask your classmates. Can the rest of the class answer your questions?

6. _____

   a. _____

   b. _____

   c. _____

7. _____

   a. _____

   b. _____

   c. _____

8. _____

   a. _____

   b. _____

   c. _____

9. Are You a Type A or Type B Personality?

Complete this chart for yourself and a partner. Check the correct column.

Do you	You			Your Partner		
	Always	Sometimes	Never	Always	Sometimes	Never
1. relax during the day?	☐	☐	☐	☐	☐	☐
2. do everything quickly?	☐	☐	☐	☐	☐	☐
3. worry a lot?	☐	☐	☐	☐	☐	☐
4. take vacations?	☐	☐	☐	☐	☐	☐
5. finish other people's sentences?	☐	☐	☐	☐	☐	☐
6. have high blood pressure?	☐	☐	☐	☐	☐	☐

Add your own questions.

7. _____	☐	☐	☐	☐	☐	☐
8. _____	☐	☐	☐	☐	☐	☐

Decide on your personality types. Give reasons. Refer to exercise 4 on page 14 to review Type A and B personality traits.

Example:
> **A:** I think we both have Type B personalities.
> **B:** I agree. We don't worry a lot, we do things slowly . . .

10. Relaxation Techniques

Work in groups. What do your classmates do when they want to relax? Use the chart below. Add as many relaxation techniques as you can. How many of your classmates use the same techniques?

Example:
> **A:** I lie down and listen to music.
> **B:** I listen to music and dance.
> **C:** I listen to music or read a book.

Things people do to relax	How many?
lie down	1
listen to music	
dance	
read a book	
_____	
_____	
_____	
_____	
_____	

Now share your findings with the rest of the class.

Example:
Three students listen to music, one student dances . . .

INTRODUCTION

Read and listen to this radio announcement about road conditions.

And now for the WXYZ traffic report. Right now the situation **is** bad on all major highways. Traffic **is moving** slowly because of the holiday weekend. A commute that usually **takes** twenty minutes **is taking** about thirty minutes. Many people who normally **use** public transportation **are driving** instead. This **is adding** to the traffic congestion. If you **don't need** to take your car, the police **recommend** public transportation. For more traffic updates, please stay tuned.

CONTRAST: SIMPLE PRESENT TENSE AND PRESENT PROGRESSIVE

SIMPLE PRESENT TENSE	PRESENT PROGRESSIVE
The trip usually **takes** twenty minutes.	The trip **is taking** longer today.

Grammar Notes

1. The present progressive describes what is happening right now or in the extended present. The simple present tense describes what generally happens (but not necessarily right now).

> Traffic **is moving** slowly today.
> Traffic **moves** slowly every holiday.

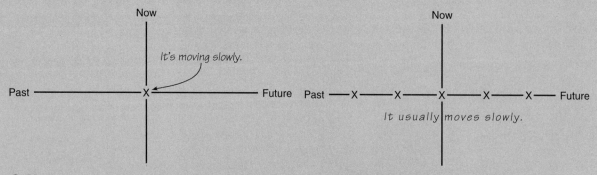

2. Non-action verbs (also called stative verbs) usually describe states or situations but not actions. Non-action verbs are not usually used in the present progressive even when they describe a situation that exists at the moment of speaking.

> I **want** to leave now.
> NOT I'm wanting to leave now.

3. Non-action verbs do the following:

   a. express emotions *(hate, like, love, want)*

   > Mike **wants** to leave right now.

   b. describe perception and the senses *(hear, see, smell, taste, feel, notice)*

   > She **feels** impatient in traffic.

   c. describe mental states *(know, remember, believe, suppose, think [believe], understand)*

   > I **don't understand** why this traffic is so bad.

   d. show possession *(have, own, possess, belong)*

   > I **have** a headache. **Do** you **have** any aspirin?

   e. describe appearance *(seem, be, appear, sound, look [seem])*

   > Traffic **looks** bad. It's not moving at all.

4. Be careful! Some verbs can have both a non-action and an action meaning.

> The soup **tastes** good. Try some.
> She**'s tasting** the soup to see if it needs more salt.

See Appendix 2 on page A4 for a list of non-action verbs.

FOCUSED PRACTICE

1. Discover the Grammar

Read the paragraph. Look at the verbs in italics. Circle the verbs that describe what is happening now. Underline the verbs that describe what generally happens.

It's 7:00 A.M. Terry Savoia (is getting) ready for work. Normally, Terry *prefers* to drive to work. Today, however, Terry *doesn't want* to take her car. She*'s listening* to the traffic report. Traffic *is moving* very slowly. A commute that normally *takes* twenty minutes *is taking* thirty minutes. Terry *has* a headache and *feels* nervous just thinking about the drive.

2. Terry's Schedule

Terry is a business executive. Look at her schedule. Complete the sentences below. Use the simple present tense or the present progressive.

8:30 – 9:00	open mail
9:00 – 12:00	meet with clients
12:00 – 1:00	~~have lunch~~ attend time management seminar
1:00 – 4:00	write reports
4:00 – 5:00	return phone calls

1. Terry usually _____ opens mail _____ between 8:30 and 9:00.

2. It's 8:45. She __ is opening mail __.

3. She __ meets with clients __ with clients for three hours every day.

4. It's 12:30. Normally, Terry __ has lunch __ between 12:00 and 1:00, but today she __ is attending time management seminar __ a seminar.

5. It's 2:00. At the moment, Terry __ is writing reports __.

6. She __ writes reports __ for three hours every day.

7. The line is busy. Terry __ is returning __ phone calls.

8. She always __ returns phone calls __ between 4:00 and 5:00.

3. Strange Sounds

*Complete this conversation between Terry and David. Use the simple present
or present progressive form of the verbs in parentheses.*

Terry: Listen! _____ Do _____ you _____ hear _____ something?

1. (hear)

David: No. I ___ am listening ___, but I ___ don't hear ___ anything. Wait a minute! It ___ sounds ___ like

2. (listen)   3. (not hear)   4. (sound)

    somebody ___ is crying ___ . Where _____ is _____ the noise ___ coming ___ from?

5. (cry)   6. (come)

Terry: I ___ think ___ it ___ is coming ___ from the apartment upstairs, but that's impossible. The

7. (think)   8. (come)

    Ortegas ___ are visiting ___ some relatives. They always _____ go _____ away in December.

9. (visit)   10. (go)

David: _____ Do _____ you _____ have _____ their phone number? Should we call them and tell them

11. (have)

    what ___ is happening ___?

12. (happen)

Terry: You know, it's strange. Every time they _____ take _____ a vacation, they _____ leave _____ me a

13. (take)   14. (leave)

    number, but not this time.

David: _____ Do _____ you _____ think _____ somebody broke into their apartment?

15. (think)

Terry: I doubt it. A robber wouldn't be crying. I ___ am thinking ___ we should go upstairs and check.

16. (think)

COMMUNICATION PRACTICE

4. Practice Listening

*A TV reporter is interviewing a commuter. Listen and write the length
of time the commute is taking today.*

    Length of today's commute: _____

Then listen again and decide if the sentences that follow are true or false. Check the correct column.

	True	False
1. The commuter feels calm right now.	✔	☐
2. She always drives to work.	☐	☐
3. The trip usually takes forty-five minutes.	☐	☐
4. The trip is taking more time today.	☐	☐
5. People are honking their horns.	☐	☐

5. Find the Differences

*Work with a partner. Look at the two pictures. Talk about Terry. What does
she usually do? What is she doing today? How many differences can you find
in two minutes? Compare your answers with your classmates'.*

USUALLY

TODAY

Example:
She usually takes the train, but today she's driving.

6. Transportation Survey

Work with a partner. Ask your partner questions to complete this survey. Check the correct answers.

1. How do you get to school?

☐ I walk ☐ by bicycle ☐ by car ☐ by bus ☐ by train

Other _____

2. Do you have a driver's license?

☐ Yes ☐ No

3. For long trips, how do you prefer to travel?

☐ by train ☐ by bus ☐ by car ☐ by plane

4. Do you want to take a long trip this year? If *yes*, where?

☐ Yes _____ ☐ No

5. Do you think a commute of forty-five minutes from home to work or

school is all right?

☐ Yes ☐ No

Add your own question.

6. _____

_____

Now report your partner's answers to the class.

Example:
Nam Sik rides his bike to school.

Put the results of the survey on the board. Talk about them.

Example:
Three students walk to school, ten take the bus . . .

7. Self-Portrait

A student drew this picture of himself.

Draw a picture of yourself. Your teacher will collect all the pictures, mix them up, and redistribute them. Work in small groups. Guess who drew each picture. Then give each picture to its correct owner.

Example:
A: This looks like Pedro.
B: I don't think so. Pedro has short hair, and he's wearing glasses today.

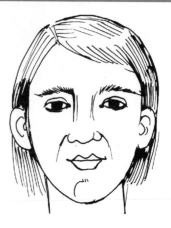

INTRODUCTION

Read and listen to the instructions an exercise teacher is giving to her class.

"**Stand up** straight. Now **bend over** and **touch** your toes. **Try** that again! OK! Good! Now, **don't bend** your knees. **Don't look down**. **Breathe deeply** and **concentrate**! **Keep** your head straight and **bend** at the hips. **Hold** it for three counts. One, two, three. **Don't curve** that spine. Good! **Relax**. And again."

IMPERATIVE

(DON'T) BASE FORM OF VERB	
Touch Don't bend	your knees.

Grammar Notes

1. Use the imperative to give directions and instructions.

   Make a right at the light.
   Breathe deeply.

2. Use the imperative to give orders or commands. An order or command can be softened by using *please*.

   Pay attention!
   Pay attention **please.**

3. Use the imperative to make requests.

   Please **bring** a towel to the next class.

4. Use the imperative to give advice or make suggestions.

   Take an umbrella.

5. Use the imperative to give warnings.

   Watch out! There's a car coming.

6. Use the imperative to extend an invitation.

   Come and **join** the class.

7. Note that the subject of an imperative statement is *you.* However, the word *you* is not said or written.

   Stand up straight!
   Don't bend your knees!

8. Be careful! The imperative form is the same in both the singular and the plural.

   John, **touch** your toes.
   John and Susan, **touch** your toes.

FOCUSED PRACTICE

1. Discover the Grammar

Match the imperative in column A with a situation in column B.

Column A

1. _f_ Don't touch that!
2. _C_ Look both ways.
3. _B_ Dress warmly!
4. _D_ Mark each answer true or false.
5. _A_ Come in. Make yourself at home.
6. _E_ Try a little more salt.

Column B

a. Someone is visiting a friend.

b. Someone is going out into the cold.

c. Someone is crossing a street.

d. Someone is taking an exam.

e. Someone is tasting some food.

f. Something is hot.

2. Who's Saying What?

Read the following instructions and guess who is speaking. Use the words in the box.

a boss	a robber	a driving instructor	a husband or wife
~~a parent~~	a receptionist	a telephone operator	

1. Come on! Hurry! Don't be late! Don't forget your lunch. Zip up your jacket. Give me a hug. Come home right after school. ____a parent____

2. Drive slowly. Turn right at the corner. Stop at the red light. Now, park the car behind the bus. _a driving instructor_

3. Don't move! Do as I say! Give me your money and don't ask any questions! _A Robber_

4. Please deposit twenty-five cents for the next five minutes. Thank you. _A telephone operator_

5. Please come in. Have a seat and make yourself comfortable. Don't worry. You won't have to wait long. _a receptionist_

6. Come to work on time. Don't leave so early. Work harder. Show me you really care about your work. _a boss_

7. Wear your best clothes. Tell them all about your work experience. Listen carefully and answer all their questions. Don't talk too much. Be very polite. Remember that the kids and I love you very much. _a husband or wife_

3. Instant Coffee

Match a verb from column A with a phrase from column B to give instructions for making a cup of coffee. Then put the sentences in order under the correct pictures.

Column A   **Column B**

Boil   the coffee
Put   the kettle with water
Add   the boiling water into the cup
Stir   a teaspoon of coffee in the coffee cup
Fill   the water
Pour   milk and/or sugar, according to taste

1. Fill the kettle with water.

2. Boil the water

3. Put a teaspoon of coffee in the coffee cup

4. Pour the boiling water into the cup

5. Add milk and/or sugar according to taste

6. Stir the coffee.

COMMUNICATION PRACTICE

4. Practice Listening

A chef is describing how to make pancakes. Listen. Then listen again and number the instructions in the correct order.

_____ Heat a frying pan and melt a piece of butter in it.

_____ Flip the pancake over when it's brown on one side.

__1__ Beat one egg in a large bowl.

_____ Add the flour to the egg.

_____ Pour some of the mixture into the preheated frying pan.

_____ Add a cup of milk.

5. Recipe Exchange

Share one of your favorite recipes with your class. Write it down and then read it to the class so everyone can try cooking something new. List the ingredients and then list the directions.

Example:
Scrambled eggs for four people
Ingredients: 6 to 8 eggs, ¼ cup milk, 1 tablespoon butter

Directions:

1. Break the eggs into a bowl.
2. Beat them well.
3. Add the milk.
4. Melt the butter in the frying pan.
5. Pour the egg mixture into the frying pan.
6. Keep mixing the eggs until they are firm.

6. Calm Down!

Work in small groups. People say many different things to themselves when they are angry and they want to calm down. Imagine you are in a traffic jam. You've been in the same spot for an hour. Someone is waiting to meet you on a street corner. How many things can you think of to calm yourself down? Share your list with the other groups.

Example:
Count to ten. Take a deep breath. Think about something else.

7. Following Directions

Work in pairs. Draw a simple picture on a blank piece of paper. Do not show your partner your picture. Take turns giving each other directions to try to draw each other's pictures. Then compare your pictures. The verbs in the box might help you.

draw	add	make	start	put

Example:
Draw a little house in the middle of the page. Put a tree on each side of the house.
Put a few flowers in front of the house. Add a little sun in the upper left-hand corner of the page.
Draw a cloud next to the sun. Don't cover the sun.

I. *Complete each sentence with the simple present tense or present progressive form of the verb in parentheses.*

1. You _____'re breathing_____ hard. Sit down and rest for a
   (breathe/are breathing)
   while.

2. Dolphins and whales are mammals. They
   _____ are breathing _____ air.
   (breathe/are breathing)

3. Fred just left. He _____ to his biology class
   (goes/is going)
   right now.

4. He _____ to biology class twice a week.
   (goes/is going)

5. In our area, it _____ a lot in March.
   (rains/is raining)

6. It _____ right now, and I don't have my
   (rains/is raining)
   umbrella.

7. We _____. Is the music too loud for you?
   (dance/are dancing)

8. We _____ every day. It's good exercise.
   (dance/are dancing)

9. The telephone _____. Could you answer it,
   (rings/is ringing)
   please?

10. The telephone _____ during dinner every
    (rings/is ringing)
    evening.

11. Greg and Tim _____ a house this semester,
    (share/are sharing)
    but Tim wants his own place soon.

12. Bill and Sue are very close. They _____ all their thoughts.
    (share/are sharing)

13. Warm air _____. Cool air _____.
    (rises/is rising)   (falls/is falling)

14. Look at that balloon. It _____ very fast. Oops! I guess it popped. Now it
    (rises/is rising)
    _____.
    (falls/is falling)

15. Karen _____ a shower. Can she call you right back?
    (takes/is taking)

16. She _____ a shower in the morning after she
    (takes/is taking)
    _____.
    (exercises/is exercising)

II. *Marcia's mother is asking about her routine at college. Put the words in parentheses in the correct order to write her questions.*

1. (what time/you/get up/do?)

   Mom: _____ What time do you get up? _____

   Marcia: I get up at about 7:00 on weekdays.

(continued on next page)

2. (exercise/do/you?)

Mom: _Do you excercise?_

Marcia: Yes, I do. I run every morning.

3. (you/when/eat/do/breakfast?)

Mom: _When do you eat breakfast?_

Marcia: I have early classes, so I usually eat at about 8:00.

4. (to school/do/walk/you?)

Mom: _Do you walk to school?_

Marcia: No, I don't. I usually ride my bike.

5. (you/how long/do/stay/at school?)

Mom: _How long Do you stay at school?_

Marcia: I stay until lunchtime. Then I come home and eat.

6. (go back/do/you/after lunch?)

Mom: _Do you go back after lunch?_

Marcia: Yes, I do. I go back and study in the library.

7. (you/have fun/do/ever?)

Mom: _Do you ever have fun?_

Marcia: Sure, I do. Ask me about my weekend schedule!

III. *Complete each conversation with the correct form of the verbs in parentheses.*

1. **A:** I ___don't understand___ this lesson. Could you help me?
   a. (not understand)
   B: Sure. What's the problem?

2. **A:** How's Treng today?

   B: She _____is_____ much better. In fact, she ___doesn't seem___ sick at all.
   a. (be)   b. (not seem)

3. **A:** That pizza ___looks___ good.
   a. (look)
   B: It ___tastes___ great. In fact, I ___ate___ my third slice right now.
   b. (taste)   c. (eat)

4. **A:** Listen. Somebody ___drives___ into the driveway.
   a. (drive)
   B: I ___don't hear___ anything.
   b. (not hear)

5. **A:** Let's go over these verb tenses together.

   B: I ___don't want___ to study anymore. Besides, I ___know___ them
   a. (not want)   b. (know)
   perfectly.

6. **A:** This _____is_____ a great movie.
   a. (be)
   B: I ___think___ so too.
   b. (think)

7. **A:** I'm sorry, but I ___don't remember___ your name.
   a. (not remember)
   B: My name's Genya. What's yours?

IV. *Rewrite each sentence to include the adverb in parentheses.*

1. John is a pleasure to have in class.

_____ John is always a pleasure to have in class. _____
(always)

2. He pays attention.

_____ He usually pays attention. _____
(usually)

3. He forgets his homework.

_____ He rarely forgets his homework. _____
(rarely)

4. Our car doesn't start on cold mornings.

_____ Our car often doesn't start on cold mornings. _____
(often)

5. It breaks down in traffic.

_____ It sometimes breaks down in traffic. _____
(sometimes)

6. It's in the repair shop when we need it.

_____ It's usually in the repair shop when we need it _____
(usually)

V. *Circle the correct adverb for each statement.*

1. Fred is an airline reservation clerk. He gets to work at 4:00 P.M. every day.
   He sometimes/(always)/never gets to work at 4:00.

2. He's only late about twice a year.
   He's (rarely)/always/often late.

3. He and his co-workers have a meeting about four mornings a week.
   They (often)/never/always have a meeting in the morning.

4. He doesn't call his friends in the afternoon because he doesn't have time.
   He always/sometimes/(never) calls his friends in the afternoon.

5. By 7:30 every evening, he's hungry.
   He's rarely/sometimes/(always) hungry by 7:30.

6. He eats dinner with his friend Carl about once a month.
   He always/never/(sometimes) eats dinner with Carl.

7. He only skips dinner about once every two months.
   He often/always/(rarely) skips dinner.

8. He stays late at work about three nights a week.
   He rarely/(often)/never stays late at work.

VI. *Complete the conversations with the present progressive or simple present tense form of the verbs in parentheses.*

1. **A:** _____ Are _____ you _____ getting _____ ready for school? It's almost 8:00.
   a. (get)

   B: Yes, I am. I _____ am brushing _____ my teeth right now.
   b. (brush)

   A: How about Sue? _____ Is _____ she _____ get _____ dressed?
   c. (get)

   B: I think so. She _____ is looking for _____ her shoes.
   d. (look for)

(continued on next page)

2. **A:** Something ___is smelling___ good. ___Are___ you ___making___ pancakes?
   a. (smell)   b. (make)

   B: No, I'm not.

   A: What ___used___ we ___eating___ then?
   c. (eat)

   B: Cereal and fruit.

3. **A:** I can't find my bookbag. ___Do___ you ___know___ where it is?
   a. (know)

   B: No, but I saw it in your room last night.

   A: I'm in my room now, but I ___am not seeing___ it. *or don't see*
   b. (not see)

4. **A:** This milk ___tastes is___ awful. I think it ___is___ sour.
   a. (taste)   b. (be)

   B: Have some juice instead. I ___am putting___ two peanut-butter sandwiches in your lunch.
   c. (put)

   Is that enough?

   A: Sure.

5. **A:** Don't pack anything for me. I ___am not___ hungry today.
   a. (not be)

   B: Why not?

   A: I ___am having___ a stomachache.
   b. (have)

   B: Your head ___seems___ a little hot too. Maybe you're sick.
   c. (seem)

6. **A:** No. I'm not. I ___am feeling___ nervous about my spelling test.
   a. (feel)

   B: Oh, no! Look at the time. I think I ___am hearing___ the school bus.
   b. (hear)

   A: Don't worry. We ___are leaving___ right now.
   c. (leave)

   B: 'Bye. Have a great day.

VII. *Complete each sentence with a negative or affirmative imperative. Use the verbs in the box. Use some verbs more than once.*

forget	enjoy	lock	call	walk	have	put

1. Please ___walk___ the dog in the morning and afternoon.

2. But ___call___ her near the Wong's house. She chases their cat.

3. Please ___lock___ the back door before you go out. The key is in the door.

4. Also, ___have___ to turn out the lights. We have high electricity bills.

5. ___put___ glass or newspaper in the garbage. They go in the green bin. We recycle them.

6. ___put___ the garbage on the sidewalk on Tuesday morning.

7. ___call___ me if you have any problems.

8. But ___have___ after 11:00. We go to bed early when we're on vacation.

9. ___enjoy___ fun, and ___forget___ the house.

PART

II

Past

UNIT 5

Simple Past Tense

INTRODUCTION

Read and listen to this excerpt from a biography of Emily Dickinson.

Emily Dickinson **was** a famous American poet. Dickinson **lived** from 1830 to 1886. She **wrote** about love, nature, and time. These **were** her favorite themes.

Emily Dickinson **led** an unusual life. She **was** a recluse—she almost never **left** her house in Amherst, Massachusetts. When she **was** at home, she **did not see** visitors, and she only **wore** white.

In addition to her poetry, Dickinson **wrote** many letters, but other people always **addressed** the envelopes for her. During her life only four of her poems **appeared** in print—and this **was** without her knowledge or permission.

SIMPLE PAST TENSE: REGULAR AND IRREGULAR VERBS

AFFIRMATIVE STATEMENTS		
SUBJECT	**VERB**	
I You He She We You They	**lived** **wrote***	in Amherst.
It (the poem)	**appeared**	in print.
	became*	famous.

Write (wrote) and *become (became)* are irregular verbs.
See Appendix 1 on page A1 for a list of irregular verbs.

NEGATIVE STATEMENTS			
SUBJECT	**DID NOT**	**BASE FORM OF VERB**	
I You He She We You They	**did not**	**live** **write**	in Amherst.
It (the poem)	**did not**	**appear**	in print.
		become	famous.

CONTRACTIONS
did not = didn't

YES/NO QUESTIONS			
DID	**SUBJECT**	**BASE FORM OF VERB**	
Did	I you he she we you they	**live** **write**	in Amherst?
Did	it	**appear**	in print?
		become	famous?

SHORT ANSWERS		
AFFIRMATIVE		
Yes,	you I he she you we they it	**did.**

SHORT ANSWERS		
NEGATIVE		
No,	you I he she you we they it	**didn't.**

WH- QUESTIONS				
WH- WORD	**DID**	**SUBJECT**	**BASE FORM OF VERB**	
Where Why	**did**	I you he she we you they	**live** **write**	in Amherst?
When		it	**appear**	in print?
			become	famous?

PAST TENSE: *BE*

STATEMENTS		
SUBJECT	**BE (NOT)** **WAS/WERE**	
I	**was (not)**	in Amherst.
you	**were (not)**	
He She It	**was (not)**	
We You They	**were (not)**	

CONTRACTIONS
was not = wasn't were not = weren't

YES/NO QUESTIONS		
WAS/WERE	**SUBJECT**	
Was	I	in Amherst?
Were	you	
Was	he she it	
Were	we you they	

SHORT ANSWERS			
AFFIRMATIVE			
Yes,	you	were.	
	I	was.	
	he she it	was.	
	you we they	were.	

SHORT ANSWERS			
NEGATIVE			
No,	you	weren't.	
	I	wasn't.	
	he she it	wasn't.	
	you we they	weren't.	

Note: Do not use *did* with *be*.

WH- QUESTIONS			
WH- WORD	**WAS/WERE**	**SUBJECT**	
Where When Why	was	I	in Amherst?
	were	you	
	was	he she it	
	were	we you they	

Grammar Notes

1. Use the simple past tense to talk about actions, states, and situations in the past that are now finished.

   > Emily Dickinson **lived** in the nineteenth century.
   > She **wrote** more than a thousand poems.
   > She **was** a poet.

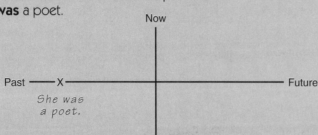

2. You can use the simple past tense with time expressions that refer to the past. Some examples of past time expressions are *last week, in 1886, 100 years ago, in the nineteenth century.*

   > She **lived** in the nineteenth century.
   > She **died** more than 100 years ago.
   > It **was** in 1886.

3. Remember: The past tense of regular verbs is formed by adding *-d* or *-ed* to the base form of the verb.

   > live → live**d**
   > appear → appear**ed**

   See page A9 in Appendix 14 for spelling rules for the simple past tense.
   See page A13 in Appendix 19 for pronunciation rules for the simple past tense.

FOCUSED PRACTICE

1. Discover the Grammar

Read part of a poem called "A bird came down the walk," by Emily Dickinson. Underline all the verbs in the simple past tense.

A bird <u>came</u> down the walk:
He did not know I saw;
He bit an angle-worm in halves
And ate the fellow, raw.

And then he drank a dew
From a convenient grass,
And then hopped sidewise to
    the wall
To let a beetle pass.

2. Another Poet

Complete this biography of another American poet, Robert Frost. Use the simple past tense form of the verbs in the boxes.

| appear | be | have | ~~live~~ | move | spend |

63
26
89

Robert Frost, one of the most popular American poets, ___lived___ from 1874 to 1963. He
___was___ originally from California, but he ___spent___ most of his life in New England. At
first, Frost ___hadn't___ much success with his poetry. In 1912 he and his family ___moved___
to England for a few years. Soon, several of his poems ___appeared___ in print.

| be | publish | read | return | say | win |

In 1915, he ___returned___ to the United States. There he ___published___ hundreds of poems and
later ___won___ four Pulitzer Prizes for poetry. Frost often ___read___ his poems in public.
He ___was___ a wonderful speaker and helped create a general interest in poetry. He once
___said___ that poetry "makes you remember what you didn't know you knew."

3. An Interview

Complete these questions about Robert Frost. Then answer them. Use the information in exercise 2.

1. When/born?
   A: _____ When was he born? _____
   B: _____ He was born in 1874. _____

2. originally from the United States?
   A: _____ where was he originally from / was he originally from United States _____
   B: _____ He was from California / yes, he was _____

3. What/write?
   A: _____ what he wrote / what did he write _____
   B: _____ He wrote poetry _____

(continued on next page)

4. successful right away?

A: _Was he successful right away_

B: _No, He wasn't_

5. Where/first become famous?

A: _Where did he first become famous_

B: _He first became famous in England_

6. How many Pulitzer Prizes/win?

A: _How many Pulitzer prizes did he win?_

B: _He won 4_

7. like to speak in public?

A: _Did he like to speak in public?_

B: _Yes, He did_

8. When/die?

A: _When did he die?_

B: _He died in 1963_

4. Life Choices

This is part of a student's journal. There are seven verb mistakes. Find and correct them.

> Today in class we read a poem by Robert Frost.
> enjoyed
> I really ~~enjoy~~ it. It was about a person who choosed
> between two roads in a forest. Many people thought
> the person were Frost. In the end, he didn't took
> the more common road. He took the one less traveled
> on. That decision change his life a lot.
>
> Sometimes I feel a little like Frost. Two years
> ago I decide to come to this country. Did I made the
> right decision?

COMMUNICATION PRACTICE

5. Practice Listening

Listen to part of a conversation between two classmates. Then listen again. Match the events in Pedro's life with the times they occurred.

___f___ 1. Pedro came to this country.   a. in 1990

_____ 2. He met his wife.   b. yesterday

_____ 3. He got married.   c. last year

_____ 4. He started his studies.   d. in 1992

_____ 5. He became an engineer.   e. in 1993

_____ 6. He became a father.   f. three years ago

6. Complete the Biography

Work with a partner. You are each going to read a different version of a short biography about an ESL student, Maria Sanchez. Each biography is missing some information.

Student A: Turn the page. Read only Biography 2. Get information from Student B. Ask questions and fill in the information.

Student B: Don't turn the page. Read only Biography 1. Get information from Student A. Ask questions and fill in the information.

Example:
  A: When was Maria born?
  B: On May 6, 1970.

When you are finished, compare your version with your partner's. Are they the same?

Biography 1

Maria Sanchez was born on May 6, 1970 in _____Mexico City_____. Her mother was a

_____, and her father made shoes. At home they spoke _____. In 1988

Maria and her family moved to _____. At first Maria felt _____. Then

she got a part-time job as a _____. She worked in a Mexican restaurant. She met

_____ at work, and they got married in 1990. They had a baby in 1992.

_____ ago Maria enrolled at the Community College. Her goal is to own her own

restaurant someday.

Biography 2

Maria Sanchez was born on _____May 6, 1970_____ in Mexico City. Her mother was a dressmaker, and

her father made _____. At home they spoke Spanish. In _____ Maria

and her family moved to California. At first Maria felt lonely. Then she got a part-time job as a cook.

She worked in a _____. She met Ricardo at work, and they got married in

_____. They had a baby in _____. A month ago Maria enrolled at the

_____. Her goal is to own her own restaurant someday.

7. What About You?

Write a short autobiography. Do not put your name on it. Your teacher will collect all the papers, mix them up, and redistribute them to the class. Read the autobiography your teacher gives you. Then ask your classmates questions to try to find its writer.

Examples:
Did you come here in 1990?
OR
When did you come here?

8. Two Poets

Work in pairs. Reread the information about Emily Dickinson (see page 36) and Robert Frost (see page 41). In what ways were the two poets similar? How were they different? With your partner write as many ideas as you can. Compare your ideas with your classmates.

Examples:
Both Dickinson and Frost were American poets.
Dickinson died in the nineteenth century. Frost died in the twentieth century.

9. Rhyming Pairs

In poetry the last word of a line sometimes rhymes with the last word of another line. For example, look at these first two lines of a famous poem by Joyce Kilmer:

I think that I shall never see
A poem lovely as a tree.

See *rhymes with* **tree.**
Work with a partner. Write down as many past-tense verbs as you can that rhyme with the verbs in the box.

sent bought drew kept spoke

Example:
Sent rhymes with bent, lent, meant, spent, and went.

Compare your lists with those of another pair of students. Who has the most rhyming pairs?
Now try to write two lines that rhyme. Use one of the rhyming pairs from the lists you made with your partner. Share your rhymes with your class.

INTRODUCTION

Read and listen to this magazine article.

Fashion
Then and Now

Isn't it interesting how fashions change? In many ways fashion **used to be** much simpler. Women **didn't use to wear** pants, and men's clothes never **used to have** such bright colors. People **used to dress** in special ways for different situations. Today you can go to the opera and find some women in evening gowns while others are in blue jeans.

Even buying blue jeans **used to be** easier. When my friends and I **used to buy** new jeans, they were always bright blue and very crisp. Today teenagers don't like new jeans—they like their jeans "worn and torn." You can get jeans pre-washed, patched-up, and even with big holes in them. Teenagers today buy new jeans in the same condition as the ones we **used to throw** away.

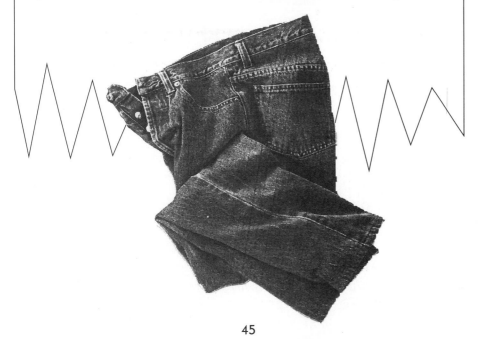

45

USED TO

STATEMENTS			
SUBJECT	*USED TO*	BASE FORM OF VERB	
I You He She It We You They	used to didn't use to	be	fashionable.

YES/NO QUESTIONS				
DID	SUBJECT	USE TO	BASE FORM OF VERB	
Did	I you he she it we you they	use to	be	fashionable?

SHORT ANSWERS		
AFFIRMATIVE		
Yes,	you I he she it you we they	did.

SHORT ANSWERS		
NEGATIVE		
No,	you I he she it you we they	didn't.

WH- QUESTIONS				
WH- WORD	DID	SUBJECT	USE TO	BASE FORM OF VERB
What	did	I you he she it we you they	use to	do?

Grammar Notes

1. Use *used to* + the base form of the verb to contrast things that happened regularly in the past with things that are happening now. *Used to* refers to repeated actions, states, or habits in the past that usually don't happen anymore.

> Teenagers **used to buy** bright blue jeans.
> Today they buy worn-and-torn jeans.

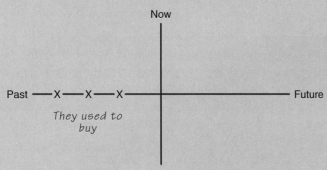

2. Be careful! Form the question for all persons with *did* + *use to* (NOT ~~did you used to~~). Form the negative with *didn't* + *use to* (NOT ~~didn't used to~~).

3. Be careful! Do not confuse *used to* + the base form of the verb with *be used to* or *get used to*.

> I**'m used to wearing** my jeans loose.
> I can't **get used to wearing** them tight.

4. *Used to* and *use to* are pronounced the same: /yu^{w}stu^w/

FOCUSED PRACTICE

1. Discover the Grammar

Read this article about the differences between married and single life. Underline
used to + *the base form of the verb only when it refers to a habit in the past.*

A re you single? Are most of your friends married? Do your married friends seem old to you? I <u>used to think</u> my married friends were old until I got married. Now I can't believe the way I used to live. When I was single, I used to go out every night. Now I prefer to stay home. I used my time very differently. I used to stay up late and get up early. I used to get very little sleep. I also used to love last-minute plans, and I never used to mind having lots of people at my house. Things are really different now. I just can't get used to those old ways again.

2. Times Change

Look at these pictures from an old magazine. Use the verbs in the box with
used to. *Write one sentence about each picture.*

wear	dance	dress	~~be~~	have

1. Women's skirts _____used to be_____ long and formal.

2. All men ____used to have____ long hair.

3. Children ___used to dress___ like adults.

4. Men and women ___used to dance___ at formal balls.

5. Women ___used to wear___ many petticoats under their skirts.

3. Teenagers Can Be Strange

Two women are talking about the strange things they used to do when they were teenagers. Complete the conversation. Use used to *and the verbs in parentheses.*

Leslie: Isn't it hard to believe some of the crazy things we ___used to do___?
1. (do)

Hillary: It sure is. Just think about jeans. Remember how tight we
___used to wear___ them?
2. (wear)

Leslie: I sure do. ___did___ you ___use to sit___ with your new jeans on in
3. (sit)
hot bath water to make them shrink?

Hillary: No, but I ___used to buy___ jeans that had patches all over them. And
4. (buy)
that's not all. ___Did___ you ___use to iron___ your hair to make it
5. (iron)
straight?

Leslie: No, I didn't. But ___Did___ you ___use to take___ your brand-new
6. (take)
sneakers and purposely get them dirty?

Hillary: I sure did. Everyone ___used to do___ that.
7. (do)

Leslie: We really ___used to have___ fun, didn't we?
8. (have)

Hillary: We sure did.

4. Progress

Look at the chart. Write five sentences describing how life used to be different. Use didn't use to *and the words in parentheses.*

1848	Chewing gum invented in the United States.
1909	First permanent hair waves given in London.
1913	Crossword puzzles appeared in an American newspaper for the first time.
1918	Daylight-saving time introduced in America.
1920	Nineteenth Amendment to the U.S. Constitution allowed women to vote.
1926	First movie with sound produced.

1. ___Before 1848 people didn't use to chew gum.___
(People/chew gum)
2. ___Before 1909 women didn't use to have P.H. waves___
(Women/have permanent hair waves)
3. ___Before 1913 crossword puzzles didn't use to appear in newspaper___
(Crossword puzzles/appear in the newspaper)
4. ___Before 1918 people didn't use to change the time___
(People/change the time)
5. ___Before 1920 women in the United States didn't use to vote___
(Women in the United States/vote)
6. ___Before 1926 movies didn't use to have sound___
(Movies/have sound)

COMMUNICATION PRACTICE

5. Practice Listening

Two friends are talking about their teenage years. Listen to their conversation. Listen again. Check the things they used to do in the past and the things they do now.

	Past	Now
1. get up very early without an alarm clock	✔	☐
2. use an alarm clock	☐	☐
3. have a big breakfast	☐	☐
4. have a cup of coffee	☐	☐
5. look at the newspaper	☐	☐
6. have endless energy	☐	☐
7. do aerobics	☐	☐

6. Before and After

Work with a partner. Look at the two pictures of Barry Tanner. Write sentences about how Barry used to look and how he looks today. Compare your sentences with your classmates' sentences.

Example:
Barry used to have long hair. Now he has short hair.

7. Things Change

Work in small groups. Think about how things used to be ten, fifteen, and twenty years ago. Think about the changes in science, business, and your daily life. Share your ideas with each other.

Example:
A local phone call used to cost ten cents everywhere. Now it costs twenty-five cents in most places.

8. The Way I Used to Be

Work in small groups. Bring in a picture of yourself when you were much younger. Talk about the differences in how you used to be and how you are now. What did you use to do? How did you use to dress?

Example:
I used to wear long skirts. Now I wear short skirts.

Past Progressive and Simple Past Tense

INTRODUCTION

The police are questioning a burglary suspect. Read and listen to part of the police interrogation.

Police: What **were** you **doing** last Tuesday between 6:00 and 9:00 P.M.?

Suspect: Well, let's see. I **was** probably **doing** what I always do. I **was** with my wife. We **were eating** dinner. We **finished** around 7:00.

Police: OK. So what **were** you **doing** between 7:00 and 9:00?

Suspect: Between 7:00 and 9:00? I **was watching** TV.

Police: And what **was** your wife **doing** while you **were watching** TV?

Suspect: I think she **was talking** on the phone. That's right. I remember, now. I **was watching** TV when the phone **rang**. That **was** at 7:30.

Police: Hmm. I thought the phone **wasn't working** because of the storm.

PAST PROGRESSIVE

		STATEMENTS	
SUBJECT	**WAS/WERE**	**NOT + BASE FORM OF VERB + -ING**	
I	was		
You	were		
He She It	was	(not) working	at 7:00. when my brother called. while he **was talking**.
We You They	were		

YES/NO QUESTIONS			
WAS/WERE	**SUBJECT**	**BASE FORM OF VERB + -ING**	
Was	I		
Were	you		
Was	he she it	**working**	at 7:00? while he **was talking?**
Were	we you they		

SHORT ANSWERS		
AFFIRMATIVE		
Yes,	you	**were.**
	I	**was.**
	he she it	**was.**
	you we they	**were.**

SHORT ANSWERS		
NEGATIVE		
No,	you	**weren't.**
	I	**wasn't.**
	he she it	**wasn't.**
	you we they	**weren't.**

WH- QUESTIONS				
WH- WORD	**WAS/WERE**	**SUBJECT**	**BASE FORM OF VERB + -ING**	
Why	**was**	I		
	were	you		
	was	he she it	**working**	at 7:00? while he **was talking?**
	were	we you they		

Grammar Notes

1. Use the past progressive (also called the past continuous) to describe an action that was <u>in progress</u> at a specific time in the past. The action began before the specific time and may or may not continue after the specific time.

> My wife and I **were eating** dinner at 6:00.

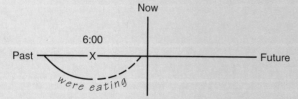

2. Be careful! Non-action verbs are not usually used in the progressive.

> I **had** a headache last night. NOT ~~I was having a headache last night~~.

3. Use the past progressive with the simple past tense to talk about an action that was <u>interrupted</u> by another action. Use the simple past tense for the interrupting action. Use *when* to introduce the simple-past-tense action.

> I **was watching** TV **when** the phone **rang**.
>
> OR
>
> **When** the phone **rang**, I **was watching** TV. (The phone call came in the middle of what I was doing.)

Notice that the time clause *(when the phone rang)* can come at the beginning or the end of the sentence. The meaning is the same. Use a comma after the time clause when it comes at the beginning.

4. Use the past progressive with *while* (or *when*) to talk about two actions in progress at the same time in the past.

Use the past progressive in both clauses.

> **While** I **was watching** TV, my wife **was talking** on the phone.
>
> OR
>
> My wife **was talking** on the phone **while** I **was watching** TV.

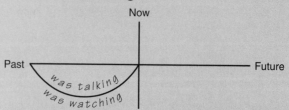

5. Be careful! Sentences with both clauses in the simple past tense have a very different meaning from sentences with one clause in the simple past tense and one clause in the past progressive.

> When the bell **rang**, I **ate** dinner. (First the bell rang; then I ate dinner.)
> When the bell **rang**, I **was eating** dinner. (First I was eating dinner; then the bell rang.)

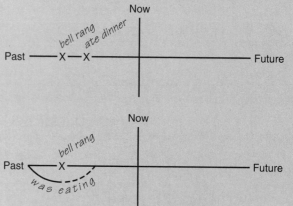

6. Use the past progressive to focus on the <u>duration</u> of an action, not its completion. Use the simple past tense to focus on the <u>completion</u> of an action.

> Paul **was reading** a book last night. (We don't know if he finished the book.)
> Paul **read** a book last night. (He probably finished the book.)

FOCUSED PRACTICE

1. Discover the Grammar

Circle the letter of the correct answer.

1. In which sentence do we know that the man died?
   a. He was drowning.
   b. He drowned.

2. Which sentence tells you that the woman finished the magazine article?
   a. She was writing a magazine article.
   b. She wrote a magazine article.

3. Which sentence talks about an interruption?
   a. When the phone rang, I answered it.
   b. When the phone rang, I was taking a bath.

4. Which sentence talks about two actions that were in progress at the same time?
   a. While Mary was painting the living room, Jeff was typing a letter.
   b. Mary put down her brush when Jeff entered the room.

5. In which sentence did the guests arrive before dinner began?
   a. When the guests arrived, we were eating dinner.
   b. When the guests arrived, we ate dinner.

2. Describe the Suspects

Look at the picture of the suspects yesterday. Write about them. Use the past progressive.

YESTERDAY

1. She ___was wearing a hat.___
   (wear/a hat)
2. He ___wasn't wearing a hat.___
   (wear/a hat)
3. They ___were wearing sunglasses___
   (wear/sunglasses)
4. She ___wasn't smiling___
   (smile)
5. He ___wasn't holding a suitcase___
   (hold/a suitcase)
6. She ___was holding a suitcase___
   (hold/a suitcase)
7. They ___were taking the subway___
   (take/the subway)
8. They ___wasn't driving___
   (drive)

3. At the Scene of a Traffic Accident

*Complete the conversation with the simple past tense or the past progressive
form of the verbs in parentheses.*

Reporter: What was the cause of the accident, Officer?

Officer: Well, it looks like there were many causes. First of all, when the accident

_____ occurred _____, the driver _____ was driving _____ much too fast. And while he
    1. (occur)   2. (drive)

_____ was driving _____, he _____ was speaking _____ to a client on his car phone. When he
    3. (drive)   4. (speak)

_____ saw _____ the pedestrian, he immediately _____ stepped _____ on the
    5. (see)   6. (step)

brakes, but it was too late. The victim wasn't paying attention, either. First of all, he didn't

wait for the traffic light to change. He _____ was crossing _____ against a red light when the
                                       7. (cross)

car _____ hit _____ him. He _____ didn't see _____ the approaching car because he
    8. (hit)   9. (not see)

_____ was talking _____ to his friend. The friend wasn't paying attention, either. He
    10. (talk)

_____ was eating _____ an ice cream cone while he _____ was crossing _____ the street. When
    11. (eat)   12. (cross)

he _____ noticed _____ the car, he _____ tried _____ to push his friend out of the
    13. (notice)   14. (try)

way, but it was too late.

Reporter: How is the victim doing?

Officer: Well, when the ambulance _____ arrived _____, he _____ was bleeding _____ from his head
                            15. (arrive)   16. (bleed)

wound, but the doctors stopped the bleeding, and they think he'll be OK.

4. Answer Carefully

*The police are questioning another suspect in the burglary last Tuesday.
Read this suspect's answers. Use the words in parentheses and the past
progressive or simple past tense to write the police officer's questions.*

1. **Police:** _____ What were you doing Tuesday night? _____
                            (What/do/Tuesday night?)

  Suspect: I was visiting a friend.

2. **Police:** _____ Who exactly were you visiting? _____
                            (Who/exactly/you visit?)

  Suspect: My girlfriend. I got to her house at 5:30 and drove her to work.

3. **Police:** _____ Was she working at 7:00? _____
                            (she/work/at 7:00?)

  Suspect: Yes, she was working the late shift.

4. **Police:** _____ Was anyone else working with her? _____
                            (anyone else/work/with her?)

  Suspect: No. She was working alone.

5. **Police:** _what were you doing while she was working_
   (What / you / do / while / she / work?)
   Suspect: I was reading the paper in her office.

6. **Police:** But there was a terrible storm Tuesday night. The lights went out.
   what were you doing when lights went out
   (What / do / when / lights go out?)
   Suspect: I was still reading the paper.

7. **Police:** _what did you do when the lights went out_
   (What / do / when / lights go out?)
   Suspect: When the lights went out, we left the building.

8. **Police:** _why were you running when the police saw you_
   (Why / run / when / the police / see you?)
   Suspect: We were running because we wanted to get out of the rain.

5. Earthquake

In 1989 a big earthquake struck the San Francisco Bay Area of California. At that time, many people were at the World Series baseball game in Candlestick Park. Combine these pairs of sentences about the earthquake. Use the simple past tense or the past progressive form of the verb.

1. a. The earthquake struck.
   b. Thousands of people sat in Candlestick Park.

   When _the earthquake struck, thousands of people were sitting in Candlestick Park._

2. a. The earthquake struck.
   b. The lights went out.

   When _the earthquake struck, the lights went out._

3. a. The crowd felt the earth move.
   b. They knew immediately it was an earthquake.

   When _____

   _____

4. a. The electric power went out.
   b. Millions of people watched the game on TV.

   When _____ were watching _____

   _____

5. a. The earth stopped moving.
   b. The police told the crowd to leave the stadium calmly.

   When _____

   _____

(continued on next page)

6. a. They got to their cars.
   b. They turned on their radios.

   When _____

   _____

7. a. They drove home.
   b. They heard about a collapsed highway ahead.

   While _____They were driving home_____

   _____

8. a. They heard the news of the collapsed highway.
   b. They got out of their cars.

   When _____

   _____

9. a. They finally got home.
   b. Their neighbors stood in the streets.

   When _____were standing_____

   _____

10. a. They entered their homes.
    b. They discovered a lot of damage.

    When _____

    _____

COMMUNICATION PRACTICE

6. Practice Listening

*The police are trying to draw a detailed picture of an accident.
Listen to a witness describe the accident. Then listen again. According
to the witness, which picture is the most accurate? Circle the number.*

1.

2.

3.

7. The Real Story

Work in groups of four. Follow these steps:

1. Three students are witnesses; the fourth is a police officer. Look at the pictures from exercise 6.

2. The police officer asks the witnesses questions to describe the accident.

3. Each of the witnesses chooses one of the sets of pictures and presents his or her version of the accident.

Examples:
A: Can you describe the accident?
B: Yes. Two men were crossing the street.

A: Were they paying attention?
B: No, they weren't; they were talking.

8. What's Your Alibi?

Work in small groups. Reread the alibi in the story on page 52. Do you think it is a good alibi? Pretend that you are a suspect in the burglary. What were you doing last Tuesday night between 6:00 and 9:00 P.M.? Give your alibi to the class. The class will decide which alibis are good and which are bad.

Example:
I work from midnight until 7:00 A.M., so between 6:00 and 9:00 P.M. I was sleeping.

9. Are You a Good Witness?

Look at this picture for ten seconds. Close your book and write down what was happening. See how many details you can remember. What were the people doing? What were they wearing?

Example:
An old woman was sitting on a bench in the park. She was wearing . . .

Compare your list with a classmate's.

10. Complete the Story

Work in pairs. Complete the story. When you read (verb), *write a verb in the past progressive or simple past tense. When you read* (when?), (who?), (what?), *or* (how?), *answer the question. Then share your story with your classmates.*

It was _____Yesterday_____. I _____was staing_____ in the _____Park_____ when all
     (when?)   (verb)   (where?)

of a sudden a big _____Bureen_____ _____came_____ in front of me. When I
       (what?)   (verb)

_____ the _____, I immediately _____. While I
 (verb)   (what?)   (verb)

_____, the _____ _____. I didn't know what to do.
 (verb)   (what?)   (verb)

All at once I saw a _____policeman_____.
       (what?)

When the _____ _____ me, I _____. When I
    (what?)   (verb)   (verb)

_____ later that day, I really felt _____.
 (verb)   (how?)

INTRODUCTION

A lawyer is questioning a crime witness. Read and listen to part of the court transcript.

Lawyer: **What happened** on the night of May 12? Please tell the court.

Witness: I went to Al's Grill.

Lawyer: **Who did you see** there?

Witness: I saw that man.

Lawyer: Let the record indicate that the witness is pointing to the defendant, Harry Adams. OK, you saw Mr. Adams. Did he see you?

Witness: No. He didn't see me.

Lawyer: But somebody saw you. **Who saw** you?

Witness: A woman. He was talking to a woman.

Lawyer: OK. **What happened** next?

Witness: The woman took out a . . .

WH- QUESTIONS: SUBJECT AND PREDICATE

QUESTIONS ABOUT THE SUBJECT		
WH- WORD	**VERB**	
Who **Which** (witnesses)	**appeared**	in court?
How many (witnesses)	**are**	

(continued on next page)

61

QUESTIONS ABOUT THE PREDICATE			
Wh- Word	Auxiliary Verb or *Be*	Subject	Verb
Who(m) **Which** (witnesses)	**did**	the lawyer	**question?**
How many (witnesses)	**is**	the lawyer	**questioning?**

Grammar Notes

1. Use *wh-* questions (also called information questions) to ask for specific information. *Wh-* questions begin with question words such as *who, what, where, when, why, which, whose, how, how many, how much,* and *how long.*

   > **Who** did you see?
   > **How long** did you stay in Al's Grill?
   > **How many** people saw you there?

2. When you are asking about the subject (usually the first part of the sentence), use a *wh-* question word in place of the subject.

   > Someone saw you.
   > ↓
   > **Who** saw you?
   > Something happened.
   > ↓
   > **What** happened?
   > Someone's lawyer is here.
   > ↓
   > **Whose** lawyer is here?

3. When you are asking about the predicate (usually the last part of the sentence), the word order is similar to a *yes/no* question, but the question begins with a *wh-* word.

   > He's going somewhere.
   > Is he going somewhere?
   > **Where** is he going?
   >
   > You said something.
   > Did you say something?
   > **What** did you say?

   Be careful! When you ask a *wh-* question about something in the predicate, you need a form of the verb *be* (*am, is, are, was, were*).

   > Who **is** Harry Adams?
   > Why **was** he at Al's Grill?
   > What **are** the witnesses saying?

   Or you need an auxiliary ("helping") verb such as *do, does, did, have, has, had, can, will.*

   > Why **does** she want to testify?
   > NOT ~~Why she wants to testify?~~
   > When **did** she arrive?
   > NOT ~~When she arrived?~~

4. In formal English, when asking about people in the predicate, *whom* is sometimes used instead of *who.*

   > Formal: **Whom** did you see?
   > Informal: **Who** did you see?

   Be careful! If the main verb is a form of *be,* you cannot use *whom.*

   > **Who** is the next witness?
   > NOT ~~Whom is the next witness?~~

FOCUSED PRACTICE

1. Discover the Grammar

Match the questions and answers.

___f___ 1. Who did you see?   a. His wife saw me.

___a___ 2. Who saw you?   b. She hit a car.

___d___ 3. What hit her?   c. Harry gave me the money.

___b___ 4. What did she hit?   d. A car hit her.

___e___ 5. Which man did you give the money to?   e. I gave the money to Harry.

___c___ 6. Which man gave you the money?   f. I saw the defendant.

2. Q and A

Read the answer. Then ask questions about the underlined words.

1. <u>The witness</u> recognized Harry Adams.

   Who recognized Harry Adams?

2. The witness recognized <u>Harry Adams</u>.

   What witness recognized Harry Adams.

3. Court begins <u>at 9:00 A.M.</u>

   When does the court begin?

4. <u>Five</u> witnesses testified.

   How many witnesses testified

5. The jury found Adams guilty <u>because he didn't have an alibi</u>.

   Why did the jury find Adams guilty?

6. <u>Something horrible</u> happened.

   What happened?

7. The trial lasted <u>two weeks</u>.

   How long did the trial last?

8. <u>The judge</u> spoke to the jury.

   Who spoke to the jury?

(continued on next page)

9. Adams paid his lawyer $2,000.

How much did Adams his lawyer?

10. The district attorney questioned the restaurant manager.

Who did the district attorney quest

3. Cross-Examination

Complete the cross-examination. Write the lawyer's questions.

1. **Lawyer:** _____What time did you return home?_____
   (What time/you/return home?)
   Witness: I returned home just before midnight.

2. **Lawyer:** _How did you get home._
   (How/you/get home?)
   Witness: Somebody gave me a ride.

3. **Lawyer:** _Who gave you a ride?_
   (Who/give/you/a ride?)
   Witness: A friend from work.

4. **Lawyer:** _What happened next?_
   (What/happen/next?)
   Witness: I opened my door and saw someone on my living room floor.

5. **Lawyer:** _Who did you see?_
   (Who/you/see?)
   Witness: Deborah Collins.

6. **Lawyer:** _Who is Deborah collins?_
   (Who/be/Deborah Collins?)
   Witness: She's my wife's boss. I mean, she *was* my wife's boss. She's dead now.

7. **Lawyer:** _What did you do?_
   (What/you/do?)
   Witness: I called the police.

8. **Lawyer:** _When did the police arrive?_
   (When/the police/arrive?)
   Witness: In about ten minutes.

9. **Lawyer:** _How many police officers came?_
   (How many police officers/come?)
   Witness: I don't remember. Why?

   Lawyer: I'm asking the questions here. Please just answer.

COMMUNICATION PRACTICE

4. Practice Listening

You are on the phone with a friend. You have a bad connection. Listen to the following sentences. Then listen again. Circle the letter of the question you need to ask in order to get the correct information.

1. a. Who did you see at the restaurant?
   b. Who saw you at the restaurant?

2. a. Which car did the truck hit?
   b. Which car hit the truck?

3. a. When did it happen?
   b. Why did it happen?

4. a. Whose mother did you call?
   b. Whose mother called you?

5. a. Who did you report it to?
   b. Who reported it?

6. a. How many people heard the shouts?
   b. How many shouts did you hear?

7. a. Who saw the man?
   b. Who did the man see?

8. a. Why do you have to hang up?
   b. When do you have to hang up?

5. What Happened Next?

Work with a partner. Look at the court transcript on page 61 again. Read it aloud. Then continue the conversation between the witness and the lawyer.

Example:
Lawyer: OK. What happened next?
Witness: The woman took out a police badge and stood up.

6. Star Reporters

Work in small groups. You are going to interview a ten-year-old child genius who is attending medical school. You have five minutes to think of as many wh- questions as you can. One student should write down all the questions.

Examples:
When did you decide to become a doctor?
Who influenced you to become a doctor?

You will be allowed to ask only six questions. Choose the best six questions. Compare questions with the rest of the class. Now work in pairs. Role play the interview. Use the six questions your group chose. Then write the interview for a magazine article.

7. Complete the Chart

Work with a partner. Look at the two charts. They are missing some information.

A: Cover Chart 1. Read only Chart 2. Get information from Student B. Ask questions and fill in the information.

B: Cover Chart 2. Read only Chart 1. Get information from Student A. Ask questions and fill in the information.

Example:
A: Where did Pascal come from?
B: France.

B: When did Pascal invent the adding machine?
A: In 1642.

When you are finished, compare your two charts. Are they the same?

CHART 1			
INVENTION	DATE	INVENTOR	COUNTRY
adding machine	1642	Pascal	France
car engine	1889	_____	Germany
bicycle	_____	Starley	England
electric battery	_____	Volta	Italy
tape recorder	1899	Poulsen	_____

CHART 2			
INVENTION	DATE	INVENTOR	COUNTRY
adding machine	1642	Pascal	France
car engine	_____	Daimler	Germany
bicycle	1885	_____	England
_____	1800	Volta	Italy
tape recorder	_____	Poulsen	Denmark

I. *Complete each sentence with the correct form of the verb in parentheses.*

1. I _____ate_____ lunch about half an hour ago.
   ('m eating/ate)

2. Chris and Bob _____are having_____ a good time on their
   (are having/had)
   vacation. They want to stay another two weeks.

3. Ouch! I just _____bit_____ my tongue.
   (bite/bit)

4. Renee sews beautifully. She _____makes_____ all her own
   (makes/made)
   clothes.

5. Last month, we _____spent_____ too much money on
   ('re spending/spent)
   entertainment. We saw six movies.

6. Bill _____won_____ first prize in the fishing contest. His
   (wins/won)
   fish was huge.

7. When Kim first moved to the United States last year, he

   _____was_____ very homesick, but now he feels much
   ('s/was)
   better.

8. I ___'m reading___ the newspaper right now, but you can
   ('m reading/read)
   have it in a few minutes.

II. *Complete the letter with the past tense form of the verbs in parentheses.*

Dear Andrea:

I just _____left_____ New York, and I'm sitting on the train to Washington.
1. (leave)
I __didn't write__ to you from New York because I _____was_____ so busy. I _____walked_____ for
2. (not write)   3. (be)   4. (walk)
miles, and I _____took_____ dozens of pictures. I _____went_____ to museums, concerts, and plays.
5. (take)   6. (go)
I also missed some things, though. I ___didn't go___ to the Bronx Zoo because it _____is_____
7. (not go)   8. (be)
such a long subway ride. And I ___didn't take___ the elevator to the top of the Empire State Building
9. (not take)
because I'm afraid of heights.

   I'll send you a postcard from Washington. Hope you're having a great summer.

                                                                    Love,
                                                                    Betsy

III. *Complete the conversation with the simple past tense form of the verbs in parentheses.*

A: Are you from Baltimore?

B: No, I'm not. I _____was born_____ in China, but I _____moved_____ here about ten
         1. (be born)   2. (move)
years ago.

A: Where _____did_____ you _____live_____ in China?
                                              3. (live)

B: In Shanghai.

A: Oh, really? I _____spent_____ three years in Shanghai.
                        4. (spend)

B: What _____did_____ you _____do_____ there?
                                          5. (do)

A: I _____taught_____ English.
           6. (teach)

B: That's interesting. _____did_____ you _____like_____ it?
                                                    7. (like)

A: Yes. Very much. It's an exciting city.

B: When _____did_____ you _____came_____ back to the United States?
                                          8. (come)

A: Let's see. I _____came_____ back two years ago.
                      9. (came)

IV. *Circle the letters of the correct verb forms to complete the conversation.*

A: When you were young, did you use to _____ in restaurants a lot?
    1.(a.) eat   c. eating
       b. ate   d. eats

B: No, not that often. We used to _____cook_____ dinner at home.
    2. a. cooking   c. cooked
       b. cook   d. did cook

A: How about prices? _____were_____ they lower when you were a kid?
    3. a. Was   c. Did
       b. Are   d. Were

B: They sure were. Let me give you an example. A movie _____used to_____ cost fifty cents.
    4. a. got used to   c. used to
       b. uses to   d. use to

A: Wow! Did you _____go_____ to the movies a lot?
    5. a. went   c. going
       b. go   d. goes

B: Yes. We _____went_____ every Saturday afternoon. Hey, how about eating that hamburger?
    6. a. were going   c. are going
       b. go   d. went

A: OK—but one last question. _____Did_____ you like everything better in those days?
    7. a. Did   c. Was
       b. Does   d. Are

B: Nope. In those days, I _____didn't use to_____ have you to talk to. I like things much better now.
    8. a. 'm not used to c. didn't use to
       b. wasn't   d. 'm not

V. *Complete the telephone conversation with the simple past or past progressive form of the verbs in parentheses.*

A: Hi, honey. I just _____had_____ a little accident with the car. Nothing serious, and no one
1. (have)
was hurt.

B: How about the car?

A: It's OK. I _____was not driving_____ fast when it happened, so there _____was not_____ much
2. (not drive)　　　　　　　　　　　　　　　　　3. (not be)
damage.

B: What _____happened_____?
4. (happen)

A: Well, I _____hit_____ the back of a bus.
5. (hit)

B: How _____did_____ you _____do_____ that?
6. (do)

A: I _____was trying_____ to find something on the radio, and I _____was not paying_____ attention to
7. (try)　　　　　　　　　　　　　　　　　　　　8. (not pay)
the road.

B: _____Did_____ you _____call_____ the police?
9. (call)

A: Yes, I did. I just _____called_____ them ten minutes ago.
10. (call)

B: I'm glad you're OK.

VI. *Find and correct a verb mistake in each sentence.*

1. I ~~weren't~~ wasn't wearing my boots when I left the house this morning.

2. It was snowing when I ~~get~~ got/went to the bus station.

3. When I was ~~arriving~~ arrived at the office, I called Bill.

4. He was taking a shower when I called.

5. I ~~discussed~~ was discussing a problem with my boss when Bill interrupted us.

6. I'm sorry I was not paying attention while you were talking.

VII. *Complete the conversation with the correct form of the verbs in parentheses.*

A: You look tired.

B: I am. There _____was_____ a street fair in my neighborhood last night.
1. (was/is/did)

A: _____Was_____ it really noisy?
2. (Was/Is/Did)

B: Yeah. A band _____was playing_____ right outside my window until midnight. People
3. (plays/was playing/play)
_____were dancing_____ in the street all night. Nobody could sleep.
4. (dance/dancing/were dancing)

A: What did you do?

B: I _____went_____ to the fair.
5. (was going/went/go)

A: _____Did_____ you have fun?
6. (Are/Did/Was)

B: I _____had_____ a great time.
7. (has/had/was having)

III

▼

Future

INTRODUCTION

Read and listen to this article from the science section of a magazine. It describes transportation in the future.

TRANSPORTATION
OF THE
FUTURE

In the next few decades people **are going to travel** very differently from the way they do today. Everyone **is going to drive** electrically operated cars. So in a few years people **won't worry** about running out of gas.

Some of the large automobile companies are really moving ahead with this new technology. F & C Motors, for example, **is holding** a press conference next week. At the press conference the company **will present** its new, electronically operated models.

Transportation in the future **won't be** limited to the ground. Many people predict that traffic **will** quickly **move** to the sky. In the coming years, instead of radio reports about road conditions and highway traffic, news reports **will talk** about traffic jams in the sky.

But the sky isn't the limit. In the future, you**'ll** probably even **be able to take** a trip to the moon. Instead of listening to regular airplane announcements, you**'ll hear** someone say, "The shuttle to the moon **leaves** in ten minutes. Please check your equipment. And remember, no more than ten ounces of carry-on baggage are allowed."

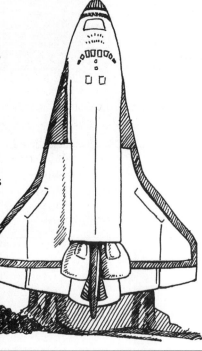

BE GOING TO FOR THE FUTURE

STATEMENTS

SUBJECT	BE	(NOT) GOING TO	BASE FORM OF VERB	
I	am			
You	are			
He She It	is	(not) going to	start	soon.
We You They	are			

CONTRACTIONS

I am	=	I'm
You are	=	You're
He is	=	He's
She is	=	She's
It is	=	It's
We are	=	We're
They are	=	They're

YES/NO QUESTIONS

BE	SUBJECT	GOING TO	BASE FORM OF VERB	
Am	I			
Are	you			
Is	he she it	going to	start	soon?
Are	we you they			

SHORT ANSWERS

	AFFIRMATIVE		
	you	are.	
	I	am.	
Yes,	he she it	is.	
	you we they	are.	

SHORT ANSWERS

	NEGATIVE		
	you're		
	I'm		
No,	he's she's it's	not.	
	you're we're they're		

WH- QUESTIONS

WH- WORD	BE	SUBJECT	GOING TO	BASE FORM OF VERB
When Where	are	you	going to	start?

PRESENT PROGRESSIVE FOR THE FUTURE

STATEMENTS		
SUBJECT + *BE*	***(NOT)* + BASE FORM OF VERB + *-ING***	
I'm	(not) starting	soon.

See pages 3 and 4 in Unit 1 for a complete presentation of the present progressive forms.

WILL FOR THE FUTURE

STATEMENTS			
SUBJECT	***WILL (NOT)***	**BASE FORM OF VERB**	
I You He She It We You They	will (not)	start	soon.

CONTRACTIONS		
I will	=	I'll
You will	=	You'll
He will	=	He'll
She will	=	She'll
It will	=	It'll
We will	=	We'll
They will	=	They'll
will not	=	won't

YES/NO QUESTIONS			
WILL	**SUBJECT**	**BASE FORM OF VERB**	
Will	I you he she it we you they	start	soon?

SHORT ANSWERS		
AFFIRMATIVE		
Yes,	you I he she it you we they	will.

SHORT ANSWERS		
NEGATIVE		
No,	you I he she it you we they	won't.

WH- QUESTIONS			
WH- WORD	**WILL**	**SUBJECT**	**BASE FORM OF VERB**
When Where	will	you	start?

THE SIMPLE PRESENT TENSE FOR THE FUTURE

STATEMENTS		
SUBJECT	**VERB**	
We	start	Monday.
It	starts	

See page 11 in Unit 2 for a complete presentation of the simple present tense forms.

Grammar Notes

1. There are several ways to talk about actions and states in the future. You can use *be going to*, the present progressive, *will*, or the simple present tense.

2. Use *be going to* or *will* to make predictions or guesses about the future.

   > Scientists believe that people **are going to travel** very differently in the future. You **will** probably **be able to take** a trip to the moon.

   Use *be going to* instead of *will* when there is something in the present that leads to the prediction.

   > Look at those cars! They**'re going to crash**!
   > NOT They'll crash!

3. We often use *be going to*, the present progressive, or *will*, to talk about future intentions or plans.

   > F & C Motors **is going to hold** a press conference.
   > F & C Motors **is holding** a press conference next week.
   > F & C Motors **will hold** a press conference next week.

   a. We often use *will* when we decide something at the moment of speaking.

   > **A:** There's going to be a lecture on transportation of the future.
   > **B:** Oh! That sounds interesting. I think **I'll go.**

   Will can also be used for making a request (see Unit 29).

   b. We often use the present progressive when we talk about future plans that have already been arranged. There is usually some reference to the future; this tells us that the event is going to happen in the future and that it is not happening now.

   > John and I **are attending** the lecture **tomorrow night**. We've already gotten tickets.

   Be careful! We usually do not use non-action (stative) verbs with the progressive.

4. Use the simple present to talk about scheduled future events (such as timetables, programs, and schedules). Verbs such as *start, leave, end,* and *begin* are often used this way.

   > The press conference **begins** at 10:00 A.M.

5. In informal speech, *going to* is often pronounced *gonna* /gənə/.

FOCUSED PRACTICE

1. Discover the Grammar

🔲 *Read this transcript and listen to a radio interview with Professor Jason Lin, a well-known researcher of the Future Watch Institute. There are fifteen forms that refer to the future. Find and underline them.*

Interviewer: For those of you who are just tuning in, this is "Looking Into the Future." I am William Bee, and we are talking with Professor Jason Lin. Good afternoon, Professor. I understand you <u>are going to tell</u> our listeners about the cars of the future.

Professor Lin: That's right. I believe there will be some surprising changes in the next century. Let me give you some examples. Cars of the future are going to have "brains." They'll start themselves, and they'll adjust the seats, mirrors, and steering wheels automatically. Luxury cars will even ask you where you want to go and tell you the best route to take.

Interviewer: That certainly is amazing! I'm sure lots of our listeners have questions for you, but, unfortunately, we only have time for a few call-ins today.

Professor Lin: Well, you know, I'm speaking at the annual Car Show next week. The show begins at 10:00 A.M. on August 11. I'm going to talk more about the plans for cars of the future. I'm also going to show some models. I hope many of your listeners will be there.

Interviewer: I'm sure they will. We have to pause for a commercial break. But don't go away, listeners. We'll be right back—and Professor Lin will be ready to answer some of your questions.

2. It's Going to Happen

Look at the pictures. Write predictions or guesses. Use the words in the box and be going to.

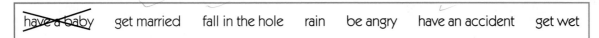

~~have a baby~~   get married   fall in the hole   rain   be angry   have an accident   get wet

1. _____ She's going to have a baby. _____

2. _____ They are going to have an accident _____

(continued on next page)

3. He is going to fall in the hole.

4. It's going to rain

5. They are going to get married

6. He is going to be angry

7. She's going to get wet

3. Professor Lin's Schedule

Write about Professor Lin's plans for next week. Use the information from his calendar and the present progressive.

	Monday	Tuesday	Wednesday	Thursday	Friday
Morning	take train to New Haven	go to Washington (8:00 A.M.)	work in research lab all day	attend annual Car Show	talk on radio show
Evening	give lecture at Yale		↓		

1. On Monday morning _____ he's taking a train to New Haven. _____
2. On Monday evening __He is going to give a lecture at yale__
3. On Tuesday morning __He is going to Washington at 8.00 AM__
4. All day Wednesday __He is going to work in research lab all day__
5. On Thursday __He is going to attend annual Carshow__
6. On Friday morning __He is going to talk on radio show__

4. Radio Call-in Questions

Radio listeners are calling in with questions for Professor Lin. Complete the questions and answers. Use the words in parentheses and will *or* won't.

Caller 1: Hello, Professor Lin. My question is this: _____ Will _____ the car of the future

_____ run _____ on gasoline?
    1. (run)

Professor Lin: No, it _____ won't _____. It _____ will _____ probably
    2.

_____ use _____ batteries. Thanks for calling. Next?
    3. (use)

Caller 2: Good morning. I had a flat tire yesterday. I was wondering, _____ will _____ we

still _____ get _____ flat tires on these future cars?
    4. (get)

Professor Lin: No, we _____ won't _____. In fact, by the year 2000, flat tires
    5.

_____ will be _____ a thing of the past. Tires _____ will have _____ a special seal
    6. (be)   7. (have)

so they _____ will repair _____ themselves automatically. Next caller, please.
    8. (repair)

(continued on next page)

Caller 3: Sounds great. In what other ways _____ *will* _____ the car of the future

_____ *be* _____ different?
9. (be)

Professor Lin: Well, instead of keys, cars _____ *will have* _____ magnetic entry systems. These
10. (have)

_____ *will look* _____ a lot like credit cards. They _____ *will open* _____ doors, and
11. (look)   12. (open)

they _____ *will adjust* _____ the seats, mirrors, and steering wheels. They
13. (adjust)

_____ *will* _____ even _____ *control* _____ inside temperature.
14. (control)

Caller 3: _____ *will* _____ they _____ *help* _____ prevent car thefts?
15. (help)

Professor Lin: Yes, they _____ *will* _____! OK, next caller?
16.

Caller 4: Hello. I'm curious. How much _____ *will* _____ these cars _____ *cost* _____?
17. (cost)

Professor Lin: I don't know exactly, but they certainly _____ *won't be* _____ cheap.
18. (not be)

5. All Aboard

Professor Lin is going to take the train from New York to New Haven on Monday. He is asking questions at the information booth. Write his questions. Then look at the train schedule and write the answers. Use the simple present tense.

NEW YORK TO NEW HAVEN

MONDAY TO FRIDAY, EXCEPT HOLIDAYS

Leave	Arrive	Leave	Arrive	Leave	Arrive
New York	New Haven	New York	New Haven	New York	New Haven
AM	AM	PM	PM	PM	PM
12:35	2:23	12:35	4:55	6:04	7:46
1:30	3:37	3:37	5:17	6:30	8:16
6:02	7:48	4:02	5:44	7:06	8:51
7:05	8:55	4:07	5:58	7:37	9:28
8:07	9:57	4:22	6:06	8:07	9:55
9:07	10:53	4:35	6:17	9:07	10:55
10:07	11:53	4:45	6:49	10:07	11:55
11:07	12:53	5:02	6:40	11:20	1:08
12:07	1:53	5:13	7:26	12:35	2:23
1:07	2:54	5:18	7:03	1:30	3:37
2:07	3:55	5:35	7:11	....	....
3:02	4:38	5:39	7:55	....	....
PM	PM	PM	PM	PM	AM

1. When/the first train to New Haven/leave New York?

Professor Lin: When does the first train to New Haven leave New York?

Information: It leaves New York at 12:35 A.M.

2. How long/the trip to New Haven/take?

Professor Lin: How long does the trip to New Haven take?

Information: It takes about two hours.

3. So, what time/the 9:07 train/arrive in New Haven?

Professor Lin: So, what time does the 9:07 train arrive in New Haven?

Information: It arrives 10:53 A.m.

4. How often/morning trains/depart for New Haven?

Professor Lin: _How often do morning trains depart for N.H._

Information: _They depart 8 times in a day_

5. And what time/the last morning train/leave New York?

Professor Lin: _And what time does the last morning train leave N.York_

Information: _The last train leaves at 11:07 Am._

6. Choose the Future

Read the conversations and circle the letter of the more appropriate future form for each one.

1. **Ari:** I just heard the weather report.
   Ben: Oh? What's the forecast?

   Ari: _____ tomorrow.
   a. It's raining
   (b.) It's going to rain

2. **Ben:** Oh, no. I hate driving in the rain. And it's a long drive to that meeting we have to attend tomorrow.

   Ari: Wait! I have an idea. _____ the train instead.
   ✓a. We'll take
   b. We're going to take

3. **Ben:** Good idea! Do you have a train schedule?

   Ari: Here's one. There's a train that _____ at 7:00 A.M.
   a. will leave
   (b.) leaves

4. **Ben:** Good. _____ some sandwiches for the trip.
   (a.) I'll make
   b. I'm making
   Ari: Great.

5. **Ben:** You know, it's a long trip. What _____ all those hours?
   a. are we doing
   (b.) are we going to do
   Ari: We can prepare for the meeting and then sleep!

6. **Ben:** Very funny. Well, we have to get up really early.
   I think _____ home now.
   a. I'm going
   (b.) I'll go

7. **Ari:** OK. I have to stay here a little longer. Mr. Smith _____ at 5:15.
   a. will call
   (b.) is calling

8. **Ben:** OK. _____ tomorrow.
   a. I'm seeing you
   (b.) I'll see you

   Ari: Good night.
   Ben: Good night.

COMMUNICATION PRACTICE

7. Practice Listening

Listen to the short conversations. Decide if the people are talking about something happening now or in the future. Listen again and check the correct column.

	Now	Future
1.	☐	✔
2.	☐	☐
3.	☐	☐
4.	☐	☐
5.	☐	☐
6.	☐	☐

8. Fortune Cookies

Most Chinese restaurants in the United States give you fortune cookies at the end of your meal. Inside each cookie is a small piece of paper with a prediction about the future.

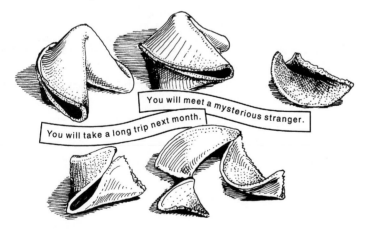

You will meet a mysterious stranger.

You will take a long trip next month.

On a piece of paper write down a fortune. Now work in small groups. Put all the fortunes in a pile and have each person take one. Discuss your fortunes with the group.

Example:
You will take a long trip next month.
  A: That's not possible. I'm starting my new job next week.
  B: That's right. I'm going back to my country for the summer.

9.   When Are You Free?

Complete your weekend schedule. If you have no plans, write free.

	Friday	Saturday	Sunday
12:00			
1:00			
2:00			
3:00			
4:00			
5:00			
6:00			
7:00			
8:00			
9:00			

Now work with a partner. Ask questions to decide on a time when you are both free to do something together.

Example:
A: What are you doing Friday afternoon? Do you want to go to the movies?
B: I'm studying at the library. How about Friday night? Are you doing anything then?

10.   Choose a Time

Work with the same partner as in exercise 9. Look at this movie schedule. Then look at your schedules from exercise 9. Decide which movie to see and when.

★★ **City Cowboy.** Sun. 12:00, 2:15, 4:30, 6:45, 9:00.

★★½ **Cracking Up.** Fri.-Sun. 2:30, 4:00, 5:30, 7:00, 8:30, 10:00.

★★★★ **Love and Kisses.** Thurs.-Fri. 5:45, 7:45, 9:45.

★★★ **Terror on Eighth Street.** Fri. 4:45, 7:15, 9:45. Sat.- Sun. 1:15, 3:45, 6:15, 8:45.

Example:
A: There are three good movies Friday night. *Terror on Eighth Street* is playing at 7:15. Is that OK?
B: That's a little early. When does the next one begin?

11.   Make Predictions

Work in pairs. What do you think the world will be like in the next few decades? What will it be like in a hundred years? Write down your ideas. Share your ideas with the class.

Example:
I think most people will have telephones in their cars.
My grandchildren are going to travel to the moon.

INTRODUCTION

▼

🔊 *Read and listen to this advertisement for a job placement agency.*

LOOKING FOR A JOB?

UNHAPPY AT WORK?

STILL IN SCHOOL?

Where **will** you **go when you decide to change** jobs? What **will** you **do when you graduate**? Here at Jobs Are Us Employment Agency, we can help you find the right job for you. Call or stop in today. **Before you know it**, an exciting new job **will be** yours.

FUTURE TIME CLAUSES

STATEMENTS				
MAIN CLAUSE			**TIME CLAUSE**	
I **will** I **am going to**			I **graduate**	
She **will** She **is going to**	get a job	**when**	she **graduates**	next June.
They **will** They **are going** to			they **graduate**	

YES/NO QUESTIONS				
MAIN CLAUSE			**TIME CLAUSE**	
Will I **Am** I **going to**			I **graduate**	
Will she **Is** she **going to**	get a job	**when**	she **graduates**	next June?
Will they **Are** they **going to**			they **graduate**	

SHORT ANSWERS		
AFFIRMATIVE		
Yes,	you	will. are.
	she	will. is.
	they	will. are.

SHORT ANSWERS		
NEGATIVE		
No,	you	won't. aren't.
	she	won't. isn't.
	they	won't. aren't.

WH- QUESTIONS					
MAIN CLAUSE			**TIME CLAUSE**		
Where	**will** I **am** I **going to**		I **graduate**	
	will she **is** she **going to**	get a job	**when**	she **graduates**	next June?
	will they **are** they **going to**		they **graduate**	

Grammar Notes

1. When a sentence about the future has two clauses, the verb in the main clause is often in the future (*will*, or *be going to*). The verb in the time clause is often in the present tense.

They**'ll look for** a job   **when they graduate**.
    main clause   time clause

OR

When they graduate,   they**'ll look for** a job.
    time clause   main clause

Be careful! Do not use the future in a time clause.

     NOT ~~when they will graduate~~

Notice that the time clause *(when they graduate)* can come at the beginning or the end of the sentence. The meaning is the same. Use a comma after the time clause when it comes at the beginning. Do not use a comma when it comes at the end.

2. Here are some common time expressions you can use to begin future time clauses:

a. *When*, *after*, and *as soon as* often introduce the event that happens first.

As soon as I graduate, I'm going to look for a job.
(First I'm going to graduate. Then I'll look for a job.)

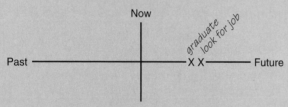

b. *Before*, *until*, and *by the time* often introduce the event that happens second.

Before I get a job, I'll finish school.
I won't get a job **until** I finish school.
By the time I get a job, I'll be out of school.
(First I'll finish school. Then I'll get a job.)

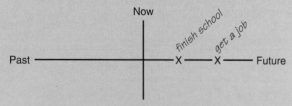

c. *While* introduces an event that will happen at the same time as another event.

While I look for a job, I'll continue to study.

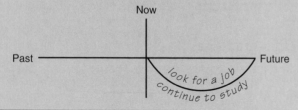

FOCUSED PRACTICE

1. Discover the Grammar

Read the first sentence in each set. Then circle the letter of the sentences whose meaning is similar.

1. Irene will open her own business when she finishes school.
   a. Irene will open her own business. Then she'll finish school.
   (b.) Irene will finish school. Then she'll open her own business.

2. Harry won't quit until he finds another job.
   (a.) Harry will find another job. Then he'll quit.
   b. Harry will quit. Then he'll find another job.

3. Jake will retire as soon as he turns sixty.
   a. Jake will retire. Then he'll turn sixty.
   (b.) Jake will turn sixty. Then he'll retire.

4. After the Morrisons sell their house, they'll move to Florida.
   (a.) The Morrisons will sell their house. Then they'll move to Florida.
   b. The Morrisons will move to Florida. Then they'll sell their house.

5. Brenda will call you when she gets home.
   a. Brenda will call you. Then she'll get home.
   (b.) Brenda will get home. Then she'll call you.

6. Janice and Bill are going to look for an apartment before they get married.
   a. Janice and Bill are going to get married. Then they'll look for an apartment.
   (b.) Janice and Bill are going to look for an apartment. Then they'll get married.

7. While Li-jing is in school, she'll work part-time.
   a. Li-jing will go to school. Then she'll get a part-time job.
   (b.) Li-jing will go to school. At the same time she'll have a part-time job.

8. By the time Marsha gets her diploma, she'll be twenty-one.
   a. Marsha will get her diploma. Then she'll turn twenty-one.
   (b.) Marsha will turn twenty-one. Then she'll get her diploma.

2. What Next?

Combine these sentences.

1. Sandy and Jeff will get married. Then Sandy will graduate.

   Sandy and Jeff will get married before Sandy graduates.

2. Jeff is going to get a raise. Then they are going to move to a larger apartment.

   to increase

   _____ as soon as _____.

3. They're going to move to a larger apartment. Then they're going to have a baby.

   After _____.

(continued on next page)

4. They'll have their first child. Then Sandy will get a part-time job.

_____ after _____ .

5. Their child will be two. Then Sandy will go back to work full-time.

By the time _____ .

6. Sandy will work full-time, and Jeff will go to school.

_____ while _____ .

7. Jeff will graduate. Then he'll find another job.

_____ when _____ .

3. Looking Ahead

Complete this student's letter to a friend. Use the correct form of the verbs in parentheses.

Dear Elise,

Hi. How are you? There's only a month before graduation.

I can't wait! I'm writing to you now because until my exams

_____**are**_____ over I _____won't have_____ any
1. (be)   **2. (not have)**

free time.

After I ___graduate___ , I ___'ll take___
    3. (graduate)   **4. (take)**

some computer classes. I want to learn word processing so I can get a job.

I really have to earn some money. As soon as I ___learn___
                                  5. (learn)

word processing, I ___will look___ for a job as a bilingual
                  6. (look)

office assistant. I'm a little worried. People say it's not easy to find

jobs now. I guess until I ___get___ a full-time job,
                       7. (get)

I ___'ll try___ to find some part-time work.
    8. (try)

What about you? What ___are___ you

___going to do___ when you ___will finish___ school?
   9. (do)   **10. (finish)**

___Are___ you ___going to take___ a vacation
                        11. (take)

before you ___look___ for a job?
        12. (look)

Write soon! I miss you.

                    Love,

                    Rosa

COMMUNICATION PRACTICE

4. Practice Listening

A woman is calling Jobs Are Us Employment Agency. Listen. Read the sentences that follow. Then listen again and number the events in order.

a. _4_ speak to job counselor

b. _2_ have interview at agency

c. _1_ send resume

d. _5_ receive more job training

e. _6_ go to companies

f. _3_ take word-processing test

5. The Next Step

Fill out this questionnaire. Check the appropriate boxes.

When I finish this course, I'm going to

☐ take another English course.

☐ apply to another school.

☐ look for a new job.

☐ take some time off.

☐ go on a vacation.

☐ move to another city.

☐ Other: _____.

Now work in small groups. Take a survey. What are your classmates going to do when they finish this course? Compare your answers with the other groups' answers.

Example:
Ten students are going to take another English course.
Two students are going to look for a new job.

6. Until Then

Complete these three sentences. Then compare your answers with your classmates' answers. How many different answers are there?

a. I'm going to continue studying English until _____

b. While I'm in this class, _____

c. I'll stay in this country until _____

Example:
I'm going to continue studying English until I pass the TOEFL® exam.

7. Interview

Work with a partner. Interview him or her about some future plans. Ask questions such as

What will you do when . . . ?

Where will you go after . . . ?

Will you . . . while you . . . ?

Take notes and then write a short paragraph about your classmate's plans.

Example:
Soo Mi is going to get married next year. Before she gets married, she's going to return home to visit her family. While she's away, she'll miss her boyfriend, but she'll write him every day.

I. *Complete the weather forecast with* will *or* won't *and the verbs in parentheses.*

There _____will be_____ heavy showers early today, so
<u>1. (be)</u>
get out your raincoat and umbrella. You ___will need___
<u>2. (need)</u>
them this morning. The rains ___won't continue___, however.
<u>3. (continue)</u>
They ___will stop___ at around 1:00, and the sky
<u>4. (stop)</u>
___will stay___ clear all afternoon. The weekend looks good too,
<u>5. (stay)</u>
so you ___won't need___ that umbrella Saturday or Sunday either. It
<u>6. (need)</u>
looks like we ___will have___ clear and sunny weather both days.
<u>7. (have)</u>

II. *Circle the letters of the correct verb forms to complete the conversation.*

A: Good morning, Sheri. This is Gloria. I _____ coming to the
office today. Did anyone call?
1. (a.)'m not   c. not
   b. don't be   d. will

B: Yes, Mr. Jenkins called. He ___'ll call___ back this afternoon.
2. a. 'll call   c. was calling
   b. calls   d. called

A: Anyone else?

B: Kim Frazer. She ___won't be___ at the meeting tomorrow.
3. a. isn't   c. won't be
   b. wasn't   d. doesn't

A: What's wrong? Is she sick?

B: No, but she ___is going to be___ out of town tomorrow.
4. a. 's going to be   c. was
   b. went   d. go

A: By the way, what time is that meeting tomorrow morning?

B: It ___starts___ at 10:00.
5. a. started   c. was starting
   b. start   d. starts

III. *There are seven verb errors related to the future. Find them and circle them.*

Dear Dana,

Here are our travel plans, so you can keep in touch. We'll be in San Juan on July 20. Our plane (arrive) at about 8:00. We are stay at the Royal Vista, Room 2010. I'm going to seeing the sights and swim, and your father is going to attends some meetings. We'll stay until he will finish his work. I send you some postcards. We'll probably go to Rio on August 1. I tell you the name of our hotel as soon as I find out.

Love,
Mom

IV. *Write a question for each answer. Put the words in parentheses in the correct order to write the questions.*

1. (where/on July 4/you/be/will?)

    A: _____ Where will you be on July 4? _____

    B: Let me look at my ticket. I'll be in Paris.

2. (you/are/leaving/when?)

    A:_____

    B: 10:00 P.M. on July 3.

3. Really? (taking/what flight/you/are?)

    A:_____

    B: Air France, flight number 888.

4. (it/arrive/does/when?)

    A:_____

    B: At 7:00 in the morning.

5. (to your hotel/you/are/a taxi/going to/take?)

    A:_____

    B: You sure ask a lot of questions!

V. *Complete the conversation with the correct words.*

1. **A:** Do you and Nora have plans for the weekend?

    B: Yes, we do. We _____ a concert on Saturday. I just bought the tickets.
    ('re going to / 'll go to)

2. **A:** I can't believe I got into medical school.

    B: You _____ a doctor in just a few years.
    (are / 'll be)

3. **A:** Oh, no! I forgot to deposit my paycheck yesterday.

   B: I _____ deposit it for you. It's on my way.
   (*'m going to / 'll*)

4. **A:** Take your umbrella. It _____ rain.
   (*'s going to / 'll*)
   B: Thanks for telling me. I didn't hear the weather report.

5. **A:** My daughter is really interested in science fiction.

   B: Maybe she _____ a career in space exploration when she grows up.
   (*has / 'll have*)

VI. *Complete the sentences with the correct form of the verbs in parentheses.*
Use will *in one clause of each sentence.*

1. Nora _____will need_____ some new furniture when she _____moves_____ into her new
   (*need*)   (*move*)
   apartment.

2. As soon as you _____ to Franklin Street, you _____ the library.
   (*get*)   (*see*)

3. We _____ here tonight until we _____ the monthly report.
   (*stay*)   (*finish*)

4. After he _____ next June, he _____ in the city.
   (*graduate*)   (*work*)

5. I _____ the newspaper while I _____ breakfast.
   (*read*)   (*eat*)

6. As soon as they _____ enough money, they _____ a computer.
   (*save*)   (*buy*)

Present Perfect

11

Present Perfect: *For* and *Since*

INTRODUCTION

Read and listen to this biographical excerpt.

West German-born Steffi Graf (1969 –   ) **has been** a tennis player **for more than twenty years**. She began playing amateur tennis at the age of four and **has played** professionally **since 1981. Since 1987** she **has won** several major tournaments including Wimbledon and the French and U.S. Opens. Today Graf is considered one of the top tennis players in the world.

PRESENT PERFECT: *FOR* AND *SINCE*

STATEMENTS				
SUBJECT	**HAVE/HAS (NOT)**	**PAST PARTICIPLE OF VERB**		**FOR/SINCE**
I You* We They	**have**	**been**† **played**	here	**for** a long time. **since** May.
He She It	**has**			

YES/NO QUESTIONS				
HAVE/HAS	**SUBJECT**	**PAST PARTICIPLE OF VERB**		**FOR/SINCE**
Have	I you* we they	**been**† **played**	here	**for** a long time? **since** May?
Has	he she it			

SHORT ANSWERS		
AFFIRMATIVE		
Yes,	you I/we you they	**have.**
	he she it	**has.**

SHORT ANSWERS		
NEGATIVE		
No,	you I/we you they	**haven't.**
	he she it	**hasn't.**

WH- QUESTIONS				
WH- WORD	**HAVE/HAS**	**SUBJECT**	**PAST PARTICIPLE**	
How long	**have**	I you* we they	**been**† **played**	here?
	has	he she it		

SHORT ANSWERS
For a few months. **Since** January.

(continued on next page)

* *You* is both singular and plural.

† *Been* is an irregular past participle. See Grammar Notes and Appendix 1 on page A1 for a list of irregular verbs.

CONTRACTIONS								CONTRACTIONS	
AFFIRMATIVE								**NEGATIVE**	
I have	=	I've	they have	=	they've	she has	=	she's
you have	=	you've	he has	=	he's	it has	=	it's
we have	=	we've						

CONTRACTIONS
NEGATIVE
have not = haven't
has not = hasn't

Grammar Notes

1. Use the present perfect with *for* or *since* to talk about something that began in the past <u>and continues into the present</u> (and may continue into the future).

> Steffi Graf **has played** tennis **since 1973**. She **has played for over twenty years**.
> (She began playing over twenty years ago, in 1973, and still plays now.)

2. Use the present perfect with *since* and a point in time <u>(since 5:00, since Monday, since New Year's Eve, since yesterday)</u> to show when something started.

> Graf **has been** a champion **since 1987**.

3. *Since* can also introduce a time clause.
Notice that the verb in the *since* clause is in the simple past tense.

> She has won many tournaments **since she began** her professional career.

Remember that a time clause can come at the beginning or end of a sentence.

4. Use the present perfect with *for* and a length of time <u>(for ten minutes, for two weeks, for years, for a long time)</u> to show how long a present condition has been true.

> Sports enthusiasts **have admired** Steffi Graf **for many years**.

5. The present perfect is formed with *have* or *has* + the past participle.

The regular form of the past participle is the base form of the verb + *-d* or *-ed*. This form is the same as the simple past form of the verb. There are many irregular past participles, however. Some common ones are listed here. There is a more complete list in Appendix 1 on page A1.

Base Form of the Verb	Past Participle	Base Form of the Verb	Past Participle	Base Form of the Verb	Past Participle	Base Form of the Verb	Past Participle
be	been	hang	hung	run	run	get	gotten
see	seen	sing	sung	come	come	give	given
bring	brought	sell	sold	do	done	take	taken
buy	bought	tell	told	go	gone	write	written
meet	met	put	put	win	won	find	found
sleep	slept	read	read	drive	driven	have	had
				eat	eaten	make	made

FOCUSED PRACTICE

1. Discover the Grammar

Read the situations. Then circle the letter of the more appropriate way to complete the sentences.

1. Sherry has played tennis since 1990. Sherry
   ⓐ still plays tennis.
   b. doesn't play tennis these days.
2. She has had long hair since she was a little girl. She
   a. has short hair now.
   b. has long hair now.
3. She's lived in the same apartment for ten years. She
   a. lived in a different apartment eleven years ago.
   b. moved a few years ago.
4. Sherry and Richard have been married for twenty-five years. They
   a. got married twenty-five years ago.
   b. are not married now.
5. They haven't been on a vacation since 1990. They
   a. were on a vacation in 1990.
   b. are on a vacation now.
6. Sherry hasn't won a tennis championship for two years. Sherry
   a. won a championship two years ago.
   b. didn't win a championship two years ago.

2. Winners

Look at these tennis sports statistics. Use short answers to answer the questions.

U.S. Open Champions—Doubles

Year	Women	Year	Men
1988	Gigi Fernandez and Robin White	1988	Sergio Casal and Emilio Sanchez
1989	Hana Mandlikova and Martina Navratilova	1989	John McEnroe and Mark Woodforde
1990	Gigi Fernandez and Martina Navratilova	1990	Pieter Aldrich and Danie Visser
1991	Pam Shriver and Natalia Zvereva	1991	John Fitzgerald and Anders Jarryd
1992	Gigi Fernandez and Natalia Zvereva	1992	Jim Grabb and Richey Reneberg

Source: The 1992 Information Please Almanac

1. Robin White won the U.S. Open Doubles Championship in 1988. Has she won again since then?

   _____ No, she hasn't. _____

2. Martina Navratilova won in 1989. Has she won again since then?

   _____

(continued on next page)

3. Sergio Casal and Emilio Sanchez won the U.S. Open Doubles Championship in 1988. Have they won again since 1988?

_____

4. Anders Jarryd won in 1987. Has he won again since then?

_____

5. Gigi Fernandez and Martina Navratilova won in 1990. Have they won as partners since then?

_____

6. Has Gigi Fernandez won since 1990?

_____

7. John McEnroe won in 1989. Has he won again since then?

_____

3. Child Genius

Read this magazine excerpt and complete it with for *or* since.

Thirteen-year-old Ronnie Segal has loved math _____*since*_____ he was a little boy. When I asked him
1.

about his passion for numbers, Ronnie replied, "I have been interested in them _____ nine
2.

years, five months, three weeks, and two days." _____ the past two years, Ronnie has
3.

attended graduate-level classes at a local university. _____ January he has taken five
4.

extremely difficult exams in number theory and has gotten 100% on all of them. _____ Ronnie
5.

began classes, he has met an average of 1.324 people a month. And what about his future plans?

Thirteen-year-old Ronnie has known _____ many years that he is going to become a famous
6.

math professor, get married, and have exactly 2.2 children.

4. A Resume

Rosa Rodriguez is applying for a job as a college sports instructor. Look at her resume and the interviewer's notes. Complete the interview. Use the words in parentheses to write questions. Then answer the questions. The year is 1994.

Rosa Rodriguez
2136 East Travis Street
San Antonio, Texas 78284

Education:

1990 Certificate (American College of Sports Medicine)
1989 MA Physical Education (University of Texas) *moved to San Antonio in 1983*

Employment:

1989–present   part-time physical education teacher
(high school)

1987–present   sports trainer (private) *teaches tennis, swimming*

Skills:

speak Spanish, English, and French

self-defense *—started classes 2 mos. ago*

Awards:

1990 Teacher of the Year Award

1987 Silver Medal in Texas Tennis Competition

Memberships:

1990–present   member of National Education Association (NEA)

1. (How long/live in San Antonio?)

Interviewer: _How long have you lived in San Antonio?_

Rosa: _I've lived in San Antoino for 11 years._

OR

I've lived in San Antonio since 1983.

2. (How long/have your MA degree?)

Interviewer: _____

Rosa: _____

(continued on next page)

3. (have any more training since you got your MA?)

Interviewer: _____

    Rosa: _____

4. (How long/be a physical education teacher?)

Interviewer: _____

    Rosa: _____

5. (How long/be a sports trainer?)

Interviewer: _____

    Rosa: _____

6. (How long/take classes in self-defense?)

Interviewer: _____

    Rosa: _____

7. (win any awards since then?)

Interviewer: I see you won a tennis award. _____

    Rosa: I won the Teacher of the Year Award in 1990.

8. (How long/be a member of the NEA?)

Interviewer: _____

    Rosa: _____

COMMUNICATION PRACTICE

5. Practice Listening

John Baker is looking for a job as an electrical engineer at Weston Industries. Listen to his interview. Listen again and circle the best way to complete the statements that follow. The date is June 1994.

1. John has been an electrical engineer for (8, (14,) 5) years.

2. He's been at the same company since (1970, 1980, 1990).

3. He's been married since (1980, 1992, he became an engineer).

4. John has lived in Los Angeles for at least (one year, two years, three years).

5. He's only seen his wife's family once since (they got married, the job interview, Christmas).

6. A Job Interview

Write a resume. Use Rosa's resume on page 101 as an example. You can use real or imaginary information. Then, role play a job interview with a partner. Take turns being the interviewer and the candidate. Use the script below to help you complete the interview.

Example:
A: How long have you been a lab technician?
B: I've been a lab technician for five years.

Interviewer: How long have you been a(n) _____?

Candidate: I've _____

Interviewer: And how many jobs have you had since _____?

Candidate: I've _____

Interviewer: I see from your resume that you live in _____
How long have you lived there?

Candidate: _____

Interviewer: Your English is quite good.
How long have you studied it?

Candidate: _____

Interviewer: How long _____?

Candidate: _____

Interviewer: Well, thank you very much. We'll be in touch with you.

7. The Best Person for the Job

A business college is going to hire a new math teacher. Look at these two resumes. In small groups, decide who to hire and why. Use for *and* since *in discussing their qualifications. Here are some things to consider: years of teaching experience, number of jobs, number and types of classes, awards, and number of published articles.*

Examples:
 A: Allen Baker has had the same job since he got his Ph.D.
 B: Erika Jones has a lot of experience. She's been a teacher since 1970.

Allen Baker	Erika Jones
Education: 1984 Ph.D. in Mathematics (UCLA) **Teaching Experience:** 1984–present Bryant College **Courses Taught:** Algebra Trigonometry Calculus Business Mathematics **Publications:** "Introducing Computers into the College Math Class" (*The Journal of Mathematics*, 1986) **Awards:** Teacher of the Year 1986 Distinguished Professor 1993	**Education:** 1970 Ph.D. in Mathematics (UCLA) **Teaching Experience:** 1990–present NYC Technical College 1985–1989 UCLA 1976–1984 University of Wisconsin, Madison 1973–1975 Brown University 1970–1972 UCLA **Courses Taught:** Mathematical Analysis 1 Mathematical Analysis 2 **Publications:** "Imaginary numbers" (*MJS*, 1975) "Number Theory" (*Mathematics*, 1976) "How real are real numbers?" (*Math Education*, 1978)

INTRODUCTION

🔊 *Read and listen to this excerpt from an article in the science section of a newspaper.*

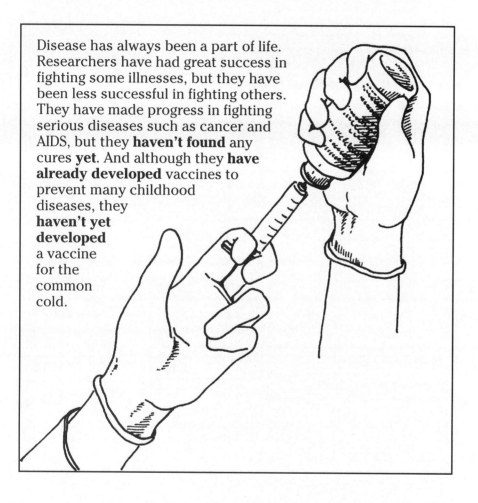

Disease has always been a part of life. Researchers have had great success in fighting some illnesses, but they have been less successful in fighting others. They have made progress in fighting serious diseases such as cancer and AIDS, but they **haven't found** any cures **yet**. And although they **have already developed** vaccines to prevent many childhood diseases, they **haven't yet developed** a vaccine for the common cold.

PRESENT PERFECT: *ALREADY* AND *YET*

AFFIRMATIVE STATEMENTS: *ALREADY*				
SUBJECT	***HAVE/HAS***	***ALREADY***	**PAST PARTICIPLE OF VERB**	
They	**have**	**already**	**developed**	a polio vaccine.
It	**has**		**helped**	a lot of people.

See pages 97 and 98 in Unit 11 for a complete presentation of present perfect forms.

NEGATIVE STATEMENTS: *YET*				
SUBJECT	***HAVE NOT/ HAS NOT***	**PAST PARTICIPLE OF VERB**		***YET***
They	**haven't**	**discovered**	a cure for AIDS	**yet.**
It	**hasn't**	**reached**	epidemic proportions	

YES/NO QUESTIONS: *YET*				
HAVE/HAS	**SUBJECT**	**PAST PARTICIPLE OF VERB**		***YET***
Have	they	**found**	a cure for AIDS	**yet?**
Has	it	**reached**	epidemic proportions	

SHORT ANSWERS		
AFFIRMATIVE		
Yes,	they	**have.**
	it	**has.**

SHORT ANSWERS		
NEGATIVE		
No,	they	**haven't.**
	it	**hasn't.**
No, not yet.		

Grammar Notes

1. We often use the present perfect with *already* in affirmative sentences to talk about events that happened some time <u>before now</u>. It is possible that the event happened earlier than expected.

  A: Is your daughter going to get her vaccination?
  B: She**'s already gotten** it.

Be careful! Do not use the present perfect with *already* when you mention a specific past point in time or a past time expression. DON'T SAY ~~They've already discovered a vaccine against measles in 1954.~~

Already usually comes between *have/has* and the main verb, but it can also come at the end of the sentence.

  Researchers **have already discovered** cures for many diseases.
  They**'ve made** a lot of progress **already**.

2. Use the present perfect with *not yet* to talk about events that have not happened <u>before now</u>. It is possible that we expected the event to have happened earlier, and it is still possible that the event will happen in the future.

  They **haven't discovered** a cure for the common cold **yet**, but they hope to discover one in the future.
  They **haven't yet discovered** a cure for the common cold.

Notice that *yet* usually comes at the end of the clause. But it can also come between *have not/has not* and the main verb.

3. We usually use *yet* in questions to find out if something has happened <u>before now</u>.

  Has your daughter **gotten** her measles vaccine **yet**?

Sometimes we use *already* in a question to express surprise that something happened sooner than expected.

  Has she **already** gotten all her shots? She's only four years old.

FOCUSED PRACTICE

1. Discover the Grammar

Match the cause with the result.

Cause	Result
_e_ 1. She hasn't met her new neighbors yet, so she	a. really hungry.
____ 2. He's already seen this movie, so he	b. can tell you all about it.
____ 3. We've already had lunch, so we	c. don't know the ending.
____ 4. She hasn't arrived at work yet, so I guess	d. aren't very hungry.
____ 5. I haven't read the book yet, so I	e. doesn't know their names.
____ 6. She hasn't had lunch yet, so she's	f. the train is late.

2. Hard to Please

David's been home with a bad cold. His friend Laura has come to visit him and is trying to cheer him up. Complete their conversation with the present perfect form of the verbs in parentheses and already *or* yet.

Laura: Would you like a cup of tea?

David: Thanks, but I __'ve already had__ four cups.
     1. (have)

Laura: _____ you _____ at today's paper _____?
                           2. (look)

I bought one for you.

David: Oh really? Thanks, but I _____ two papers and three magazines this morning.
                    3. (read)

Laura: OK. How about renting a video, then? I hear that *Red Velvet* is available now.

David: No, I don't think so. I _____ it.
                    4. (see)

Laura: Are you hungry? We can order a pizza.

David: No, thanks. I'm not hungry. I _____.
                    5. (eat)

Laura: Well, is there anything you _____?
                    6. (not do)

David: Yes. I _____ a nap _____, and I'd really love to do that.
              7. (not take)

Laura: OK, I'm out of here. I'll call you later.

3. | Medical Record

Look at this baby's immunization chart. Use the words in parentheses to write sentences with the present perfect and already *or* yet.

LIFETIME IMMUNIZATIONS

NAME: Mary West

		(2 mos.)	(4 mos.)	(6 mos.)	(15–18 mos.)	(4–6 yrs.)
		Date Given	Date Given	Date Given	Date Given	Date Given
D P T	Diphtheria Pertussis Tetanus	8/14/92	10/2/92	12/16/92		
P O L I O		8/14/92	10/2/92	12/16/92		

(12–15 mos.)		Date Given		Date Given		(18–24 mos.)		Date Given
M M R	Measles Mumps Rubella	6/19/93				Hemophilus Influenzae Type B (Hib)		

(Booster every 10 yrs.)		Date	Date	Date
Tetanus Diphtheria				

1. (Mrs. West/take Mary to the doctor)

   Mrs. West has already taken Mary to the doctor.

2. (The doctor/give/Mary her 15–18-month DPT injection)

   The doctor hasn't given Mary her 15–18-month DPT injection yet.

3. (Mary/get her 6-month DPT injection)

   _____

4. (Mary/receive/15–18-month polio immunization)

   _____

5. (Mary/be to the doctor for her MMR immunization)

   _____

6. (She/get a tetanus booster)

   _____

7. (The doctor/vaccinate Mary against the mumps)

   _____

8. (Mary/receive /Hib vaccine)

   _____

COMMUNICATION PRACTICE

4. Practice Listening

🎞 *David and Laura are going to watch a movie on TV. Listen to their conversation. Listen again and check the movies Laura has already seen.*

Laura has seen:

1. ✔ *Superman*
2. ☐ *Ghostbusters*
3. ☐ *E.T.*
4. ☐ *Annie Hall*
5. ☐ *Crocodile Dundee*
6. ☐ *Rambo*

5. Chores

Laura wanted to do these things in her bedroom.

1. make the bed
2. vacuum the carpet
3. wash the windows
4. put her clothes away
5. hang some pictures
6. paint the walls
7. fix the doorknob
8. buy a new lamp

Work in pairs. Look at the picture. Ask and answer questions about Laura's chores.

Example:
A: Has she vacuumed the carpet yet?
B: No, not yet. OR No, she hasn't.

6. What About You?

Write a list of things that you planned or wanted to do by this time (for example: find a new job, paint the apartment). Include things that you have already done and things that you haven't done yet. Exchange lists with a classmate and ask and answer questions about the items on the lists.

Example:
A: Have you found a new job yet?
B: No, not yet. I'm still looking.
OR
Yes, I have.

7. Inventions and Discoveries

Work in pairs. Decide together if the following things have already happened or have not happened yet. Check the appropriate column. Discuss your answers with your classmates.

Example:
A: They haven't discovered a cure for the common cold yet.
B: They've already found a test for the virus that causes AIDS, but they haven't found a cure yet.

	Already	Not Yet
1. a cure for the common cold	☐	✔
2. a test for the AIDS virus	✔	☐
3. a successful heart transplant (animal to human)	☐	☐
4. a successful heart transplant (human to human)	☐	☐
5. a vaccine to prevent tooth decay (cavities)	☐	☐
6. a pillow that prevents snoring	☐	☐
7. liquid sunglasses (in the form of eyedrops)	☐	☐
8. electric cars	☐	☐
9. flying cars	☐	☐
10. light bulbs that can last fourteen years	☐	☐

Add your own inventions and discoveries.

	Already	Not Yet
11. _____	☐	☐
12. _____	☐	☐
13. _____	☐	☐

INTRODUCTION

Read and listen to a short excerpt from a movie star's journal entry.

I've just won the National Acting Award! Now I'm famous! I cannot believe it! Newspaper reporters ask, *"Have you ever had* doubts about your success?" Of course, I *have.* Even though I*'ve been* on every talk show at least twice in the last few months, and my face *has appeared* on the cover of ten major magazines, I still ask myself, "Is it really me standing in front of all those cameras?"

I've worked very hard, but I*'ve* also *done* many wonderful things. *I've traveled* all over the world and *met* many famous people. *I've been* to five of the seven continents. I*'ve* even *eaten* dinner with the president of the United States and the queen of England. It*'s been* great, but I have many more dreams.

PRESENT PERFECT: INDEFINITE PAST

STATEMENTS			
SUBJECT	**HAVE/HAS (NOT)**	**PAST PARTICIPLE OF VERB**	
They	**have (not)**	**appeared**	**on TV.**
It	**has (not)**	**been**	

See pages 97 and 98 in Unit 11 for a complete presentation of present perfect forms.

YES/NO QUESTIONS			
HAVE/HAS	**SUBJECT**	**PAST PARTICIPLE OF VERB**	
Have	they	**appeared**	**on TV?**
Has	it	**been**	

SHORT ANSWERS	
AFFIRMATIVE	
Yes,	they **have.** it **has.**

SHORT ANSWERS	
NEGATIVE	
No,	they **haven't.** it **hasn't.**

WH- QUESTIONS				
WH- WORD	**HAVE/HAS**	**SUBJECT**	**PAST PARTICIPLE OF VERB**	
How often	**have**	they	**appeared**	**on TV?**
	has	it	**been**	

Grammar Notes

1. Use the present perfect to talk about things that happened at an <u>indefinite time</u> in the past. You can use the present perfect when you don't know when something happened, when you do not want to be specific, or when the specific time is not important.

>   I**'ve traveled** all over the world.

2. You can use *ever* with the present perfect to ask questions. It means at <u>any time up until the present</u>.

>   Have you **ever** seen a Broadway show?

Use *never* to answer negatively.

>   No, I've **never** seen one.
>   OR
>   No, **never**.

3. Use the present perfect with certain adverbs of time to emphasize that something happened in the <u>very recent</u> (but still indefinite) <u>past</u>.

>   I've **recently** won the National Acting Award.
>   We've **just** returned from a trip around the world.
>   She hasn't had much leisure time **lately**.

Note that in spoken American English people often use *just* and *recently* with the simple past tense to refer to indefinite time.

>   I **just returned** from a trip around the world.

4. Use the present perfect to talk about repeated actions at some <u>indefinite</u> time in the past.

>   She**'s been** on a lot of talk shows
>   over the past few weeks.
>   I**'ve seen** her movies many times.

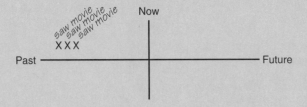

FOCUSED PRACTICE

1. Discover the Grammar

Read the first sentence. Then decide whether the second sentence is true (T) or false (F).

_T_   1. I've recently come to this country.
          I am a newcomer.

_____   2. I have never been to Switzerland.
          I went to Switzerland a long time ago.

_____   3. I've just finished the book.
          I finished it a little while ago.

_____   4. John asks, "Have you ever seen this movie?"
          John wants to know when you saw the movie.

_____   5. Debbie asks you, "Have you read any good books lately?"
          Debbie wants to know about a book you read last year.

_____   6. She's visited New York several times.
          This is her first visit to New York.

_____   7. She has become very pretty.
          She is pretty now.

2. Blind Date

Marge and Bill are on a blind date—they have never met before. Complete the sentences, using the present perfect form of the verbs in the box. The verbs can be used more than once.

want	be	travel	live	take

Marge: I'm not sure about this. I __'ve___ never ___been___ on a blind date like this
1.

        before. I mean I don't even know you, and here we are all alone.

Bill: Well, does it make you feel better to know that I _____ never _____ a
2.

        woman to such a fancy restaurant on a first date?

Marge: I guess so. It's really a lovely restaurant! Tell me about yourself, Bill.

Bill: OK. I _____ in Philadelphia all my life.
3.

Marge: _____ you ever _____ to live outside of Philadelphia?
4.

Bill: No. I _____ never _____ to try any other place. I like it here.
5.

(continued on next page)

Marge: Well, _____ you _____ a lot?

6.

Bill: No, traveling is definitely not for me. I really like it here, don't you?

Marge: It's OK here, but I _____ in many different countries. It's a big world out there,

7.
you know.

Bill: Philadelphia is good enough for me. I don't want to go anywhere else, but I do want to see you again. How about dinner tomorrow night? Same time, same place.

Marge: Well . . .

3. Mother's Day

A brother and sister are making plans for Mother's Day. They want to do something different this year, so they are trying to remember what they did in past years. Use the words below to write questions and answers. Use ever *with the questions and, when appropriate, use* never *with the answers.*

1. we/have/a picnic in the park?

   Have we ever had a picnic in the park?

   No, we've never had a picnic in the park.

2. Mom/go/to that new restaurant on Charles Street?

   Has Mom ever gone to that new restaurant on Charles Street?

   Yes, she has.

3. we/bring/her/breakfast in bed?

   _____

   No, _____

4. we/buy/her tickets for a show?

   _____

   No, _____

5. Mom/take/a boat trip?

   _____

   Yes, _____

6. we/forget/about Mother's Day?

   _____

   No, _____

7. Mom/complain/about her present?

   _____

   No, _____

4. All in a Day's Work

Look at the pictures of moments in the life of a movie star. Write a sentence describing each picture. Use the words in the box.

- just/return from a trip
- not have/much rest/lately
- see/this movie/many times before
✔ just/finish her exercise class
- win/the National Acting Award/many times
- recently/film her first TV talk show

1. ___She's just finished her exercise class.___   2. _____

3. _____   4. _____

5. _____   6. _____

5. Interview with a Movie Star

Read the short excerpt from a movie star's journal on page 112. Imagine you are interviewing the star. Ask and answer questions about her recent life.

1. **Interviewer:** I understand you've received some awards recently.

   Which awards have you won?
   _____
   (Which awards/win?)

   Star: Well, I've just won the National Acting Award.

2. **Interviewer:** And you've appeared on so many talk shows lately.

   _____
   (Which shows/be on?)

   Star: Oh, I can't remember all their names,

   but _____

3. **Interviewer:** I've seen your face on so many magazine covers.

   Exactly_____
   (how many covers/appear on?)

   Star: _____

4. **Interviewer:** _____
   (Where/travel?)

   Star: _____

5. **Interviewer:** _____
   (What famous people/meet?)

   Star: _____

6. **Interviewer:** _____
   (How many continents/visit?)

   Star: _____

COMMUNICATION PRACTICE

6. Practice Listening

🔲🔲 *Lynette Long is a movie star. She is talking to her travel agent about different vacation possibilities. The travel agent is asking questions about where she has traveled before. Read the choices that follow. Listen to their conversation. Then listen again and check the best travel package for her.*

a. _____ Switzerland—$1,220 includes: round-trip ticket, five nights in a beautiful hotel, day trips in the mountains, fresh air, and lots of exercise

b. _____ Jamaica—$600 includes: round-trip ticket, six days and five nights in a beautiful hotel, all meals, lots of beaches

c. _____ Egypt—$2,500 includes: eight days and seven nights, beautiful hotel, all meals, bus tours to the pyramids

7. Have You Ever?

Ask your classmates questions. Find out how many people have ever done any of the following things. If the answer is yes, *ask more questions. Get the stories behind the answers. Share your answers and stories with the class.*

• Meet a famous movie star
• Take a long trip by car
• Climb a mountain
• Dream in a foreign language
• Walk in the rain
• Drive cross-country

Add your own:

• _____

• _____

• _____

Example:
A: Have you ever met a famous movie star?
B: Yes, I have. I was visiting Hollywood, and I saw . . .

Contrast: Present Perfect and Simple Past Tense

INTRODUCTION

🔊 *Read and listen to this excerpt from an article in* Modern Day *magazine.*

COMMUTER MARRIAGES

Many modern marriages are finding interesting solutions to difficult problems. Take Joe and Maria Smith, for example. Joe and Maria **married** in June 1990. They **lived** in Detroit for three years. Then in 1993 Joe **got** a great job offer in Chicago. At the same time, Maria's company **moved** to Boston. They are still married, but they **have lived** apart ever since. They **have decided** to travel back and forth between Boston and Chicago until one of them finds a different job. Sociologists call this kind of marriage a "commuter marriage." "It **hasn't been** easy," says Maria. "Last month I **saw** Joe three times, but this month I**'ve** only **seen** him once."

CONTRAST: PRESENT PERFECT AND SIMPLE PAST TENSE

PRESENT PERFECT	SIMPLE PAST TENSE
She **has been** here since 1980.	She **arrived** here in 1980.

Grammar Notes

1. The present perfect is used to talk about things that started in the past, continue up to the present, and may continue into the future.

> They **have lived** apart for the past three years. (They started living apart three years ago and are still living apart.)

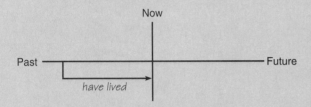

The simple past tense is used to talk about things that happened in the past and have no connection to the present.

> They **lived** in Detroit for three years. (They lived in Detroit until 1990. They no longer live in Detroit.)

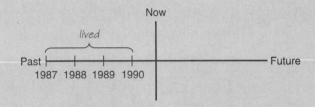

2. The present perfect is also used to talk about things that happened at an <u>unspecified</u> time in the past.

> They **have decided** to travel back and forth. (We don't know exactly when the decision was made, or the timing of the decision is not important.)

The simple past tense is used to talk about things that happened at a <u>specific</u> time in the past. The exact time is known and sometimes stated.

> They **lived** in Detroit **in 1990.**

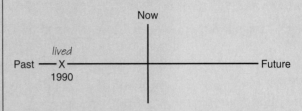

Be careful! Do not use specific past time expressions with the present perfect.

> I've lived in Detroit. NOT ~~I've lived in Detroit in 1990~~.

3. Use the present perfect to talk about things that have happened in a period of time that is not finished, such as *today, this month, this year*.

> She**'s had** three cups of coffee **this morning.** (It's still this morning, and it is possible that she will have some more.)

Use the simple past tense to talk about things that happened in a time period that is finished, such as *yesterday, last month, last year*.

> She **had** three cups of coffee **yesterday.** (Yesterday is finished.)

Be careful! Some time expressions like *this morning, this month,* or *this year* can refer to a finished or unfinished time period. Use the present perfect if the time period is unfinished. Use the simple past tense if the time period is finished.

> It's 10:00 A.M. She**'s had** three cups of coffee **this morning.** (The morning is not over.)
>
> It's 1:00 P.M. She **had** three cups of coffee **this morning.** (The morning is over. It is now afternoon.)

FOCUSED PRACTICE

1. Discover the Grammar

Read the information about Joe and Maria. Then circle the letter of the sentence (a or b) below that best describes the situation.

1. It's 1994. Joe's family moved to Houston in 1984. They still live there.
   a. Joe's family lived in Houston for ten years.
   b. Joe's family has lived in Houston for ten years.

2. Last year Joe and Maria enjoyed their vacation in Canada.
   a. They had a good time.
   b. They've had a good time.

3. Joe is telling his friend about his wife, Maria.
   a. His friend asks, "How long were you married?"
   b. His friend asks, "How long have you been married?"

4. Joe is telling Maria that the weather in Chicago has been cloudy and hot for the past five days.
   a. Five days ago the weather started to be cloudy and hot, and it is still that way.
   b. Sometime in the past year the weather was cloudy and hot for five days.

5. Joe studied the piano for ten years, but he doesn't play anymore.
   a. Joe has played the piano for ten years.
   b. Joe played the piano for ten years.

6. Maria wants to move to Chicago from Boston but must find a job first. She is interviewing for a job in Chicago.
   a. She says, "I lived in Boston for two years."
   b. She says, "I've lived in Boston for two years."

7. This month Maria and Joe have met once in Boston and once in Chicago and will meet once more in New York.
   a. They've seen each other twice.
   b. They saw each other twice.

2. Phone Conversation

Use the words in parentheses to complete the phone conversation between Maria and Joe. Use the present perfect or the simple past tense.

Joe: Hi, honey! How are you?

Maria: I'm OK—a little tired, I guess. I only _____slept_____ a few hours last night.
1. (sleep)

Joe: Why's that?

Maria: Oh, it's just work. I'm writing this big report for tomorrow's meeting, and I _____ worrying about it all week.
2. (not stop)

Joe: You need to rest. Listen—maybe I'll come see you this weekend. We _____
3. (only see)

each other twice this month. I think it might help you.

Maria: It might. But I really have to work. Remember the last time you _____ here? I
4. (come)

_____ any work at all.
5. (not do)

Joe: I know. But work isn't everything. I miss you, and I really want to come. OK?

Maria: Well . . .

Joe: Good! Now, why don't you go make yourself a cup of coffee and just relax.

Maria: Coffee! You must be kidding! I _____ five cups today. And yesterday I
6. (already have)

_____ at least six. No more coffee for me.
7. (drink)

Joe: Well then, get some rest, and I'll see you tomorrow.

Maria: OK. Good night!

3. An Interview

Read the magazine article on page 120 again. Pretend you wrote the article. You asked Joe and Maria questions to get your information. What were they? Use the words below and write the questions.

1. How long/be married?

_____How long have you been married?_____

2. How long/have your job?

_____

3. How long/live in Detroit?

_____

4. When/you get a job offer?

_____

(continued on next page)

5. When/your company move?

_____

6. How long/live apart?

_____

7. How often/see each other last month?

_____

8. How often/see each other this month?

_____

4. Changes

Joe and Maria met in the 1970s. Since then Joe has changed.
Use the words below and write down how Joe has changed.

In the 1970s	Since then
1. have/long hair	become/bald
2. be/skinny	grow/heavy
3. be/a student	become/successful businessman
4. work/factory	buy/his own business
5. live/in England	live/in Detroit and Chicago

1. In the 1970s Joe had long hair. _____

   Since then, he has become bald. _____

2. In the 1970s _____

   Since then, _____

3. _____

   _____

4. _____

   _____

5. _____

   _____

COMMUNICATION PRACTICE

5. Practice Listening

🔲🔲 *Listen to the radio talk show and read the transcript. Then listen again and circle the correct choice to complete the transcript.*

Host: Hello everyone, and thank you for tuning in to "Issues of the 90s."
_____We invited/We've invited_____ Dr. June Eastheimer to speak with us about issues in
1.
personal relationships. Get ready to call in with your questions. Caller Number 1, you're on
the air.

Caller 1: Hello, Dr. June. _____I had/I've had_____ three different girlfriends in one month. I
2.
only wanted to have one. What am I doing wrong?

Dr. June: ___Did you like/Have you liked___ any of your three girlfriends?
3.

Caller 1: No.

Dr. June: Then I hope you have a few more this month.

Caller 2: Dr. June, _____I was/I've been_____ married twelve times and . . .
4.

Dr. June: Did you say twelve times?

Caller 2: Yes, I did, and . . .

Dr. June: Next caller, please.

Caller 3: Hello, Dr. June. I always wanted/I've always wanted to ask you—How many times
5.
___were you/have you been___ married?
6.

Dr. June: I don't ask personal questions, and I don't answer them. Did you have any other questions?

Caller 3: Yes, I ___wasn't/haven't been___ happy for a long time. I think the last time I smiled was . . .
7.

Dr. June: ___Did you see/Have you seen___ a therapist to discuss this?
8.

Caller 3: No.

Dr. June: I think you should.

Now discuss these questions with your classmates.

Have you ever heard a personal advice talk show or read a personal advice column in the newspaper?
What kinds of questions did people ask?
What answers did the advisors give?
Do you think the callers were serious about these problems?
Do you think Dr. June has given helpful answers?

6. Marriage and Divorce

Look at the chart. Work in pairs and discuss the marriage and divorce statistics in the United States. Use the words in the box.

↑	increase get higher go up	decrease get lower go down ↓

	1980	1990
Marriage rate	2,406,708	1,182,000
Divorce rate	2,244,000	1,175,000

**Percentage of
    men (20–24)
    never married**
	68.8%	79.7%

**Percentage of
    women (20–24)
    never married**
	50.2%	64.1%

**Average age of
    first marriage:**
    men
    women
	
	24.7
	22.0
		
		26.1
		23.9

Source: Department of Commerce, Bureau of the Census and the Department of Health and Human Services, National Center for Human Statistics.

Example:
The marriage rate has decreased. In 1980, 2,406,708 people got married. In 1990 only 1,182,000 got married.

7. Looking Back

Work in pairs. Look at Maria's records from last year and this year. It's now the beginning of August. Compare what Maria did last year with what she's done this year.

LAST YEAR					
Jan.	Feb.	March	April	May	June
business trip to N.Y. Chicago–2x	Chicago–2x 1 seminar	business trip to L.A. Chicago–1x	Chicago–3x 1 lecture	10 vacation days Jay's wedding	2 seminars Chicago–2x
July	Aug.	Sept.	Oct.	Nov.	Dec.
Chicago–1x Sue's wedding	Chicago–1x	Chicago–2x 1 lecture	business trip to Little Rock	1 seminar	10 vacation days

THIS YEAR					
Jan.	Feb.	March	April	May	June
Chicago–1x	business trip to L.A. 1 lecture	Chicago–1x Nan's wedding	Chicago–1x	business trip to Miami Chicago–1x	5 vacation days 1 seminar
July	Aug.	Sept.	Oct.	Nov.	Dec.
Barry's wedding	Chicago–1x 1 lecture				

Example:
Last year she went on three business trips.
So far this year she's only gone on two.

8. A Country You Know Well

Work in small groups. Talk about a country you know well. Use the words or expressions in the box. Add your own dates.

for the past century	never	unemployment
since (1975)	(twenty) years ago	inflation
between (1980) and (1985)	for (fifty) years	civil war
ever	in (1992)	epidemic
already		Olympics
since I can remember		earthquake
when I was born		stock market crash
		peace

Examples:
When I was born, my country was in the middle of a civil war.
Since I can remember, there has never been serious inflation in my country.

INTRODUCTION

▶️ *A journalist **has been writing** a series of articles about the problem of homelessness in the United States. Read and listen to this second in a series of five articles.*

It **has been raining**. The ground is still wet. John Tarver **has been sitting** on the same park bench for hours. His clothes are soaked. A while ago someone gave him a cup of hot coffee. It's no longer warm, but John **has been drinking** it anyway.

John is just one of a possible three million Americans who **have been making** their homes in the streets, parks, and subway stations of our cities. The number of homeless men, women, and children **has been climbing** steadily since 1980 and will continue to rise until the government takes action.

PRESENT PERFECT PROGRESSIVE

STATEMENTS					
SUBJECT	**HAVE/HAS (NOT)**	**BEEN**	**BASE FORM OF VERB + -ING**		**(FOR/SINCE)**
I You* We They	**have (not)**	**been**	**sitting**	here	(**for** hours).
He She It	**has (not)**				(**since** 12:00).

* You is both singular and plural.

YES/NO QUESTIONS					
HAVE/HAS	SUBJECT	BEEN	BASE FORM OF VERB + -ING		(FOR/SINCE)
Have	I you* we they	been	sitting	here	(**for** an hour)? (**since** 12:00)?
Has	he she it				

SHORT ANSWERS		
AFFIRMATIVE		
Yes,	you I/we you they	have.
	he she it	has.

SHORT ANSWERS		
NEGATIVE		
No,	you I/we you they	haven't.
	he she it	hasn't.

WH- QUESTIONS					
WH- WORD	HAVE/HAS	SUBJECT	BEEN	BASE FORM OF VERB + ING	
How long	have	I you* we they	been	sitting	here?
	has	he she it			

SHORT ANSWERS
For a few hours. **Since** 9:00.

* *You* is both singular and plural.

Grammar Notes

1. Use the present perfect progressive (also called the present perfect continuous) to talk about an action or situation that began in the past and <u>continues to the present</u>. The action or situation is usually not finished. It is continuing, and it will probably continue into the future.

> It**'s been raining** all day. When is it going to stop?

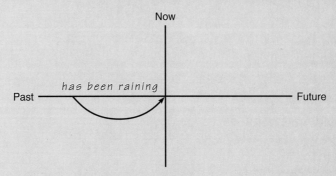

2. Also use the present perfect progressive for repeated actions that started in the past and continue up to the present time. Verbs that are frequently used in this way are: *hit, punch, knock, cough, jump, nod,* and *kick.*

> John **has been kicking** an empty can all morning.

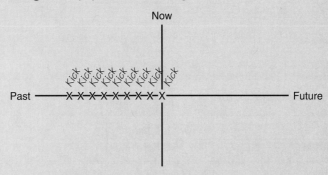

3. Use the present perfect progressive to describe actions that have stopped in the recent past. The action is not happening right now, but there are results of the action that <u>you can still see</u>.

> It**'s been raining.** The streets are still wet.
> John **has been** fighting. He has a black eye.

4. Use the present perfect progressive to talk about an action that is temporary or about to change.

> —Where do you live?
> —Well, I**'ve been living** in San Antonio, but I plan to move soon.

Be careful! Remember that non-action (stative) verbs are not usually used with the progressive (see page 20).

FOCUSED PRACTICE

1. Discover the Grammar

Read the first sentence in each set. Then circle the letter of the sentence (a *or* b) *that is true.*

1. John has been sitting on that park bench for hours.
   (a) He is still sitting on the park bench.
   b. He is no longer sitting on the park bench.
2. We've been living in San Antonio for ten years.
   a. We used to live in San Antonio.
   b. We still live in San Antonio.
3. It's been snowing since 8:00.
   a. It's still snowing.
   b. It stopped snowing a little while ago.
4. Someone looks out the window and says, "It's been snowing." We know that
   a. it is definitely still snowing.
   b. it is possible that it stopped snowing a little while ago.
5. Bill has been living with his sister.
   a. Bill's living arrangement is probably only temporary.
   b. Bill's living arrangement is probably permanent.
6. He's been coughing.
   a. He coughed several times.
   b. He coughed only once.

2. An Interview

The newspaper interviewed John Tarver, a homeless man. Complete the interview. Use the present perfect progressive form of the words in the box.

ask	eat	~~live~~	look
read	sleep	think	worry

Interviewer: How long ___have___ you ___been living___ on the streets, Mr. Tarver?

1.

Mr. Tarver: For almost two years now.

Interviewer: Where do you sleep?

Mr. Tarver: It's been pretty warm, so I _____ in the park. But winter will be here soon, and

2.
it's too cold to sleep in the park. I _____ about that.

3.

Interviewer: What do you do about food?

Mr. Tarver: I _____ much lately. Sometimes someone gives me money, and I buy a

4. (not)
sandwich and something to drink.

(continued on next page)

Interviewer: And how do you spend your time?

Mr. Tarver: I do a lot of thinking. Recently, I _____ a lot about my past and how I ended up
5.
without a home.

Interviewer: Do you see any way out of your present situation?

Mr. Tarver: I want to work, so I _____ for a job. I _____ the want ads every day in
6.   7.
the paper, and I _____ everyone I know for a job.
8.

Interviewer: Any luck?

Mr. Tarver: So far, no.

3. What's Been Happening?

*Look at the two pictures. Complete the sentences. Use the present perfect
progressive form of the verbs in parentheses.*

1. _____ They've been watching TV. _____
(watch TV)

2. _____
(read the newspaper)

3. _____
(drink coffee)

4. _____
(drink tea)

5. _____
(smoke)

6. One woman _____
(cry)

7. _____
(rain)

COMMUNICATION PRACTICE

4. Practice Listening

🔲🔲 *Listen to Martha talk to her friend about driving lessons. Listen again and check the things Martha is still doing.*

Martha is still

1. ✔️ driving a car
2. ☐ taking driving lessons
3. ☐ giving driving lessons
4. ☐ teaching her daughter to make a U-turn
5. ☐ teaching her daughter to park

5. Explanations

Work in pairs. Think of as many explanations as possible for the following situations.

Example:
Janet's eyes are red.
   A: Maybe she's been crying.
   B: Or maybe she's been suffering from allergies.
   A: She's probably been rubbing them.

1. John looks exhausted.

2. Sally's face is all dirty.

3. Gloria and Tom look angry.

4. The streets are all wet.

5. Gina's wallet is stuffed with $100 bills.

6. Randy lost five pounds.

6. What About You?

Complete the chart with information about your present life.

address: ——————————————————————————

job: ——————————————————————————

hobbies/interests: ——————————————————

school subjects: ——————————————————

plans: ——————————————————————————

concerns: ——————————————————————

(continued on next page)

Work in pairs. Look at each other's charts. Ask and answer questions with
How long + the present perfect progressive. The verbs in the box can help you.

> **Example:**
> **A:** How long have you been working as a cook?
> **B:** For two years. OR Since I moved here.

live at	study
work at/as	plan to
play/collect/do	worry about

7. Employment Statistics

Work in pairs. Look at these government statistics. Discuss them with your
partner. Make sentences using the present perfect progressive. Use the words
in the boxes below.

decrease	fall	get worse
improve	increase	rise

unemployment
the situation
the number of

Employed and Unemployed Workers
(in thousands)

	1988	1989	1990	1991
Total 16 years old and over:				
Employed	114,968	117,342	117,914	116,877
Unemployed	6,701	6,528	6,874	8,426
Men 20 years old and over:				
Employed	59,781	60,837	61,198	60,174
Unemployed	2,987	2,867	3,170	4,109
Women 20 years old and over:				
Employed	40,383	49,745	50,455	50,535
Unemployed	2,487	2,467	2,555	3,028
Both sexes 16–19 years old:				
Employed	6,805	6,759	6,261	5,628
Unemployed	1,226	1,194	1,149	1,290

Source: U.S. Dept. of Labor, Bureau of Labor Statistics

> **Example:** The total number of unemployed workers has been increasing.

8. Homelessness

Reread the article on page 128. Is homelessness a problem in your city or
country? Has it been increasing or decreasing? What has the government
been doing about it? Discuss the problem with your classmates.

U N I T

16

Contrast:
Present
Perfect
and Present
Perfect
Progressive

INTRODUCTION

*Professor Jane Owen **has been writing** about environmental problems for several decades. Read and listen to this excerpt from her latest article on elephants in* Science Today, *a popular science magazine.*

Elephants, which are among the largest animals in the world, **have been roaming** this earth for hundreds and hundreds of years. They **have** always **been** an important link in the African wildlife chain. But today they are in danger of becoming extinct. Local ivory-factory owners **have been killing** elephants and **removing** their very valuable tusks, leaving the rest of the animals to rot. Over half of the estimated 1.5 million elephants that existed in 1979 **have died** for their tusks. People **have used** their ivory to make jewelry, sculptures, and other ornaments. Some environmental groups **have been protesting** this situation. They want to prevent the extinction of the elephant.

CONTRAST: PRESENT PERFECT AND PRESENT PERFECT PROGRESSIVE

PRESENT PERFECT
Almost a million elephants **have died** since 1979.

PRESENT PERFECT PROGRESSIVE
Elephants **have been roaming** the earth for hundreds of years.

135

Grammar Notes

1. The present perfect progressive often shows that an activity or state is <u>unfinished</u>. It started in the past and is still continuing.

> I**'ve been reading** a book about elephants.
> (I'm still reading it.)

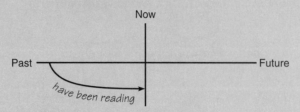

The present perfect often shows that an activity or state is <u>finished</u>. The emphasis is on the result of the action.

> I**'ve read** a book about elephants.
> (I finished the book.)

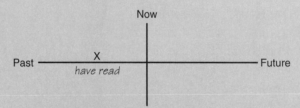

2. Sometimes you can use either the present perfect or the present perfect progressive. The choice of tense shows a difference in emphasis.

   a. The present perfect progressive places more emphasis on the continuation of the action into the present.

> She **has been trying** to save the elephants. (The emphasis is: She is still trying.)
> She **has tried** to save the elephants. (The emphasis is: She tried over a period of time in the recent past.)

   b. The present perfect progressive can also emphasize the <u>temporary</u> nature of the action.

> They**'ve been living** in Africa for three years, but they are returning to the States next month.

   c. The present perfect places more emphasis on the <u>permanence</u> of the action or state.

> They**'ve** always **lived** in Africa.

3. We often use the present perfect to talk about how much someone has done, how many times someone has done something, and how many things someone has done.

> I**'ve read** five books on elephants.
> I**'ve read** that book **many times.** NOT ~~I've been reading that book many times.~~

We often use the present perfect progressive to talk about how long something has been happening.

> I**'ve been reading** books on elephants **for two months.**

FOCUSED PRACTICE

1. Discover the Grammar

Read the first sentence. Then decide whether the second sentence is true (T) *or false* (F).

1. Professor Owen has been reading a book about African wildlife.

___F___ She finished the book.

2. She's read a book about African wildlife.

_____ She finished the book.

3. She's written a magazine article about the rain forest.

_____ She finished the article.

4. She's been waiting for some supplies.

_____ She received the supplies.

5. They've lived in Uganda since 1992.

_____ They are still in Uganda.

6. They've been living in Uganda since 1992.

_____ They are still in Uganda.

7. We've been discussing environmental problems with the leaders of many countries.

_____ The discussions are probably over.

8. We've discussed these problems with many leaders.

_____ The discussions are probably over.

2. Professor Owen's Work

Read these statements. Complete the sentences. Circle the correct form. In some cases, both are correct.

1. Professor Owen is working on two articles for the *National Wildlife Magazine*. She
   has written /(has been writing) these articles since Monday.

2. *The National Wildlife Magazine* ___has published / has been publishing___ its annual report on the
   environment. It is an excellent report.

3. Hundreds of African elephants ___have already died / have been dying___ this year.

4. Professor Owen ___has given / has been giving___ many talks about wildlife preservation in past
   lecture series.

(continued on next page)

5. She <u>has spoken / has been speaking</u> at our school many times.

6. Congress <u>has created / has been creating</u> a new study group to discuss the problem of endangered animals. The group has already met twice.

7. The new group has a lot of work to do. Lately, the members <u>have studied / have been studying</u> the problem of the spotted owl.

8. Professor Owen was late for a meeting with the members of Congress. When she arrived the chairperson said, "At last, you're here. We <u>have waited / have been waiting</u> for you."

9. Professor Owen <u>has lived / has been living</u> in England for the last two years, but she will return to the United States in January.

10. She <u>has worked / has been working</u> with environmentalists in England and France.

3. Tuna or Dolphin?

Complete the sentences. Use the present perfect or the present perfect progressive form of the verb. In many cases, either form is acceptable, depending on your point of view.

Tuna fish sandwich, anyone? American families __have been eating__ large numbers of tuna fish
1. (eat)
sandwiches for a very long time. Just ask typical American parents how many times their children

_____ tuna fish in the last week. And yet, not many people know that this year alone
2. (eat)
the fishing industry _____ nine thousand dolphins in the nets they use to catch tuna.
3. (kill)
The nets catch lots of tuna, but they also trap the dolphins swimming nearby.

Environmentalists are very concerned about this. They _____ to "save the
4. (fight)
dolphins" for many years. As a result, many tuna companies _____ to stop using large,
5. (decide)
dangerous nets to catch fish. Instead, the fishing industry _____ to find safer ways to
6. (try)
catch tuna fish. Environmentalists say that all this effort _____ a big difference. Fewer
7. (make)
dolphins _____ this year than ever before.
8. (die)

But many in the fishing industry say they are having trouble. Lately they _____ as
9. (not catch)
many tuna, and they _____ as much money. In the past few years it
10. (not make)
_____ difficult for some of them to make a good living. They also aren't meeting the
11. (become)
demands for tuna of all those tuna-loving families.

Everyone _____ to solve this environmental problem. But the solutions are not
12. (try)
always easy.

4. Ask the Farmer

Use the words below to ask the farmer questions.

1. How often/you/check/the quality of the water/this year?

   How often have you checked the quality of the water this year?

2. How many times/you/spray/your corn fields this past month?

   _____

3. How long/you/permit/people to fish on your property?

   _____

4. How much water/you/use/for the animals this past year?

   _____

5. What pesticides/you/apply/to your crops?

   _____

COMMUNICATION PRACTICE

5. Practice Listening

🎧 *Listen to the conversations. Then listen again and circle the letter of the pictures that illustrate the situations.*

1.

a.

(b.)

2.

a.

b.

3.

a.

b.

4.
         a.   b.

5.
         a.   b.

6.
         a.   b.

6. Giving Advice

Sometimes we are asked to give advice, but we don't have enough information. Read the following situations and list the questions you might ask to get the information you need. Work with a partner. Take turns asking and answering questions and giving advice. Try to use the present perfect or the present perfect progressive. Then role play these situations.

Your friend calls you. He says that he is tired of waiting for his girlfriend. She is always late. This time he wants to leave to teach her a lesson.

Questions:

How long have you been waiting?

How often . . .

How many times . . .

Have you ever . . .

Advice:

Your father is trying to quit smoking. He's having a hard time and tells you that he needs to have just one more cigarette.

How long . . .

How many times . . .

Have you ever . . .

Advice:

Your friend is an author. She has published several books and is working on a new one. She is getting very frustrated and feels like she will never finish.

How many pages . . .

How long . . .

Have you ever . . .

Advice:

7. What Has Your Country Been Doing to Protect the Environment?

In small groups, discuss what your country's government has done or has been doing to protect the environment. Then talk about what you and your family or neighbors have been doing.

Examples:
The government has passed a law about recycling.
In my building, we've been recycling since 1988.

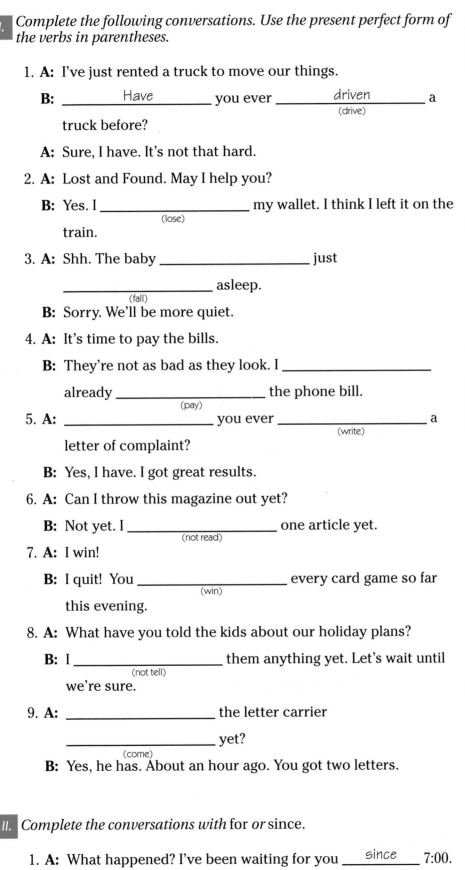

I. *Complete the following conversations. Use the present perfect form of the verbs in parentheses.*

1. **A:** I've just rented a truck to move our things.

   B: _____ Have _____ you ever _____ driven _____ a
   (drive)
   truck before?

   A: Sure, I have. It's not that hard.

2. **A:** Lost and Found. May I help you?

   B: Yes. I _____ my wallet. I think I left it on the
   (lose)
   train.

3. **A:** Shh. The baby _____ just

   _____ asleep.
   (fall)

   B: Sorry. We'll be more quiet.

4. **A:** It's time to pay the bills.

   B: They're not as bad as they look. I _____

   already _____ the phone bill.
   (pay)

5. **A:** _____ you ever _____ a
   (write)
   letter of complaint?

   B: Yes, I have. I got great results.

6. **A:** Can I throw this magazine out yet?

   B: Not yet. I _____ one article yet.
   (not read)

7. **A:** I win!

   B: I quit! You _____ every card game so far
   (win)
   this evening.

8. **A:** What have you told the kids about our holiday plans?

   B: I _____ them anything yet. Let's wait until
   (not tell)
   we're sure.

9. **A:** _____ the letter carrier

   _____ yet?
   (come)

   B: Yes, he has. About an hour ago. You got two letters.

II. *Complete the conversations with* for *or* since.

1. **A:** What happened? I've been waiting for you _____ since _____ 7:00.

   B: My train broke down. I sat in the tunnel for an hour.

2. **A:** How long have you lived in San Francisco?

   B: _____ I was born. How about you?

   A: I've only been here _____ a few months.

3. **A:** When did you and Alan meet?

   B: I've known Alan _____ ages. We went to elementary school together.

4. **A:** Has Greg worked at Cafe Fidelio for a long time?

   B: Not too long. He's only been there _____ 1992.

5. **A:** Why didn't you answer the door? I've been standing here ringing the doorbell _____ five minutes.

   B: I didn't hear you. I've been on the telephone.

6. **A:** How long have you had trouble sleeping, Mr. Yang?

   B: _____ March. It started when I moved.

7. **A:** Celia has been studying English _____ she was ten.

   B: That's why she speaks so well.

8. **A:** Did you know that Gary plans to change jobs?

   B: He's been saying that _____ the past two years. He never does anything about it.

III. *Complete the conversation with the present perfect or present perfect progressive form of the verbs in parentheses.*

A: _____ Have _____ you ever _____ appeared _____ on a game show?
1. (appear)

B: No, but I _____ always _____ to.
2. (want)

A: Why did you decide to try out for "Risk"?

B: Actually, it was my wife's idea. She _____ your show for years. She
3. (watch)
_____ always _____ me to apply. Finally, I did it.
4. (tell)

A: It says on your application that you're a librarian. How long _____ you
_____ that kind of work?
5. (do)

B: I _____ as a reference librarian for fifteen years.
6. (work)

A: What's the strangest question that a reader _____ ever _____
7. (ask)
you?

B: That's hard to say. My readers have _____ always _____
8. (have)
interesting questions. But last week a little boy wanted a book about how to kill snakes.

A: Most of our contestants read a lot. Do you?

B: Yes, I do. I _____ five books so far this month.
9. (read)

A: What do you like to read about?

B: Lately, I _____ interested in the environment. I _____ just
       _{10. (be)}

_____ a book on the Brazilian rain forest.
_{11. (finish)}

A: You sound like the perfect "Risk" contestant, Mr. Smith.

IV. *Complete this letter to a landlord with the correct form of the verbs in parentheses.*

Dear Mr. Jones,

I _____*am writing*_____ this letter to complain about noise from
   _{1. (write / will write / am writing)}

Apartment 3C. I _____ into Apartment 2C on November 1. Since
   _{2. (moved / am moving / have moved)}

I _____ in, my upstairs neighbors have played their stereo
   _{3. (moved / have moved / am moving)}

loudly every night. I _____ them to turn it down several times
   _{4. (am asking / have asked / ask)}

already. However, they _____ the noise yet. I am a student, and
   _{5. (didn't stop / haven't stopped / don't stop)}

I _____ every night. I _____ my
   _{6. ('m studying / study / have studied)}   _{7. (will fail / failed / fail)}

final exams next month unless this noise stops. Please _____ to my
   _{8. (talk / talking / have talked)}

neighbors, and ask them to turn down their stereo after 9:00.

Sincerely yours,

Sattar Mukadam

V. *Complete the conversation by choosing the correct words in parentheses.*

A: How may I help you?

B: I'm planning a vacation. I want to go somewhere new.

A: Have you been to Hawaii _____*yet*_____?
       _{1. (yet / ever)}

B: Oh, yes. I went last year.

A: How about Tahiti?

B: I've _____ vacationed there several times.
       _{2. (never / already)}

A: I know! Rio de Janeiro!

B: I've been to Rio every year _____ 1985. I go to the Carnival.
       _{3. (for / since)}

A: OK. I've got the perfect spot for you. You've _____ been to this place. I
       _{4. (never / ever)}

guarantee it.

B: Where is it?

A: Fairbanks, Alaska.

B: Alaska! Of course I've _____ been to Alaska. I love sunshine.
5. (yet/never)

A: Then you're going to love Fairbanks. The sun shines twenty hours a day in the summer. And it

has beautiful wildlife.

B: Have *you* _____ been to Fairbanks?
6. (never/ever)

A: Of course. I've vacationed there every year _____ the last ten years. I
7. (for/since)

recommend it.

VI. *Circle the letter of the correct verb form to complete each sentence.*

1. Rosemary Dare is a wildlife photographer. She _____ in Uganda for
many years.
   - a. lives
   - b. will live
   - ⓒ 's been living
   - d. doesn't live

2. She _____ elephants for twenty years.
   - a. 's been photographing
   - b. photographs
   - c. is photographing
   - d. photograph

3. She _____ thousands of pictures since the 1970s.
   - a. 's taking
   - b. 'll take
   - c. has taken
   - d. takes

4. Last year, she _____ an international prize for nature photography.
   - a. won
   - b. 's winning
   - c. has won
   - d. has been winning

5. She _____ many prizes over the years.
   - a. won
   - b. is winning
   - c. 's won
   - d. wins

6. Recently, Ms. Dare _____ interested in rhinos.
   - a. has become
   - b. becomes
   - c. will
   - d. become

7. She _____ them for the last few months.
   - a. tracks
   - b. will track
   - c. has been tracking
   - d. tracking

8. I'm sure we _____ some interesting photos soon.
   - a. 'll see
   - b. saw
   - c. have been seeing
   - d. have seen

VII. *Find and correct the error in each sentence.*

1. I ~~am~~ *have* applied for the position of junior accountant in my department.

2. I have been working as a bookkeeper in this company since four years.

3. I have did a good job.

4. I has gained a lot of experience in retail sales.

5. In addition, I have took several accounting courses.

6. Since February my boss liked my work a lot.

7. She has gave me more and more responsibility.

8. I have already show my accounting skills.

VIII. *Complete each conversation with the correct form of the verb in parentheses.*

1. (see)

   A: _____Have_____ you _____seen_____ *Triassic Park* yet?
   a.

   B: Yes, I have. I _____ it last night. Why?
   b.

   A: I'm seeing it on Friday. Is it good?

2. (drink)

   A: Who _____ all the soda?
   a.

   B: Not me. I _____ any soda at all since last week. I _____ water
   b.   c.

   all week. It's much healthier.

3. (write)

   A: Susan Jack _____ a lot of books lately.
   a.

   B: _____ she _____ *Wildest Dreams?*
   b.

   A: Yes, she did. She _____ that one about five years ago.
   c.

4. (cook)

   A: You _____ for hours. When are we eating dinner?
   a.

   B: I just finished. I _____ something special for you. It's called "ants on a tree."
   b.

   A: Gross!

   B: Actually, I _____ it for you many times before. It's just meatballs with rice.
   c.

PART

V

Adjectives
and Adverbs

INTRODUCTION

A young couple is going to look at an apartment for rent. Read and then listen to their conversation with the apartment owner.

Owner: As you can see, this is a **nice, quiet** building. We've never had any trouble with **noisy** neighbors here. You're both **serious** students, aren't you?

Maggie: Oh, yes.

Luis: Isn't this apartment a **little small** for two people?

Owner: Definitely not. I think this **beautiful** apartment is **perfect** for the two of you. **Small**? It's not **small!** It's **warm** and **cozy.**

Maggie: You've described it **perfectly**. It looks **great**. It's a **lovely** apartment.

Owner: Yes, it is. It's **absolutely perfect**. I know I'll rent this apartment **very quickly**. Take it before it's **too late** or you'll be **sorry**.

Maggie: OK.

Luis: Not so **fast**. How much does it cost?

Owner: Oh, well, that's a **very good** question. Please sit down.

EAST SIDE 2 BR w/priv grdn, $578/mo Ideal for shares, immediate occupancy 555-8453	PARK SLOPE Several 2 BR, 2 bth apts avail for immed occup from $599/mo. Excel building. 555-4956
EAST SIDE Studio w/separate kitchen in excellent building. $250 per month 555-2335	PARK SLOPE 1 BR in newly renov house. Nr all transportation/shopping. No pets. $350/mo 555-3256
EAST SIDE Attractive elevator building, laundry rooms, 1 BR $454, Studios $265, utilities included 555-5436	SUNNYSIDE Cozy 1BR on quiet street. Perfect for students. Reasonable rent. Call owner 555-3428
MIDDLE VILLAGE Large 1 BR + den, in owner occupied house. $432/mo Utilities included. No pets. 555-3209	SUNNYSIDE Beautiful, bright 1 BR + study, near trains, shopping, $362/mo + utilities 555-5460
MIDDLE VILLAGE Spacious, renov 2BR/2bth, lots of closets, express bus to city, wlk to school and shops 555-7665	SUNNYSIDE 3 BR, very modern, near transp/shopping $775/mo + util/heat. NO PETS. Call owner 555-7769

ADJECTIVES AND ADVERBS

ADJECTIVES	ADVERBS
They are **quiet** students. It's a **fast** elevator. The building looks **nice**. It's absolutely **perfect**.	They work **quietly**. It moves **very fast**. She described it **nicely**. It's **absolutely** perfect.

PARTICIPIAL ADJECTIVES	
-ING ADJECTIVE	**-ED ADJECTIVE**
The kitchen is **disgusting**. The **disgusting** kitchen is full of cockroaches.	The tenant feels **disgusted**. The **disgusted** tenant left the kitchen.

Grammar Notes

1. Use adjectives when you are describing or giving more information about nouns (people, places, or things). Adjectives usually come before the nouns they are describing.

> It's a **quiet** building. (*Quiet* tells you more about the building.)

Sometimes adjectives come after the verbs and the nouns they describe. This can happen with non-action (stative) verbs such as *feel*, *look*, *smell*, *sound*, *taste*, and *be*.

> You'll feel **warm** and **safe**. (*Warm* and *safe* describe how you will feel.)
> This apartment is **warm** and **cozy**. (*Warm* and *cozy* describe the apartment.)

2. Use adverbs of manner when you are describing or giving more information about verbs (actions). These adverbs often answer the question "how."

> She described the apartment **perfectly**. (*Perfectly* tells you how she described the apartment.)

3. Also use adverbs when describing or giving more information about other adjectives or adverbs.

> This place is **absolutely** perfect. (*Absolutely* [an adverb] tells you just how *perfect* [an adjective] the place really is.)
> This apartment will rent **very** quickly. (*Very* [an adverb] tells just how *quickly* [another adverb] the apartment will rent.)

4. See Unit 2 for a discussion of adverbs of frequency.

5. Adverbs of manner are often formed by adding *-ly* to adjectives. See Appendix 16 on page A10 for spelling rules for forming *-ly* adverbs. These adverbs usually come after the verbs they are describing.

> You should decide **quickly**. (*Quickly* [quick + ly] describes how to decide.)

6. Some adverbs of manner have two forms: one with *-ly* and one without *-ly*.

> cheaply OR cheap
> slowly OR slow
> quickly OR quick
> loudly OR loud
> clearly OR clear

> Don't speak so **loudly**; the neighbors will hear. OR
> Don't speak so **loud**; the neighbors will hear. (In informal speech only.)

Be careful! Not all words ending in *-ly* are adverbs. Some adjectives also end in *-ly*—for example, *silly*, *friendly*, *lovely*, and *lonely*.

Be careful! Some common adverbs do not end in *-ly*—for example, the adverb form of *good* is *well*.

7. Participial adjectives are adjectives that end with *-ed* and *-ing*. The two forms have different meanings. *Disgusting* and *disgusted* are examples of participial adjectives.

> The cockroach is **disgusting** (causes the feeling of disgust).
> The woman looks **disgusted** (feels disgust).

Some examples of participial adjectives follow:

fascinated	fascinating
interested	interesting
bored	boring
amazed	amazing
annoyed	annoying

See Appendix 4 on page A5 for a more complete list of participial adjectives.

8. A few adjectives and adverbs have the same form.

Adjective	Adverb
The visitor was **late**.	He woke up **late** this morning.
She is a **hard** worker.	She works **hard**.

Some other common examples are: *early, far, fast,* and *wrong.*

9. Be careful! In some cases, forming an adverb by adding *-ly* to an adjective changes the meaning of the word. For example, *hardly* is not the adverb for *hard.* It means something completely different—"almost not."

I have **hardly** shown anyone this apartment. You are one of the first to see it.

FOCUSED PRACTICE

1. Discover the Grammar

Read this notice the owner of an apartment for rent put on a bulletin board at the local university. Underline the adjectives and circle the adverbs. Then draw an arrow from the adjective or adverb to the word it is describing.

APT. FOR RENT

Students! Are you looking for a <u>special</u> place to live? Come to 140 Grant Street, Apt. 4B. This apartment is (absolutely) perfect for two serious students who are looking for a quiet neighborhood, just 15 minutes from town. This lovely apartment is in a new building. It is a short walk from the bus stop. The express bus goes directly into town. At night the bus hardly makes any stops at all. You can walk peacefully through the wonderful parks on your way home. The rent is very affordable. Call for an appointment: 555-5050. Don't wait! This apartment will rent fast.

---

2. Did You Like It?

Many different people went to see the apartment described in exercise 1. Complete their comments about the apartment. Use the correct form of the words in parentheses.

1. I am very interested. I think the apartment is ____extremely nice____.
   (extreme/nice)

2. I was expecting much bigger rooms. I was _____.
   (terrible/disappointed)

3. I thought it would be hard to find the apartment, but it wasn't. It was _____.
   (surprising/easy)

4. I think it's a great place—and the price is very reasonable. I am sure it will rent

   _____.
   (incredible/fast)

5. I thought the notice said it was a quiet place. I heard the neighbors _____.
   (very/clear)

6. I heard them, too. I thought their voices were _____.
   (unusual/loud)

3. Writing Home

Complete this letter. Choose the correct word in parentheses.

Dear Mom and Dad,

Life in Chicago is very ___*exciting*___ . I wasn't sure I

1. (exciting / excitingly)

would like living in a _____ city, but I do. I love it!

2. (large / largely)

You'd be surprised to see me. I walk _____ down the

3. (happy / happily)

busy streets, and the noise doesn't bother me at all.

There is always something to do. Yesterday, when I left class, I saw

a street musician. He played the violin so _____ . I

4. (beautiful / beautifully)

couldn't believe he was on the street and not in a big concert hall.

My new roommate is very _____ . She seemed

5. (nice / nicely)

_____ at first and _____ said

6. (shy / shyly)   **7. (hard / hardly)**

anything, but now we are very _____ friends,

8. (good / well)

and we can't stop talking.

I hope you are both well. Please give my love to everyone

and write back soon!

Maria

4.	**Student Evaluation**

Read this evaluation one student wrote about his teacher. Fill in the blanks.
Use either the adjective or adverb form of the word in parentheses.

Please write your _____*general*_____ impression of your teacher
　　　　　　　　　　　1. (general)
this year. All information will be _____
　　　　　　　　　　　　　　　　　　2. (strict)
_____ .
3. (confidential)

　　This English teacher was _____ .
　　　　　　　　　　　　　　　4. (exceptional)
He was always ready with an _____ lesson.
　　　　　　　　　　　　　　　5. (interesting)
Obviously, he prepared _____ for
　　　　　　　　　　　　6. (careful)
each class.

　　His class was not _____ , but the time
　　　　　　　　　　　　　7. (easy)
always passed _____ because it was so
　　　　　　　　　　8. (quick)
_____ .
9. (interesting)

　　In conclusion, I recommend this teacher _____ .
　　　　　　　　　　　　　　　　　　　　　　　10. (high)
I did very _____ in his class, and I'm sure
　　　　　　　11. (good)
other students will too.

5.	**It's Hard to Tell with Alice**

Maggie and Luis are talking about Maggie's sister. Read their conversation.
Circle the correct adjectives to complete the sentences.

Maggie: What's the matter with Alice?

　Luis: Who knows? She's always (annoyed)/annoying about something.
　　　　　　　　　　　　　　　　　　　1.

Maggie: I know. But this time I'm really puzzled/puzzling.
　　　　　　　　　　　　　　　　　　　2.

Luis: Really? Why is this time so <u>puzzled/puzzling</u>?
    3.
Maggie: Oh, I don't know. I thought things were going so well for her. You know, she met an

   <u>interested/interesting</u> man last week .
        4.
Luis: That's nice. Was she <u>interested/interesting</u> in him?
                    5.
Maggie: I thought she was. I mean, she said they had a good time together. She said they saw a

   <u>fascinated/fascinating</u> movie together. So I thought . . .
        6.
Luis: Maybe she was <u>fascinated/fascinating</u> by the movie, but it sounds to me like she might be
                7.
   <u>disappointed/disappointing</u> with the guy.
        8.
Maggie: Maybe you're right. It's hard to tell with Alice. Her moods are always very <u>surprised/surprising</u>.
                                                            9.

COMMUNICATION PRACTICE

6. Practice Listening

Listen to a conversation between Sandra and her teacher. Then listen again and mark the statements true (T) or false (F).

1. Sandra's test results were good. ___F___

2. Sandra said she hardly studied. _____

3. Sandra is disappointed. _____

4. Sandra is friendly to others. _____

5. Sandra admits she's been late to class a lot. _____

7. Your Evaluation

Read the student's evaluation of his teacher in exercise 4 again. Now write your own evaluation of your teacher, your class, or this grammar book. Use as many adjectives and adverbs as you can. Share your evaluation with a classmate. Do you agree or disagree with your classmate's evaluation?

Example:
My terrific teacher explains new grammar very clearly.
She tries extremely hard and seems quite happy with her work.

8. Where Do You Live?

Work in small groups. Describe where you live. Tell each other how you found the place. Tell how you first felt about it (pleased, disappointed, etc.). Describe what it looks like. Tell how you decorated it. What is special about your place?

Example:
I found my apartment last summer when I was walking down the street. I saw an "Apartment for Rent" sign. I knocked on the door.
At first, I was disappointed. It's a small apartment . . .

9. Home Sweet Home

Work with a partner. There are many different types of housing. Describe the different types listed below. How are they similar? How are they different? Use your dictionaries to help you. Do these types of housing exist in other places you have lived?

apartment
boarding house
dorm (dormitory)
mansion
private home
rented room in someone's house
studio apartment
trailer

Example:
A mansion is a very large, expensive house. It's much bigger than an ordinary private home. There are a lot of old mansions in my country. Usually only very wealthy people own them.

10. Your Ideal Living Partner

Work in small groups. Take turns describing your ideal roommate or living partner. Describe the person and his or her activities. Here are some words you might want to use:

Adjectives	Adverbs
cheerful	early
considerate	easily
gloomy	happily
loud	late
messy	loudly
neat	noisily
reliable	quietly
serious	seriously

Example:
My ideal roommate is not **messy** and doesn't get up too **early**.

INTRODUCTION

Read and listen to this restaurant review from a neighborhood newspaper.

The COUNTRY INN has just reopened under new management. The new owners have done a wonderful job redecorating the inn. The dining room looks **bigger**, **brighter**, and **prettier than** the old one. The food is just **as good as** before, but, unfortunately, the menu is **less varied**, and **more expensive**. Good choices are the roast chicken with mashed potatoes and the spaghetti with fresh tomatoes and olives. Be sure to leave room for the desserts. The selection keeps getting **better and better**. The homemade apple pie is **as good as** you can get, and the chocolate soufflé is **as light as** air.

The staff is friendly but not able to handle large numbers of people—**the more crowded** the restaurant, **the slower** the service. At dinner time the lines outside this popular restaurant are getting **longer and longer**. Try lunch for a **quieter, less rushed** meal.

159

ADJECTIVES: EQUATIVES AND COMPARATIVES

EQUATIVE:

	(NOT) AS + **ADJECTIVE**	*AS*
The new restaurant is	(not) as good	**as** the old restaurant.

COMPARATIVE:

	COMPARATIVE ADJECTIVE FORM	*THAN*
The new room looks	brighter prettier	**than** the old one.
The new menu is	more expensive less varied	**than** the old menu.

	COMPARATIVE ADJECTIVE FORM	*AND*	**COMPARATIVE ADJECTIVE FORM**
The lines are getting	longer	and	longer.

THE	**COMPARATIVE ADJECTIVE FORM**		*THE*	**COMPARATIVE ADJECTIVE FORM**	
The	more crowded	the restaurant,	the	slower	the service.

Grammar Notes

1. Use the equative, *as* + adjective + *as*, to talk about two or more things that are <u>equal</u> in some way.

   The new menu is **as good as** the old menu.
   (The new and old menus are equally good.)

   Use *not as* + adjective + *as* to talk about two or more things that are <u>different</u> in some way.

   The new menu is**n't as expensive as** the old menu. (The new and old menus have different prices. The items on the new menu cost less.)

   Note that it is not always necessary to name the second thing. Sometimes it is clear from the context.

   I liked the old menu. The new one isn't **as varied**.
   (The new menu isn't as varied as the old menu.)

   (continued on next page)

2. Use the comparative form of adjectives to focus on a difference between two things.

> The new room looks **bigger than** the old room.
> The new waiters are **friendlier than** the old waiters.

3. There is more than one way to form the comparative of adjectives.

a. For one-syllable adjectives or two-syllable adjectives ending in *-y*, use adjective + *-er*.

> bright → brighter   nice → nicer
> big → bigger   pretty → prettier

Be careful! There are often spelling changes when you add *-er*. See Appendix 15 on pages A9 and A10 for spelling rules for the comparative form of adjectives.

b. For most other adjectives of two or more syllables, use *more/less* + adjective.

> comfortable → more comfortable
> expensive → less expensive

Be careful! Some adjectives have irregular comparative forms.

> good → better   bad → worse

See Appendix 3 on page A4 for a list of irregular adjectives.

c. Note that some adjectives use either *-er* or *more/less*.

> pleasant → pleasanter or more/less pleasant
> friendly → friendlier or more/less friendly
> quiet → quieter or more/less quiet

See Appendix 5 on page A5 for a list of more of these adjectives.

4. Use the comparative with *than* when you mention the things you are comparing.

> The Country Inn is **better than** the Parker House.

Use the comparative without *than* when it is clear from the context which things you are comparing.

> The restaurant is **more expensive** under the new management. (The restaurant is more expensive under the new management than under the old management.)

5. Use the same comparative form of the adjective joined by *and* to talk about change—an increase or decrease. These statements often use the verbs *get, become,* and *grow.*

> It's getting **harder and harder** to find an inexpensive restaurant.
> It's becoming **more and more difficult**. (Both sentences mean the difficulty is increasing.)
> I'm **less and less** interested in eating out. (My interest is decreasing.)

6. Use *the* + comparative form of the adjective + *the* + comparative form of the adjective to show a cause-and-effect relationship.

> **The more crowded** the restaurant, **the slower** the service. (When the restaurant gets more crowded, the service gets slower.)
> **The riper** the peach, **the better** it tastes.

FOCUSED PRACTICE

1. Discover the Grammar

Read part of an article from a health food magazine. Underline all the comparative and equative forms.

There are about 40,000 varieties of rice in the world. When long-grain rice is cooked, it is <u>drier than</u> medium-and short-grain rice. It's also fluffier. This makes long-grain rice more common in such foods as curries, pilafs, and salads. Medium-and short-grain rice are stickier. They are better than the long-grain variety for desserts.

Be careful when you cook rice. The procedure isn't as easy as it first seems. The longer the cooking time, the softer the rice becomes. Some people think there is nothing worse than mushy rice. Besides, overcooking rice makes it tasteless and less nutritious. So follow the cooking instructions on the box, and remember the Chinese New Year's greeting, "May your rice never burn."

2. Not All Rice Is Equal

Look at this consumer magazine chart comparing three brands of rice. Complete the sentences. Use as . . . as *or* not as . . . as *and the correct form of the words in parentheses.*

RICE		Better ●——○ Worse	
Brand	**Price (per serving)**	Taste	Smell
X	7¢	◓	●
Y	3¢	◓	◓
Z	3¢	○	◓

1. Brand Z ___is as expensive as___ Brand Y.
   (be/expensive)

2. Brand Y _____ Brand X.
   (be/expensive)

3. Brand X _____ Brand Y.
   (taste/good)

4. Brand Z _____ Brand Y.
   (taste/good)

5. Brand Y _____ Brand X.
   (smell/nice)

6. Brand Y _____ Brand Z.
   (smell/good)

3. Menu

Look at the menu. Then complete the comparisons. Use -er, more, less *and* than *in your comparisons.*

```
                MENU
 ★ Broccoli with Garlic Sauce . . . . . . . . . . . . .$6.25

   Beef with Broccoli . . . . . . . . . . . . . . . . . . $7.75

 ★ Beef with Dried Red Pepper . . . . . . . . . . . $7.75

   Chicken with Broccoli . . . . . . . . . . . . . . . . $7.25

 ★ Chicken with Orange Sauce . . . . . . . . . . . $7.25

   Sweet and Sour Shrimp . . . . . . . . . . . . . . $8.25

   Pork with Scallions . . . . . . . . . . . . . . . . . . $6.25

 ❤ Steamed Mixed Vegetables . . . . . . . . . . . $5.50

 ❤ Steamed Scallops with Broccoli . . . . . . . . $7.75

   ★ HOT AND SPICY
   ❤ NO SUGAR, SALT, OR OIL
```

1. The sweet and sour shrimp is ____more expensive than____ the steamed scallops with broccoli.
(expensive)
2. The beef with dried red pepper is _____ the beef with broccoli.
(hot)
3. The pork with scallions is _____ the sweet and sour shrimp.
(expensive)
4. The steamed scallops with broccoli is _____ the chicken with orange sauce.
(spicy)
5. The steamed mixed vegetables are _____ the pork with scallions.
(salty)
6. The chicken with broccoli is _____ the chicken with orange sauce.
(mild)
7. The steamed mixed vegetables are _____ the beef with dried red pepper.
(healthy)
8. The broccoli with garlic sauce is _____ chicken with broccoli.
(cheap)

4. City or Country

Read this student's essay. There are six mistakes in making comparisons. Find and correct them.

> Some people like the city. Some like the country. I like the city because it is
> more interesting ~~from~~ than the country. The city is expensive than the country, but it's worth it. The restaurants are more better, and entertainment is more available. Store hours are convenienter, so you can go shopping any time, day or night.
>
> I enjoy walking around the city. It is true that the country is clean than the city, and it is also more quiet. But city streets are more exciting. There is always something happening.
>
> For me the city is definitely nicer that the country, and I hope to remain here.

5. The More the Merrier

Complete these comments about a restaurant. Use the comparative forms of the words in parentheses to show cause and effect.

1. **A:** I can't believe the size of this menu. It's going to take me forever to make up my mind.

   B: I know what you mean. _____The longer_____ the menu,
   (long)
   _____the more difficult_____ the choice.
   (difficult)

2. **A:** People say this restaurant is getting better and better.

   B: Yes, and _____ the restaurant, _____ the
   (good)   (high)
   prices.

3. **A:** The cigarette smoke in here is really bothering me.

   B: Me, too. And I have a cold. Our table is too close to the smoking section.

   _____ the room, _____ my cough gets.
   (smoky)   (bad)

4. **A:** It's pretty loud in here. I can hardly hear myself think.

   B: That can happen when a restaurant becomes popular. _____ the
   (crowded)

   restaurant, _____ the room.
   (noisy)

5. **A:** Why do they have to put so much salt in the soup?

   B: Well, _____ the food, _____ it tastes.
   (salty)   (good)

   A: Oh, I don't agree. Besides, you can always add your own salt.

6. **A:** They certainly give you a lot of food. I can't eat another bite.

   B: _____ the portions, _____ it is to finish.
   (big)   (hard)

6. More and More

Look at the statistics about life in the United States. Read the statements. Write That's right _or_ That's
wrong. _Then write a true statement. Use_ get, _the words in parentheses, and the comparative form to talk
about change._

Life in the United States	1970	1980	1990
1. Cost of food per week (family of three)	$28.80	$62.90	$91.70
2. Cost of hospital care	$28.0 billion	$101.6 billion	$250.4 billion
3. Population	203,302,031	226,542,518	248,709,873
4. Life expectancy at birth	70.8 years	73.7 years	75.3 years
5. Cost of average one-family home	$23,000	$62,200	$95,500

Sources: The 1993 World Almanac, The 1993 Information Please Almanac, and Statistical Abstracts of the United States.

1. The cost of food is rising.

   _____That's right. It's getting higher and higher._____
                                    (high)

2. The cost of hospital care in the United States is decreasing.

   _____
                              (expensive)

3. The U.S. population is increasing.

   _____
                              (large)

4. Life expectancy in the United States is decreasing.

   _____
                              (long)

5. The cost of an average one-family home is increasing.

   _____
                              (expensive)

COMMUNICATION PRACTICE

7. Practice Listening

A couple is trying to choose between two new cars. Listen to their conversation. Then listen again and check the car that is better in each category.

	Ranger	Speedster
1. cheap	✓	☐
2. safe	☐	☐
3. comfortable	☐	☐
4. big	☐	☐
5. fuel efficient	☐	☐
6. fast	☐	☐

8. What About You?

Work with a partner. Pretend you are going to rent a car. Look again at the information about the Ranger and the Speedster in exercise 7.

Compare the two cars.

Example:
A: I think I'll get the Ranger. It's cheaper.
B: But the Speedster is better. It's . . .

9. Quiz

Complete the questions. Use the comparative form of the adjectives in parentheses. Then answer the questions. Compare your answers with a classmate's.

1. Which planet is _____farther_____ from the Earth: Mars or Jupiter? _____
   (far)
2. Which city is _____, Vancouver or Toronto? _____
   (big)
3. Which flavor of ice cream is _____, vanilla or chocolate? _____
   (popular)
4. Which animal is _____, a lion or a tiger? _____
   (heavy)

5. Which is _____, white rice or brown rice? _____
   (nutritious)
6. Which food is _____, a baked potato or a cup of cooked rice? _____
   (fattening)
7. Which type of transportation is _____, the bus or the train? _____
   (dangerous)

Now add three of your own quiz questions. Ask your partner.

8. _____?

9. _____?

10. _____?

10. As Popular as These Expressions

Some popular expressions make comparisons with as + *adjective* + as—*for example,* **as white as snow** *and* **as busy as a bee**. *Work with a partner. Match the adjectives in the first column with the nouns in the second to complete these common English expressions.*

1. __e__ as white as   a. gold

2. _____ as pretty as   b. pie

3. _____ as gentle as   c. a mouse

4. _____ as hot as   d. sugar

5. _____ as timid as   e. snow

6. _____ as good as   f. fire

7. _____ as sweet as   g. a lamb

8. _____ as easy as   h. a picture

Compare your answers with your classmates' answers. Then give examples of people or things that these expressions can describe.

Example:
My grandmother's hair is as white as snow.

11. Things Change

Think of how something in your life is changing. Tell a partner. Use the comparative form and get, become, *or* grow. *Here are some ideas you can talk about.*

Your: city or town

English

job

apartment

Example:
A: My English is getting more and more fluent.

Adjectives: Superlatives

INTRODUCTION

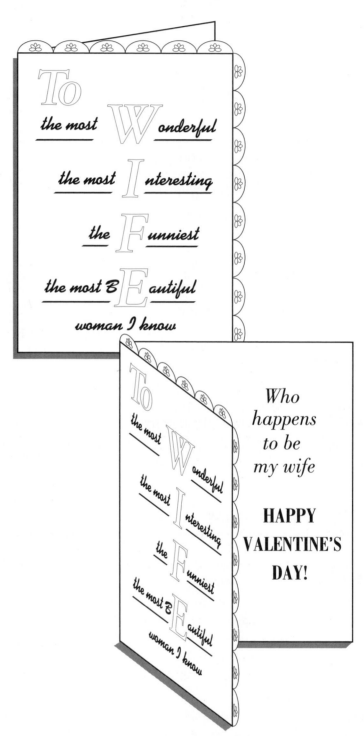

Read and listen to the Valentine's Day card.

To the most **W**onderful
the most **I**nteresting
the **F**unniest
the most **B**eautiful
woman I know

To the most **W**onderful
the most **I**nteresting
the **F**unniest
the most **B**eautiful
woman I know

Who happens to be my wife

HAPPY VALENTINE'S DAY!

ADJECTIVES: SUPERLATIVES

	SUPERLATIVE ADJECTIVE FORM	
You are	the sweetest the funniest the most wonderful the best	person in the world.
You have	the nicest the loveliest	smile I've ever seen.

Grammar Notes

1. Use the superlative form of adjectives to single out one thing from two or more things.

    You are **the sweetest person** in the world.
    You are **the most wonderful** companion I've ever had.

2. There is more than one way to form the superlative.

    a. For one-syllable adjectives or two-syllable adjectives ending in -y, use *the* + adjective + -est.

    sweet → the sweetest
    funny → the funniest
    nice → the nicest
    pretty → the prettiest

    Be careful! There are often spelling changes when you add -est. See Appendix 15 on pages A9 and A10 for spelling rules for the superlative form of adjectives.

    b. For most other adjectives of two or more syllables, use *the most/the least* + adjective.

    wonderful → the most wonderful
    interesting → the least interesting

    Be careful! Some adjectives have irregular superlative forms:

    good → the best
    bad → the worst
    little → the least
    far → the farthest/the furthest

    See Appendix 3 on page A4 for a list of irregular adjectives.

    c. Some adjectives form the superlative with -est or *the most/the least*.

    pleasant → the pleasantest
    OR
    the most/the least pleasant

    friendly → the friendliest
    OR
    the most/the least friendly

    See Appendix 5 on page A5 for a list of more of these adjectives.

3. The superlative is often used with expressions beginning with *in* and *of*, such as *in the world* and *of all*.

    You're **the best** mother **in the world**.

4. The superlative is sometimes followed by a clause. Often the clause uses the present perfect with *ever*. (See page 114 for the present perfect with *ever*.)

    You have **the loveliest** smile **I've ever seen**.

FOCUSED PRACTICE

1. Discover the Grammar

Read this Mother's Day card written by a young child. Underline all the superlative adjectives.

To my mother,

You are <u>the best</u> mother in the whole
   wide world.
You are the smartest, the brightest, and
   the funniest of all moms I've ever known.
You are the nicest mom I've ever had.
You are the most wonderful and definitely
   the least mean.
No mom in the whole wide world is
   better than you .
You are the greatest mother of all.
   I love you very, very much !

Happy
Mother's Day!

Love,
Erin

2. Valentine's Day

In Canada and the United States, Valentine's Day (February 14) is a day when many people think about the special friends and relatives in their lives. They send cards and letters and tell these people their feelings. Complete the sentences from Valentine's Day cards. Use the superlative form of the adjectives in parentheses and the expressions in the box.

in the world	of my life	in the school
of the year	of all	in our family

1. You are so good to me. I am ___the luckiest___ person ____in the world____.
   (lucky)
2. The day we were married was _____ day _____.
   (happy)
3. You are a terrific teacher. You are _____ teacher _____.
   (good)
4. You make me feel warm, even in _____ months _____.
   (cold)
5. You are _____ cousin _____.
   (nice)
6. Grandma, you are _____ person _____. Maybe that's why I love you
   (wise)
   the most.

3. A Special Gift

Look at the pictures. Write sentences about the gift items. Use the words in parentheses and the most, the least, *or* -est.

1. The painting _____ is the most unusual gift. _____
   (unusual)
2. The scarf _____
   (practical)
3. The book _____
   (expensive)
4. The scarf _____
   (expensive)
5. The book _____
   (small)
6. The painting _____
   (big)

4. What About You?

Write questions. Use the words in parentheses with the superlative and the present perfect with ever.

1. _____ What's the strangest gift you've ever received? _____
   (What/strange/gift/you/receive?)
2. _____
   (What/funny/thing/you/do?)
3. _____
   (Who/smart/person/you/know?)
4. _____
   (What/nice/place/you/see?)
5. _____
   (Where/hot/place/you/be?)
6. _____
   (What/bad/experience/you/have?)
7. _____
   (What/silly thing/you/say?)
8. _____
   (What/long/book/you/read?)
9. _____
   (What/valuable/lesson/you/learn?)
10. _____
    (What/difficult/thing/you/do?)
11. _____
    (What/enjoyable/thing/you/do?)

COMMUNICATION PRACTICE

5. Practice Listening

Timothy is trying to pick a gift for his wife. Listen to the conversation. Then listen again and check the appropriate column.

	Bracelet	Winter Coat	Picture Frame	Soap and Bubble Bath
1. least expensive	✓	☐	☐	☐
2. most practical	☐	☐	☐	☐
3. silliest	☐	☐	☐	☐
4. most romantic	☐	☐	☐	☐
5. sweetest	☐	☐	☐	☐

6. The Most . . .

Work in small groups. Take turns. Answer the questions in exercise 4. Talk about your answers.

Example:
The smartest person I've ever known is my father.

7. Your Own Cards

Read the Valentine's Day card in the introduction again. Write your own card for a special day (for example, Mother's Day, a birthday, an anniversary). Use as many superlatives as you can.

Now work in small groups. Read the cards. Decide which card is

the funniest
the most original
the most artistic
the most serious
the most sentimental

Example:
Sam's card is the funniest, but Juan's card is definitely the most sentimental.

8. What About Your Holidays?

Work in small groups. Talk about holidays. What are some of the most important holidays for you? What are some of the things you do on those holidays? Do you send cards? What is the best card you've ever received?

Adverbs: Equatives, Comparatives, Superlatives

INTRODUCTION

Read this transcript and listen to the radio sportscast.

Today in the world of sports we turn our attention to the amazing tennis player, Sergio Cortes of Chile. He is playing **better and better** every year. Think back to the days when he beat Tom Nijssen of Sweden, for example. Sure, he won that match, but he just wasn't playing **as well as** he could. In fact, while Cortes returned serves **more forcefully than** usual, everyone agreed that Nijssen served **the most forcefully** of any player in the competition. Cortes was just not moving quickly enough. Well, things have changed since then. Cortes is definitely playing **more aggressively** these days. And **the harder** he plays, **the better** he does. Keep your eyes on him. He's playing **the best** he has in a very long time.

ADVERBS: EQUATIVES, COMPARATIVES, SUPERLATIVES

EQUATIVE

	As + Adverb	*As*
He played didn't play	as well	(as his opponent).

COMPARATIVE

	Comparative Adverb Form	*Than*
Cortes played	harder more aggressively	(than Nijssen).

	Comparative Adverb Form	*And*	Comparative Adverb Form
They're going to play	better	and	better.

The	Comparative Adverb Form		*The*	Comparative Adverb Form	
The	harder	he played,	the	better	he performed.

SUPERLATIVE

	Superlative Adverb Form	
He handled the ball	the most skillfully	of anyone in the match.

Grammar Notes

1. Use the equative, *as* + adverb + *as*, to talk about actions that are the same or equal.

> Cortes served **as well as** most players. (He and the other players served equally well.)

Use *not as* + adverb + *as* to talk about actions that are not the same or equal.

> Cortes did**n't** serve **as forcefully as** Nijssen.
> (Cortes and Nijssen served differently. Cortes served forcefully, but he served less forcefully than Nijssen.)

2. Use the comparative form of adverbs to focus on the differences between actions.

> Cortes played **better than** Nijssen.　　Nijssen played **worse.**

3. Note that it is not always necessary to name the second person or thing. Sometimes it is clear from the context who or what that is.

> Nijssen played **hard.** Cortes played **as hard** (as Nijssen).
> Cortes played **aggressively.** Nijssen didn't play **as aggressively** (as Cortes).
> Cortes hit the ball **farther** (than Nijssen).

4. Use the superlative form of adverbs to single out something about an action. We often use the superlative with expressions beginning with *in* and *of*, such as *in the match* or *of any player.*

> Nijssen served **the most forcefully** of any player in the competition.

5. There is more than one way to form the comparative and superlative of adverbs.

   a. For one-syllable adverbs or for adverbs whose forms are the same as adjectives, use *-er* or *-est.*

Adverb	Comparative	Superlative
fast	faster	the fastest
hard	harder	the hardest

Be careful! There are often spelling changes when you add *-er* or *-est.* See Appendix 15 on pages A9 and A10 for rules for spelling changes.

   b. For other adverbs of two or more syllables, use *more/less* or *the most/the least.* Most of these adverbs end in *-ly.*

Adverb	Comparative	Superlative
aggressively	more/less aggressively	the most/the least aggressively
forcefully	more/less forcefully	the most/the least forcefully

Be careful! Some adverbs have irregular comparative and superlative forms.

Adverb	Comparative	Superlative
badly	worse	the worst
well	better	the best
little	less	the least

See Appendix 3 on page A4 for a list of irregular adverbs.

(continued on next page)

Note that some adverbs of manner have two forms.

Adverb	Comparative	Superlative
quickly	more quickly OR quicker	the quickest OR the most quickly
slowly OR slow	more slowly OR slower	the most slowly OR the slowest

Please speak **more slowly.** OR Please speak **slower.**

Be careful! Although *more quickly, more slowly,* and *the most quickly* and *the most slowly* are the traditional comparative and superlative forms of these adverbs, *quicker, slower,* and *the quickest,* and *the slowest* are often heard in informal speech.

6. Use the same comparative form of the adverb joined by *and* to talk about change.

Cortes is playing **better and better** every year.

7. Use *the* + comparative form of the adverb + *the* + comparative form of the adverb to show a cause-and-effect relationship.

The harder he played, **the better** he performed.

FOCUSED PRACTICE

1. Discover the Grammar

Read this feature story from the sports section of the newspaper. Underline all the words that make comparisons with adverbs.

In the first soccer game of the season, the Golds beat the Silvers, 6 to 3. The Silver team played a truly fantastic game, but its defense is still weak. The Golds defended the ball much <u>more aggressively than</u> the Silver team did. Of course, Ace Jackson certainly helped win the game for the Golds. The Golds' star player was back on the field today to the delight of his many fans. He was hurt badly at the end of last season, but he has recovered quickly. Although he didn't play as well as people expected, he still handled the ball like the old Ace. He certainly handled it the most skillfully of anyone on the team. He controlled the ball the best, kicked the ball the farthest, and ran the fastest of any of the players on either team. He played hard and helped the Golds look good. In fact, the harder he played, the better the Golds performed. Watch Ace this season.

And watch the Silvers. They have a new coach, and they're training more seriously this year. I think we'll see them play better and better as the season progresses.

2. Not All Bikes Are Equal

Read this chart comparing several models of bicycles. Complete the sentences. Use (not) as + *adverb* + as *and the words in parentheses. Change the adjectives to adverbs.*

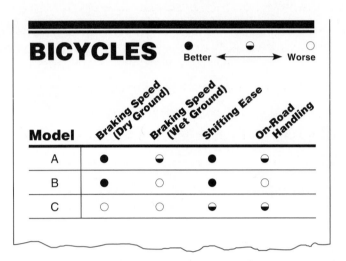

1. Model C <u>doesn't stop as quickly as</u> Model A.
   (stop/quick)
2. On wet ground, Model B _____ Model C.
   (stop/quick)
3. On dry ground, Model C _____ Model B.
   (stop/quick)
4. Model A _____ Model B.
   (shift/easy)
5. Model C _____ Model B.
   (shift/easy)
6. On the road, Model B _____ Models A and C.
   (handle/good)
7. Model A _____ Model C.
   (handle/good)

3. Speed Reading

Two friends are talking about a new speed-reading course. Use the equative, comparative, and superlative form of the words in parentheses to complete their conversation. Add as *or* than *where necessary.*

Sara: Did you hear about the new speed-reading course? It helps you read _____<u>faster</u>_____
1. (fast)

and _____ .
2. (well)

Laura: That's impossible. The _____ you read, the _____ you
3. (fast)   4. (little)

understand.

Sara: That's what I thought. But the course description says that after this course you can read

ten times _____ and understand five times more. It says you won't work
                 5. (rapidly)

any _____.
    6. (hard)

Laura: I'd like to see that. I read _____ most people, but I remember details
                                       7. (slowly)

_____ and _____ most people do.
       8. (clearly)   9. (long)

Sara: But, just think—maybe you could read _____ and still remember
                                                10. (quickly)

everything.

Laura: Did you read the course description completely?

Sara: I read it _____ I always read things.
                    11. (completely)

Laura: Uh-oh! Remember when you read the advertisement for a business in your home? You

spent $500 for nothing. I think you'd better read everything a lot _____
                                                                    12. (carefully)

from now on—and forget about taking a speed-reading class!

4. The All-around Athlete

*Look at the chart. Then complete the sentences. Use the comparative or
superlative form of the adverbs in the box.*

far	good	fast	bad	slow	high

	Broad Jump	Pole Vaulting	5-mile Run
Athlete 1	14.3 feet	7 feet 3 inches	24 minutes
Athlete 2	14.1 feet	7 feet 2 inches	28 minutes
Athlete 3	15.2 feet	7 feet 8 inches	30 minutes
Athlete 4	15.4 feet	8 feet 2 inches	22 minutes

1. Athlete 1 jumped _____ farther than _____ Athlete 2.

2. Athlete 4 vaulted _____ the highest _____ of all.

3. Athlete 3 ran _____.

4. Athlete 2 ran _____ Athlete 4.

5. Athlete 4 jumped _____.

6. Athlete 1 ran _____ Athlete 2.

7. Athlete 4 vaulted _____ than Athlete 2.

8. All in all, Athlete 4 did _____.

9. All in all, Athlete 2 did _____.

COMMUNICATION PRACTICE

5. Practice Listening

Listen to the radio announcer. He is describing a horse race. Then listen again and rank the horses from first place (1) to last place (5).

_____ Exuberant King

___1___ Get Packin'

_____ Inspired Winner

_____ Señor Speedy

_____ Wild Whirl

6. Sports around the World

Work as a class. Name several famous athletes for one sport. Compare their abilities. Use the comparative and superlative forms of adverbs. Use your own ideas or the ideas in the box to help you.

Activities	Adverbs
catch	carefully
hit	defensively
kick	easily
play	powerfully
race	regularly
run	seriously
throw	straight
train	successfully

Example:
Ricky Henderson is a baseball player.
He runs faster than most other players.

7. A Questionnaire

Answer the questionnaire.

1. How many hours do you work every week? _____

2. How many books have you read this month? _____

3. When did you last see a movie? _____

4. How many hours a week do you study? _____

5. How many trips have you taken in the last year? _____

6. How many countries have you visited? _____

Compare your answers with those of your classmates.

Find out:

1. Who works the hardest?

2. Who reads the most?

3. Who has seen a movie the most recently?

4. Who studies the most diligently?

5. Who has traveled the most frequently?

6. Who has traveled the most extensively?

Now add your own questions.

Example:
Sharif works the hardest. He works 45 hours every week.

I. *Complete the advertisements by choosing the correct words in parentheses.*

1. FOR RENT. Live _____comfortably_____ in this
   a. (comfortable/comfortably)

   _____ studio apartment.
   b. (cozy/cozily)

   _____ rent makes it a
   c. (Cheap/Cheaply)

   _____ home for one student.
   d. (perfect/perfectly)

2. FOR SALE. Woman's bicycle. I'm asking the

   _____ low price of $65 for this
   a. (incredible/incredibly)

   _____ five-speed bike. I've
   b. (new/newly)

   _____ used it at all. Don't miss this
   c. (hard/hardly)

   _____ bargain.
   d. (terrific/terrifically)

3. Free to a _____ family. Skipper is a
   a. (good/well)

   _____ and friendly puppy. He behaves
   b. (beautiful/beautifully)

   _____ with children, and he is very
   c. (good/well)

   _____. We are moving very soon, so Skipper
   d. (obedient/obediently)

   needs a new home _____.
   e. (quick/quickly)

II. *Complete each conversation with the comparative form of the words in parentheses.*

1. **A:** How do those shoes fit?

   B: They're very loose. I need a _____smaller_____ size.
   (small)

2. **A:** Did you pass your driving test?

   B: Yes, I did. It seemed much _____ this time.
   (easy)

3. **A:** I'm out of breath.

   B: Then let's walk a little _____.
   (slowly)

4. **A:** You look great. What happened?

   B: I'm watching my diet more closely, and I'm exercising

   _____.
   (regularly)

5. **A:** Could you keep the noise down? I'm trying to work.

   B: Sorry. We'll talk _____.
   (quietly)

6. **A:** I feel awful. I'm staying home from work.

   B: Good idea. Your cold seems a lot _____ today.
   (bad)

7. **A:** Which team plays _____, the Cowboys or the Knicks?

(well)

   B: The Knicks. They've won every game this season.

8. **A:** How was your dinner at the Country Inn?

   B: The food was delicious, but dinner was much _____ than it used to be. Our bill

(expensive)

   was almost eighty dollars.

9. **A:** Tomi's English has improved a lot.

   B: I know. She's studying a lot _____ this year.

(hard)

10. **A:** It's 9:30. How come you're so late?

   B: Your place is _____ than I thought. I just didn't leave enough time. Sorry.

(far)

III. *Complete each sentence with the participial adjective that comes from the underlined verb.*

1. Bob and Ray didn't rent that apartment. The garbage in the hallway <u>disgusted</u> them.

   a. The garbage was _____disgusting_____.

   b. Bob and Ray were _____disgusted_____.

2. The subway ride <u>exhausts</u> Maria. She prefers to ride the bus.

   a. Maria feels _____ after she rides the subway.

   b. The subway ride is _____.

3. Let's order dinner. Those appetizers didn't <u>satisfy</u> me.

   a. The appetizers weren't _____.

   b. I'm not _____.

4. John's travel stories always <u>amaze</u> us. Do you think they're true?

   a. We're _____.

   b. His stories are _____.

5. I don't speak Spanish well at all. My mistakes <u>embarrass</u> me.

   a. I'm _____.

   b. My mistakes are _____.

6. This verb <u>confused</u> the class.

   a. The verb was _____.

   b. The class was _____.

IV. *Complete the sentences with the comparative form of the adjectives and adverbs. Use the information in parentheses to help you.*

1. Ann's criticism was very unfair.

   (I thought about it thoroughly. I became angry.)

   The ____more thoroughly____ I thought about it, the ____angrier____ I became.

2. My teacher tried to explain the lesson, but she talked very fast.

   (She talked fast. I felt confused.)

   The _____ she talked, the _____ I felt.

3. Bruce gets really silly when he's tired. Last night he studied until midnight.

   (It got late. He became silly.)

   The _____ it got, the _____ he became.

4. Sylvia studied hard for her French course last semester.

   (She studied hard. She spoke fluently.)

   The _____ she studied, the _____ she spoke.

5. Greg takes good care of his garden.

   (He often waters his tomatoes. They get big.)

   The _____ he waters his tomatoes, the _____ they get.

6. My neighbors' dog always barks at me when I run near their house.

   (He barks loud. I run fast.)

   The _____ he barks, the _____ I run.

7. Sal felt guilty when his girlfriend apologized for their argument.

   (She apologized profusely. Sal felt bad.)

   The _____ she apologized, the _____ he felt.

V. *Complete each paragraph with the words from the box. Use each word once.*

the	best	of	~~successful~~	hard

1. Pat's the most ____successful____ salesperson in her office, and she deserves to be. She

a.

   works the longest hours. Sometimes she works until 10:00 at night. She also works the

   _____. When she works with a client, she talks _____ most

b.   c.

   persuasively _____ all our salespeople. She's really the _____.

d.   e.

big	sooner	than	many	much	exciting

2. Communications equipment used to be only for _____ companies, but recently

a.
   more and more small offices are buying it. Fax machines are cheaper _____ they

b.
   used to be, and _____ home offices have them now. Car telephones are also

c.
   becoming _____ more common. The most _____ new

d.　　　　　　　　　　　　　　　　　　　　　　　e.
   development is the videophone. It will be available for offices _____ than you

f.
   think—probably in the next two or three years.

VI. *There are six errors with comparisons in the diary entry. Find and correct them.*

　　　　　　　　　　　　　　　　　　worst
　　I think today has been the ~~bad~~ day of my life. My car broke down on the Expressway during rush

hour this morning—a busiest time of day. I sat there for an hour waiting for a tow truck. The longer I

sat, the nervous I got. I was a wreck when I got to work. Of course, this was the day we were closing

biggest deal of the year. My boss called me five times about one letter. And more frequently he called,

the worse I typed. My next worry is the repair bill for the car. I hope it isn't as expensive the last time.

VI

Gerunds and Infinitives

Gerunds: Subject and Object

INTRODUCTION

▸ *Read and listen to this sign in a doctor's office.*

NO SMOKING

SMOKING is bad for your health!
NOT SMOKING
is a matter of Life & Breath.

For information on how to stop **smoking**, phone for our free pamphlet
Taking Control of Your Health:
Quit **Smoking** Before It's Too Late.

GERUNDS AS SUBJECTS AND OBJECTS

GERUND AS SUBJECT		
GERUND (SUBJECT)	**VERB**	
Smoking Not exercising	is	bad for your health.

GERUND AS OBJECT		
SUBJECT	**VERB**	**GERUND (OBJECT)**
You	should quit	**smoking.**
I	suggest	**not smoking** for a week.

Grammar Notes

1. Gerunds (base form of verb + *-ing*) are verbs that function like nouns. The gerund can be the subject of a sentence.

    Smoking is bad for your health.

    Notice that the gerund is always singular and is followed by the third-person-singular form of the verb.

    Smoking in public places **is** often against the law.
    Smoking cigarettes **is** dangerous to your health.

    Be careful! Don't confuse the gerund with a progressive form of the verb.

    Smoking isn't healthy. (gerund)
    He **is smoking** now. (progressive)

2. Gerunds are also used as the object of certain verbs. The following verbs can be followed by gerunds. A more complete list is included in Appendix 6 on page A6.

admit	deny	practice	risk
appreciate	enjoy	prohibit	suggest
avoid	finish	quit	
can't stand	mind	recall	
consider	miss	resent	
delay	postpone	resist	

    I **enjoy exercising**.
    I've **considered joining** a gym.

3. There are many common expressions with *go* + the gerund. These expressions usually describe activities, such as shopping, fishing, skiing, swimming, and camping.

    We often **go swimming** or **hiking**.
    Yesterday I **went shopping** for a new pair of running shoes.

FOCUSED PRACTICE

1. Discover the Grammar

Read part of an article from a health newsletter. Underline the words ending in -ing *that are gerunds.*

YOUR HEALTH

SWIMMING is great exercise. It's healthy, fun, and relaxing. Because swimming is a "low-impact" sport, most people enjoy participating in this activity without fear of injury to bones or muscles. Jogging, a "high-impact" activity, is sometimes harmful. I know this from personal experience. Last year while I was jogging, I injured my right knee. I don't go jogging anymore. After a painful month of recovery, I stopped running and switched to water sports. I'm now considering joining a club and competing in races.

2. Health Issues

Complete these statements with gerunds. Use the verbs in the box.

increase	eat	do
walk	~~smoke~~	swim
run	go	

1. _____Smoking_____ is bad for your heart and lungs.

2. _____ too much fat and sugar is also unhealthy.

3. Doctors suggest _____ the number of fruits and vegetables in your diet.

4. Avoid _____ too many high-impact sports such as jogging and jumping rope. Instead, consider _____ in a pool every day. It's an excellent low-impact sport.

5. Many health experts think that _____ is better than _____ because there is less stress on your body when your feet come into contact with the ground.

6. Many people postpone _____ to the doctor or dentist, but regular checkups are important.

3. A Question of Health

Read these conversations. Write a summary sentence for each conversation. Choose the appropriate verb from the box and use the gerund form of the verb in parentheses.

admit	avoid	consider	deny
~~enjoy~~	go	mind	quit

1.   **Ann:** Do you want to go jogging with me before work?

     Tom: No, thanks. I really don't like that kind of exercise.

SUMMARY: Tom doesn't _____ enjoy jogging. _____
                              (jog)

2.   **Ralph:** Would you like a cigarette?

     Marta: Oh, no, thanks. I don't smoke anymore.

SUMMARY: Marta _____ .
                        (smoke)

3.   **Chen:** What are you doing after work?

     An-ling: I'm going to that new swimming pool on Park Place. Would you like to go with me?

SUMMARY: An-ling is going to _____ .
                                   (swim)

4.   **Jim:** I smell smoke in here. You had a cigarette, didn't you?

     Ellen: No, I didn't.

SUMMARY: Ellen _____ .
                     (smoke)

5.   **Irene:** You're lazy. You really need to exercise more.

     Mike: You're right. I *am* lazy.

SUMMARY: Mike _____ lazy.
                      (be)

6.   **Monica:** Would you like a piece of chocolate cake?

     Phil: No, thanks. I try to stay away from sweets.

SUMMARY: Phil _____ sweets.
                     (eat)

7.   **Craig:** The doctor says that exercise is really important, but I just hate it. What about you?

     Vilma: Well, I don't *love* it, but it's OK.

SUMMARY: Vilma doesn't _____ .
                       (exercise)

8.   **Erik:** I'm exhausted.

     Alice: Me, too. We've been working too hard. Maybe we need a vacation.

     Erik: A vacation? Hmm. That's an interesting idea. Do you think we can afford it?

SUMMARY: Erik and Alice _____ a vacation.
                        (take)

COMMUNICATION PRACTICE

4. Practice Listening

A doctor is giving advice to a patient. Some things are OK for this patient to do, but other things are not. Listen to the conversation. Listen again and check the correct column.

	OK to do	Not OK to do
1. smoking	☐	✓
2. drinking coffee	☐	☐
3. losing more weight	☐	☐
4. eating more complex carbohydrates	☐	☐
5. running every day	☐	☐
6. riding a bike every day	☐	☐
7. working eight hours a day	☐	☐

5. A Questionnaire

Complete the questionnaire. Use the key to mark your likes and dislikes. Add your own activities. Find out about your classmates. Then in small groups discuss your likes and dislikes.

Example:
I enjoy participating in sports, but Park prefers watching sports.

Key: + = enjoy
✓ = don't mind
− = dislike

Activities	Me	_____ (classmate)	_____ (classmate)	_____ (classmate)
1. participate in sports				
2. watch sports				
3. do exercises				
4. walk				
5. jog				
6. clean the house				
7. dance				
8. _____				
9. _____				
10. _____				

6. Learning English

Complete the sentences with information about your English-language-learning experience. Discuss your responses with a classmate.

Example:
 A: I enjoy reading magazines in English.
 B: I enjoy listening to songs in English.

1. I enjoy _____

2. I don't enjoy _____

3. I sometimes avoid _____

4. I don't mind _____

5. I dislike _____

6. I keep _____

7. I sometimes consider _____

8. I often practice _____

9. I miss _____

10. _____ is the best way to improve your English.

11. _____ doesn't really help improve your English.

7. No Smoking

Many people think there should be laws that prohibit smoking in all public places. Work in small groups. Think of arguments for and against allowing smoking in public places. Take notes.

Discuss the topic with your classmates, and then take a class vote on whether or not to prohibit smoking in all public places.

Example:

For	Against
	Breathing other people's cigarette smoke is unhealthy.

INTRODUCTION

Many schools have bulletin boards for notices to students. Read and listen to this notice about the Student Council.

GET INVOLVED

Are you **interested in meeting** new friends?
Do you have ideas **about improving** student life at school?
Are you **used to organizing** large groups of people?
Are you **tired of hearing** complaints and not **finding** solutions?

If you answered

YES

to any of these questions,
join the Student Council.
We need your help!

Come to our next meeting on
Monday, March 25 at 8:00 P.M.
in the Main Auditorium.
We **look forward to seeing** you there.

You CAN make a difference!

ART EXHIBIT
THURS
thru
SAT
5:00 P.M.
to
8:00 P.M.
1st Floor
Campus
LIBRARY

Geometry
STUDY GROUP
with
Ms. Green
Room 205
Hale Hall
2:15 P.M.
M, W, F

LOST:
Black-and-white dog,
goes by the name of
"Smokey"
Call: Joe 595-2350

GERUNDS AFTER PREPOSITIONS

PREPOSITION + GERUND		
Do you have ideas	**about improving**	life at school?
Are you tired	**of hearing**	complaints?
They insist	**on coming**	to the meeting.
She is used	**to organizing**	large groups.

Grammar Notes

1. Prepositions are words such as *about, at, by, for, in, instead of, of, on, to, with,* and *without.* Prepositions can be followed by nouns or pronouns.

> The organization is **for students.**
> The organization is **for them.**

Since gerunds (the base form of the verb + *-ing*) act as nouns, they can follow prepositions too.

> These are recommendations **for improving** life at school.

2. Many common expressions are made up of a verb or an adjective followed by a preposition.

advise against	be afraid of	be famous for
believe in	be bored with	be fond of
count on	be concerned about	be good at
insist on	be crazy about	be interested in
look forward to	be excited about	be nervous about

These expressions can be followed by a gerund.

> We **look forward to seeing** you.
> He **is afraid of getting** involved.
> She**'s interested in improving** student life.

See Appendices 10 and 11 on page A7 for more expressions followed by prepositions.

3. Be careful! In the following expressions, *to* is a preposition, not part of an infinitive form. For this reason it can be followed by the gerund.

> be accustomed to
> be opposed to
> be used to
> admit to
> look forward to
> object to

> I'm looking forward **to seeing** you at the meeting.
> NOT I'm looking forward to see you at the meeting.

See Unit 23 for a full discussion of infinitives.

Be careful! *Be used to* + gerund means "be accustomed to."

> I **am used to getting up** at eight o'clock.

Get used to + gerund means "get accustomed to."

> If I change jobs, I'll have to **get used to getting up** earlier.

Remember that *used to* + the base form of the verb describes repeated past actions, states, or habits.

> Before joining the council, I **used to complain** a lot.

See Unit 6 for a full discussion and practice of *used to.*

FOCUSED PRACTICE

1. Discover the Grammar

The Student Council wrote a letter to Ana Rivera, the president of the college. Read the letter and underline all the preposition + gerund combinations.

October 4, 1994

Dear President Rivera:

We, the members of the Student Council, would like to share with you the thoughts and concerns of the general student body. As you probably know, many students are complaining about life on campus. We are interested <u>in meeting</u> with you to discuss our ideas for dealing with these complaints.

We know that you are tired of hearing students complain, and that you are not used to working with the Student Council. However, if you really believe in giving new ideas a try, we hope you will think about speaking with our representatives soon.

We look forward to hearing from you soon.

Respectfully submitted,

The Student Council

2. Spring Break

The school newspaper surveyed students. Reporters asked, "What do you like to do, and what are your plans for spring break?" Complete the student responses below. Choose the appropriate preposition from the box. (You will use one of the prepositions several times.) Add the gerund form of the verb in parentheses.

at	on	of	against	instead of
in	to	about	for	

1. I'm very interested ____*in listening*____ to jazz. I'm going to attend the Spring Jazz Festival.
   (listen)

2. We're driving all the way to Quebec City. It's famous _____ great food.
   (have)

3. I don't have any plans, but I'm not concerned _____ bored. I can always take a
   (get)
   walk in the woods or something.

4. I love languages, but I'm not good _____ them. I'm worried _____
   (learn)   (not do)
   well in my regular Japanese class, so I'm going to take a crash course in Japanese over the break.

5. My friends and I are driving to Canada. I always get excited _____ on a trip, but
   (go)
   I'm a little nervous _____ at night.
   (drive)

6. My friends and I are going camping, but my little brother insists _____ with us. A
   (come)
   lot of fun that'll be!

7. I'm really looking forward _____ at home and _____ .
   (stay)   (relax)

8. My girlfriend's very fond _____ and _____ to the movies, so I
   (read)   (go)
   guess I'll read a lot and see a lot of movies over the vacation.

9. I'm crazy _____. I'm going to experiment with a bunch of new recipes.
   (cook)

10. Everyone advised _____ to the beach at this time of year. So
    (go)
    _____ my vacation at the shore, I'm going hiking in the mountains.
    (spend)

3. Making Changes

Larry Jones quit school after high school and had various jobs. Then he decided to go to college. Now he is a full-time student. This is a big change for him. Complete the sentences about Larry. Use the appropriate form of the verb in parentheses.

1. Larry used to _____be_____ a student, but then he quit after high school.
   (be)
2. He used to _____ a job.
   (have)
3. In fact, he used to _____ a lot of different jobs.
   (have)
4. When he went back to college, he had to get used to _____ a student again.
   (be)
5. He wasn't used to _____ to school every day.
   (go)
6. He had to get used to _____ homework again and _____ for tests.
   (do)   (study)
7. When Larry was working, he used to _____ quite a bit of money. He used to
   (earn)
   _____ everything he earned, too. Now he has to get used to
   (spend)
   _____ less on food and entertainment.
   (spend)
8. It hasn't been easy, but now Larry has gotten used to _____ a student's life again.
   (live)

4. School Issues

Combine the following pairs of sentences to make statements about school life. Use the prepositions in parentheses.

1. You can't walk on campus late at night. You have to worry about your safety.

   You can't walk on campus late at night without worrying about your safety.
   (without)
2. In some cases, students just complain. They don't make suggestions for improvements.

   _____
   (instead of)
3. Students get annoyed with some teachers. Some teachers come late to class.

   _____
   (for)
4. You can improve your grades. Study regularly.

   _____
   (by)
5. We can make changes. We can tell the administration about our concerns.

   _____
   (by)
6. The administration can help. It can listen to our concerns.

   _____
   (by)

COMMUNICATION PRACTICE

5. Practice Listening

Megan is a new student. She is looking for a studio apartment. Listen to her conversation with a real estate agent, and mark the following statements true (T) or false (F).

___T___ 1. Megan wants to rent an apartment.

_____ 2. She knows the neighborhood she wants to live in.

_____ 3. Megan has looked for an apartment before.

_____ 4. Megan has not made many decisions about the kind of apartment she wants.

_____ 5. Noise doesn't bother Megan.

_____ 6. The agent thinks Megan can find everything she wants in one apartment.

6. Stress

Below are some life events, both positive and negative, that can lead to stress. Work by yourself and rank them from most stressful (1) to least stressful (7). Then in small groups compare and discuss your lists. Use be used to *and* get used to *to explain your choices.*

_____ moving to a new city

_____ changing jobs

_____ marriage

_____ divorce

_____ gaining a new family member (through birth or adoption)

_____ death of a close family member

_____ getting fired at work

Example:
I think marriage is the third most stressful life event.
You have to get used to living with another person.

7. Vote for Me

Pretend you are running for president of the Student Council. Prepare your campaign speech and read it to the class. Answer some of these questions.

If you are elected, what can students look forward to?

What are you most interested in?

What do you believe in?

What will you insist on?

What are you opposed to?

What are you excited about?

What are you good at?

Example:
Vote for me. I'm interested in making our lives better.

Then, have an election.

INTRODUCTION

Infinitives after Certain Verbs

Read and listen to this letter to the newspaper advice column, "Ask Annie."

ASK ANNIE

Dear Annie,

I never thought having a teenage daughter would be so difficult. It seems everything I say and do is wrong. I **want to know** where she's going with her friends, but she **refuses to tell** me. I **encourage her to bring** her friends home once in a while, but she always **decides to go** somewhere else. I even **invited her friends to celebrate** her birthday at a restaurant last month, but she planned her own party.

I don't think I am unreasonable, do you?

Exasperated

VERBS FOLLOWED BY INFINITIVES

STATEMENTS				
SUBJECT	**VERB**	**(OBJECT)**	**INFINITIVE**	
She	**decided**		**to go**	somewhere else.
I	**wanted**	(them)	**to celebrate**	her birthday.

Grammar Notes

1. Certain verbs can be followed by an infinitive (*to* + the base form of the verb).

   > I want **to know** where she's going.
   > I asked her **to help** me.

2. Some of these verbs are followed directly by infinitives.

   > His daughter **decided to go** somewhere else.
   > She **refused to tell** me her friend's name.

   The following verbs can be followed directly by infinitives.

   > decide
   > hope
   > learn
   > plan
   > refuse

   See Appendix 8 on page A6 for a more complete list of verbs that are followed by the infinitive.

3. Some verbs require a noun object or a pronoun object before the infinitive.

   > noun object
   > I invited **Mary** to celebrate with us.

   > pronoun object
   > I can't force **him** to listen to me.

   The following verbs require an object before the infinitive.

   > advise   order
   > allow   remind
   > encourage   tell
   > force   urge
   > invite   warn

   See Appendix 9 on page A7 for a more complete list of verbs that require an object before the infinitive.

4. Some verbs can be followed directly by the infinitive (without an object):

   > He **would like to leave**.

   or by an object and then the infinitive.

   > He **would like you to leave**.

   The following verbs can be followed directly by the infinitive or by an object and then the infinitive:

   > ask
   > expect
   > help
   > promise
   > want
   > would like

   See Appendix 9 on page A7 for a more complete list of these verbs.

FOCUSED PRACTICE

1. Discover the Grammar

Read this entry in a personal diary. Underline all the verbs + infinitives and the verbs + object + infinitives.

Dear Diary,

    We had another fight today. I try to be nice to my mother, but she wants me to tell her everything. Sometimes I just need to talk to my friends. She refuses to understand that!

    I think tonight I'd like to have a talk with her. I'll tell her that sometimes I just want to be alone. Maybe I'll ask her to think about when she was a teenager. Maybe that will force her to understand me better. Maybe she'll remember how it feels. Yes, I've decided to talk to her tonight. I'll tell you about it soon.

2. Talking to Your Teenager

Read the letter on page 201 again. Annie wrote an answer to "Exasperated" in her advice column. Read her answer. Fill in the blanks with the correct form of the verbs in parentheses.

Dear Exasperated,

    Your letter sounds so familiar. There really is nothing quite like being the parent of a teenager!

When we _____decide to have_____ children, we think of the cute little ones running around in
               1. (decide/have)

diapers. I guess most of us _____ that all those cute bundles grow up to be
                                 2. (would like/forget)

teenagers—exhausting, wonderful young people.

(continued on next page)

Believe me, I know! I have a sixteen-year-old daughter. She _____
_____ 3. (refuse/do)
anything I say. She tells me I don't understand her. She sometimes _____
_____ 4. (force/me/be)
much stricter than I'd like. At this stage of development, parents _____ all
_____ 5. (need/have)
the patience in the world—and then some. I always _____ that as with all
_____ 6. (tell/them/remember)
stages, this one will eventually pass. As much as we _____ that we are their
_____ 7. (would like/our children/think)
friends, we often _____ that they follow certain rules. Try to set those rules
_____ 8. (forget/insist)
straight, and I hope life will be easier for you.

Sincerely,

Annie

3. In Summary

Write a summary statement for each short conversation. Use a verb from the box, followed by an infinitive or an object + infinitive.

remind would like need in~~vi~~te warn ~~refuse~~ promise advise

1. **Mother:** Do the dishes.

   Daughter: No, I won't.

   SUMMARY: The daughter _____ refused to do the dishes. _____

2. **Father:** Come in. Make yourself comfortable.

   Teenage boy: Thank you.

   The father _____ invited the boy to come in. _____

3. **Father:** You must be home by 10:00 P.M. If you're not, I won't let you go out for two weeks. Do you understand me?

   Daughter: Yes, I understand.

   SUMMARY: The father _____

4. **Mother:** It would make me so happy if you would celebrate your birthday at home.

   Son: We'll see.

   SUMMARY: The mother _____

5.   **Mother:** Call me as soon as you get home.

Daughter: OK, OK.

SUMMARY: The daughter _____

6.   **Son:** Can I use the car tonight?

Mother: Sorry, I'm picking up your grandmother at the airport.

SUMMARY: The mother _____

7.   **Daughter:** Don't forget to bring my lunch to school.

Mother: I won't forget.

SUMMARY: The daughter _____

8.   **Daughter:** I'm so confused. Should I get a job now or finish school first? What do you think?

Father: I think you should definitely finish school.

SUMMARY: The father _____

COMMUNICATION PRACTICE

4. Practice Listening

Listen to a teenager talk about his parents. Listen again and circle the letter of the sentences that you hear.

1. (a.) I often need to explain what I am doing over and over.

   b. I often need them to explain what I am doing over and over.

2. a. She's OK. It's just that she wants to behave like an adult all the time.

   b. She's OK. It's just that she wants me to behave like an adult all the time.

3. a. It's unreasonable. They expect to be perfect.

   b. It's unreasonable. They expect me to be perfect.

4. a. OK. I'll try to understand better, but I refuse to do everything they say.

   b. OK. I'll try to understand them better, but I refuse to do everything they say.

5. a. Sometimes I'd just like to run away.

   b. Sometimes I'd just like them to run away.

6. a. Life isn't easy. Would you like to be a teenager again?

   b. Life isn't easy. Would you like him to be a teenager again?

5. Describe Your Parents

Work in pairs. Tell each other about your parents.

What did they encourage you to do?

How did they encourage you to do that?

What didn't they allow you to do?

What did they force you to do?

What did they advise you to do?

Why did they advise you to do that?

What would they like you to do?

What do they expect you to do?

What would *you* prefer to do?

Example:
My parents encouraged me to learn languages.

Add your own questions.

6. Role Play

Work in pairs. Read the situations that follow and take turns being the parent and the teenage child. Use infinitives.

1. *Parent:* You want your teenager to be home by 10:00 P.M.

2. *Parent:* You refuse to allow your teenager to drive.

3. *Parent:* You want to know how your teenager is planning to come home after the party.

4. *Parent:* It's 11:00 P.M. You asked your teenager to call you at 9:00 P.M.

Teenager: All of your friends can stay out until midnight.

Teenager: You would like to borrow your parents' car for the night.

Teenager: You've decided to go to a school party.

Teenager: You forgot to call your parents at 9:00. You're calling them now.

Can you think of some other situations? Share them with the class.

7. What Do You Think?

Work in pairs. Write your own response to the letter on page 201. Use infinitives. Then read your letter to your classmates. Decide on the best advice.

INTRODUCTION

Read and listen to this ad for an electronic pocket organizer.

DATALATOR 534 F

DATALATOR 534 F

Rick Smith
555-2786

$34.95*

*Batteries not included

Fifteen years ago, you bought your first calculator **to help** balance your checkbook. Today's new Datalator looks like a calculator but does much more than add two plus two. You can use it **to store** fifty names and phone numbers, **to tell** you the date and time, or **to convert** foreign currencies. (Of course you can still use it **to add** and **subtract**, if you want.) Buy the new Datalator 534 F and put the whole world at your fingertips.

Available at all Lacy's Department Stores

207

INFINITIVE OF PURPOSE

AFFIRMATIVE
I went to Lacy's **(in order) to buy** an electronic organizer. Give me some batteries **to put** in my Datalator.

NEGATIVE
You can use it **in order not to waste** time.

Grammar Notes

1. Use an infinitive to explain the purpose of an action. It often answers the question *Why?*

   A: I went to Lacy's Department Store.
   B: Why did you go there?
   A: I went there **to buy** an electronic organizer.

   You can also use the longer form, *in order to*, but *to* + the base form of the verb is more common in informal speech and writing.

   I bought a calculator **in order to balance** my checkbook.
   OR
   I bought a calculator **to balance** my checkbook.

2. In spoken English, you can answer the question *Why?* with an incomplete sentence beginning with *To*.

   A: Why are you going to Lacy's?
   B: **To buy** an electronic organizer.

3. Use *in order not to* to express a negative purpose.

   I use a calculator **in order not to make** mistakes. (I don't want to make mistakes.)

4. You can also use the infinitive after a noun or pronoun to express the purpose of an object.

   I need **something to help** me balance my checkbook.
   Give me a **battery to put** in my calculator.

FOCUSED PRACTICE

1. Discover the Grammar

Read the conversation. Underline all the infinitives that express a purpose.

Yoko: It's 5:00. Aren't you going home?

Lee: No. I'm staying late <u>to finish</u> this report. What about you? Are you going straight home?

Yoko: No. I'm going to stop at the bank to get some cash. Then I'm going to Lacy's Department Store to take advantage of the sale they're having.

Lee: Oh, what do you want to buy?

Yoko: One of those new electronic organizers they're advertising. I've been looking for something to help me with my work.

Lee: What's wrong with a regular calculator?

Yoko: Nothing. But sometimes I have to convert other currencies to dollars.

Lee: What else are you going to use it for?

Yoko: Oh, to store important names and phone numbers and to balance my checkbook.

Lee: What did we do before they invented all these electronic gadgets?

Yoko: We made a lot of mistakes!

2. Tell Me Why

Look at Yoko's list of things to do. Then write a phrase to answer each question.

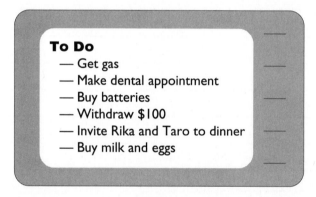

To Do
— Get gas
— Make dental appointment
— Buy batteries
— Withdraw $100
— Invite Rika and Taro to dinner
— Buy milk and eggs

1. Why did she call Dr. Towbin's office?

   To make a dental appointment.

2. Why did she go to the bank?

3. Why did she call Mrs. Watanabe?

4. Why did she go to the supermarket?

5. Why did she go to the electronics store?

6. Why did she go to the service station?

3. The Reason Is

Match each action with its purpose.

Action	Purpose
_g_ 1. He enrolled in Chinese 101 because he	a. didn't want to get any phone calls.
____ 2. She took a bus because she	b. wanted to get more exercise.
____ 3. She went to Lacy's Department Store because she	c. didn't want to be late.
____ 4. We disconnected our phone because we	d. wanted to listen to the news.
____ 5. They started jogging because they	e. didn't want to worry me.
____ 6. He turned on the radio because he	f. needed to buy some dishes.
____ 7. He didn't tell me he was sick because he	g. wanted to learn the language.

Now combine the sentences. Use the infinitive of purpose.

1. He enrolled in Chinese 101 to learn the language.
2. She took a bus in order not to be late.
3. _____
4. _____
5. _____
6. _____
7. _____

COMMUNICATION PRACTICE

4. Practice Listening

You are calling Lacy's Department Store to get information. Read the list below. Listen to Lacy's automatic telephone message. Then listen again and write the number of the telephone key that you should press for each of the following purposes.

1. place an order [3]
2. find out when the store opens [ ]
3. report a lost or stolen credit card [ ]
4. ask about a bill [ ]
5. ask about a delivery [ ]
6. speak to a customer service representative [ ]
7. listen to the message again [ ]

5. What's the Use?

Work in groups. Think of uses for the following objects. Use the infinitive of purpose and your imagination!

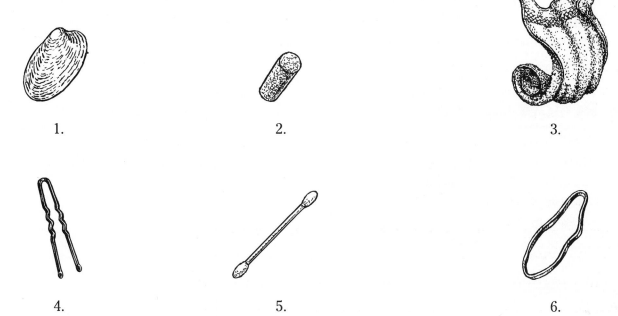

1.

2.

3.

4.

5.

6.

Example:
You can use a shell to hold coins, to keep soap in, or to eat from.

6. What Are Their Motives?

Work in groups. Read the following situations. Think of as many reasons as possible to explain the people's actions. Use the infinitive of purpose.

1. Sally doesn't speak or understand a word of Italian. However, last night she went to see an Italian movie. Why?

   Example:
   A: Perhaps she went there to meet someone in secret.
   B: Maybe she went there to get some sleep.

2. John lives a block away from a supermarket. However, when he wanted to buy a container of milk, he went to another store located ten minutes from his home. Why?

   Perhaps he went to the other store . . .

3. Fran usually drives home from work. However, this month she decided to walk. Why?

   Perhaps she's walking home from work . . .

4. George grew a beard and changed the color of his hair.

   Perhaps he . . .

7. The Datalator

*Reread the ad on page 207. Would you like to have an electronic organizer?
What would you use it to do? What wouldn't you use it to do? Discuss your
answers with a partner.*

Example:
I'd use it to keep a record of my appointments.
I wouldn't use it to add two plus two!

8. Remote Control

Read this ad for a remote control.

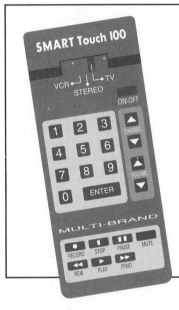

The SMART Touch 100

You can program this powerful remote
to operate up to six video and audio
components—your TV, VCR, stereo,
cassette deck, and more. It's easy and
convenient to use. So, get smart, get
the SMART Touch.

*Work in small groups. Discuss the Smart Touch 100. Would you like to have
one? Imagine that it could control everything in your house—not only
electronic equipment. What would you use it to do?*

Example:
A: I'd use it to turn on my shower.
B: I'd use it to open and close my windows.

INTRODUCTION

Infinitives with *Too* and *Enough*

Read and listen to this letter to the editor of the Herald Weekly *newspaper.*

To the Editor:

Take away the vote? No way! I am referring to the *Herald's* editorial of last Sunday about taking the vote away from 18-year-olds. I am an 18-year-old high school senior, and I am very angry about the results of your survey. Perhaps people answered your survey **too quickly to consider** all the issues.

In 1971, the 26th Amendment to the U.S. Constitution lowered the voting age from 21 to 18. We, the 18-year-olds of America, were **old enough to vote** then; why are we **too young to vote** now? Perhaps we have not voted **often enough for people to understand** our role in politics.

According to your editorial, most Americans feel we are **mature enough to be** in the army but we are **not responsible enough to vote** in national elections. Does that make any sense? Are we really **not too young to die** for our country but still **too young for older people to want** us to make important decisions about our future? I don't understand it. Do you?

INFINITIVES WITH *TOO* AND *ENOUGH*

INFINITIVES WITH *TOO*				
	TOO	ADJECTIVE/ ADVERB	(*FOR* + NOUN/ OBJECT PRONOUN)	INFINITIVE
We're (not)	too	young	(for people)	**to trust.**
People answered		quickly	(for them)	**to consider** all the issues.

INFINITIVES WITH *ENOUGH*				
	ADJECTIVE/ ADVERB	*ENOUGH*	(*FOR* + NOUN/ OBJECT PRONOUN)	INFINITIVE
They're (not)	old	enough	(for people)	**to trust.**
We have(n't) voted	often		(for them)	**to understand** our role.

Grammar Notes

1. Use *too* + adjective/adverb + infinitive to give a reason. Remember that *too* often has a negative meaning.

> I'm **too young to vote.** (I'm too young, so I can't vote.)
> I arrived **too late to vote**. (I arrived too late, so I couldn't vote.)

2. You can also use adjective/adverb + *enough* + infinitive to give a reason. Remember that *enough* usually has a positive meaning.

> I'm **old enough to go** into the army. (I'm old enough, so I can go into the army.)
> I ran **fast enough** to pass the physical. (I ran fast enough, so I passed the physical.)

3. Notice that you don't need to use the infinitive when the meaning is clear from the context.

> I'm 17 years old, and I can't vote yet. I'm **too young**. I'm **not old enough**.

Be careful! Note the placement of *too* and *enough*. *Too* comes before the adjective or adverb. *Enough* comes after the adjective or adverb.

> She's **too old.**
> I'm not **old enough**.

4. Sometimes we use *for* + a noun or a pronoun in front of the infinitive.

> We are too young **for many Americans** to trust us. (Many Americans don't trust us.)
> We are too young **for them** to trust us. (They don't trust us.)

FOCUSED PRACTICE

1. Discover the Grammar

People have different opinions about women in military combat. Read the sentences that follow. Then choose the sentence that summarizes each opinion.

1. Women are not too delicate to fight.
   - (a.) Women can fight.
   - b. Women can't fight.

2. Women are strong enough to carry modern weapons.
   - a. Women can carry modern weapons.
   - b. Women can't carry modern weapons.

3. Women are too emotional to go to war.
   - a. Women can go to war.
   - b. Women can't go to war.

4. Women run fast enough to keep up with men.
   - a. Women can keep up with men.
   - b. Women can't keep up with men.

5. Women have worked too hard to give up the fight for equal rights now.
   - a. Women can stop fighting for equal rights now.
   - b. Women can't stop fighting for equal rights yet.

6. Women don't command aggressively enough for soldiers to follow their orders.
   - a. Soldiers will follow women's orders.
   - b. Soldiers won't follow women's orders.

7. Public opinion isn't supportive enough to allow women in combat.
   - a. Public opinion doesn't support women in combat.
   - b. Public opinion supports women in combat.

8. Men are too afraid to accept women as equals.
   - a. Men can accept women as equals.
   - b. Men cannot accept women as equals.

Read the sentences again. Write the number of the sentences that support the idea of women in military combat. Write the number of the sentences that are against the idea of women in military combat.

In Favor	Against
1	

2. Can You Get By?

Match the pictures with the sentences below.

1. __e.__

2. _____

3. _____

4. _____

5. _____

6. _____

7. _____

8. _____

a. The buttons are too high for him to reach.

b. The buttons are low enough for him to reach.

c. The step is too steep for her to get up.

d. The box is too heavy for him to lift.

e. The street is too busy for them to cross.

f. The traffic is slow enough for them to cross.

g. She is old enough to join the army.

h. She is too old to join the army.

3. Attention!

Complete these conversations that take place on a military base. Use the words in parentheses with the infinitive and too *or* enough.

1. **A:** Can we use this road?

   B: No. It's _____ too dangerous to drive _____ on. Take that other one.
   (dangerous / drive)

2. **A:** Can't you drive any faster?

   B: Sure. What's the problem?

   A: You're not going _____ there on time.
   (fast / us / get)

3. **A:** Do you think we can carry these boxes of ammunition back to the barracks?

   B: Sure. They're _____.
   (light / us / carry)

4. **A:** Have you seen the new sergeant?

   B: Yes. I can't believe he's a sergeant.

   A: I know. He looks _____ a sergeant.
   (young / be)

5. **A:** Hey, guys! Keep your voices down! It's _____.
   (noisy / me / sleep)

   B: Sorry.

6. **A:** Do you think we'll get there before the sun sets?

   B: I'm afraid not. It's _____ before dark.
   (far / us / reach)

7. **A:** Ugh! This tastes awful!

   B: What do you expect from army food?

   A: Well, it should at least be _____!
   (good / eat)

8. **A:** Try some of this coffee.

   B: Ow! It's _____.
   (hot / drink)

COMMUNICATION PRACTICE

4. Practice Listening

Listen to the description of a new community center. It is built so that people in wheelchairs can get around easily. Then listen again and circle the number of the picture that best fits the description.

1.

2.

3.

5. Is It Fair?

Read the letter on page 213 or the Discover the Grammar on page 215. Discuss one of these questions.

Should 18-year-olds vote?

Should women be in combat?

Share your opinions. Be sure to use too *and* enough *in your discussion.*

6. Common Expressions

What do you think these expressions mean? When would you use them?
Discuss your ideas in small groups.

1. She's old enough to know better.
2. Life is too short to worry about every little thing.
3. You're never too old to try.
4. It looks good enough to eat.
5. It's too hot to handle.

7. What's Your Opinion?

Complete the following sentences. In small groups, compare your opinions.

1. Elderly people are too . . .

   Example:
   A: People over seventy are too old to drive.
   B: Oh. I don't agree. Some elderly people drive better than young people.

2. The president of the United States is powerful enough . . .
3. Teenagers are too crazy . . .
4. Guns are too dangerous . . .
5. Taxes aren't high enough . . .
6. Women are strong enough . . .
7. Radio and TV broadcasters speak (or don't speak) clearly enough . . .
8. Time goes by too quickly . . .

UNIT
26

Contrast: Gerunds and Infinitives

▼

INTRODUCTION

▼

 Read and listen to this excerpt from a magazine article entitled "Stop Forgetting."

[STOP] Forgetting

Sonia **wanted to go** to the party. She's friendly and **enjoys meeting** people. But as Sonia looked at the invitation, part of her **kept saying,** "I can't go! I'll make a fool of myself." Sonia's problem is not unusual — she can't remember people's names. What can Sonia do? Here are some tips from memory experts.

- **Decide to remember. Making** an effort can really help.

- Listen carefully when you hear someone's name for the first time. It's important **to pay** attention.

- **Keep repeating** the name. **Calling** the person by name more than once will help fix the name in your mind.

- Write the name down. **Putting** things in **writing** is the most common memory aid.

- Don't **hesitate to ask** the person **to repeat** the name. Most people won't **mind doing** this.

And last, but not least,

- **Stop worrying.** Anxiety only makes the problem worse.

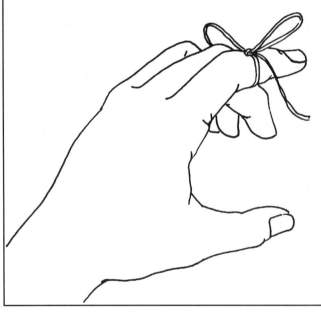

220

CONTRAST: GERUNDS AND INFINITIVES

GERUNDS
Sonia **enjoys meeting** people.
She **loves meeting** new people.
She **stopped buying** ice cream.
She's worried **about forgetting** people's names.
Meeting new people is fun.

INFINITIVES
Sonia **wants to go** to the party.
She **loves to meet** new people.
She **stopped to buy** ice cream.
It's fun **to meet** new people.

Grammar Notes

1. Some verbs are followed by the gerund. (See Appendix 8 on page A6 for a list of these verbs.)

   Sonia **enjoys meeting** people.
   She **avoids going** to parties.

2. Some verbs are followed by the infinitive. (See Appendix 7 on page A6 for a list of these verbs.)

   She **wanted to go** to the party.
   She **decided to improve** her memory.

3. Some verbs can be followed by either the gerund or the infinitive. Some of these include *begin, hate, like, love,* and *prefer*. (See Appendix 8 on page A6 for a list of these verbs.)

   Sonia **loves meeting** new people.
   OR
   Sonia **loves to meet** new people.

4. Be careful! A few verbs (for example, *stop, remember,* and *forget*) can be followed by either the gerund or the infinitive, but the meanings are very different.

   Sonia **stopped eating** ice cream. (She doesn't eat ice cream anymore.)
   Sonia **stopped to eat** ice cream. (She stopped another activity **in order to** eat some ice cream.)

   Frank **remembered mailing** the invitation. (First he mailed the invitation. Then he remembered that he did it. He can picture it in his mind.)
   Frank **remembered to mail** the invitation. (First he remembered. Then he mailed the invitation. He didn't forget.)

   Sonia **forgot to meet** John. (Sonia had plans to meet John, but she didn't meet him because she forgot about the plans.)
   Sonia **forgot meeting** John. (Sonia met John, but afterwards she didn't remember the event.)

5. The gerund is the only verb form that can follow a preposition. (See page 195 in Unit 22.)

   Sonia's worried **about forgetting** people's names.

6. You can use the gerund as the subject or *it* + the infinitive to make general statements.

   Meeting new people is fun.
   OR
   It's fun **to meet** new people.

FOCUSED PRACTICE

1. Discover the Grammar

Read the first sentence. Then decide if the second sentence is true (T) *or false* (F).

1. Sonia remembered meeting Mr. Jackson.

   __T__ Sonia has already met Mr. Jackson.

2. Frank stopped smoking.

   _____ Frank doesn't smoke anymore.

3. She didn't remember to buy a cake for the party.

   _____ She bought a cake.

4. She stopped eating desserts.

   _____ She used to eat desserts.

5. Frank forgot to invite his boss to the party.

   _____ Frank invited his boss.

6. Frank forgot inviting his neighbor to the party.

   _____ Frank invited his neighbor.

7. Frank thinks giving a party is fun.

   _____ Frank thinks it's fun to give a party.

8. Sonia likes going to parties.

   _____ Sonia likes to go to parties.

2. Super Memory

Complete these ideas from a book called Super Memory* *by Douglas J. Herrmann, Ph.D. Use the gerund or infinitive form of the verb in parentheses.*

1. Get in the habit of _____repeating_____ things aloud.
                          (repeat)

2. Never rely on someone else's memory.

   Learn _____ your own.
              (trust)

3. It's easy _____ what you don't want _____.
                (forget)   (learn)

4. Study immediately before _____ to sleep. You'll remember a lot more the next day.
                                  (go)

5. Our memories are filled with a lot of things we never even meant _____.
                                                                      (remember)

6. Make it a habit to pass in front of your car every time you get out, and you'll never forget

   _____ your headlights.
        (turn off)

7. _____ games is a fun way of _____ your memory skills.
       (Play)   (improve)

*Herrmann, Douglas J.: *Super Memory: A Quick Action Program for Memory Improvement,* 1991, Wings Book, N.J.

3. Party Talk

Read these conversations that took place at Frank's party. Complete the summary statements. Use the gerund or the infinitive.

1. **Frank:** Hi, Roger. Did you bring the soda?

    Roger: Yes. Here it is.

    Roger remembered _____ *to bring the soda* _____.

2. **Frank:** Sonia, do you remember Alicia and Roger?

    Sonia: Oh, yes. We met last year.

    Sonia remembers _____.

3. **Alicia:** Oh, no. Somebody spilled grape juice all over the couch.

    Roger: Don't look at me! I didn't do it!

    Roger denied _____.

4. **Sonia:** What do you do in your free time, Alicia?

    Alicia: I listen to music a lot.

    Alicia enjoys _____.

5. **Adam:** Would you like to go dancing some time?

    Sonia: Sure. I'd like that very much.

    Adam suggested _____.

    Sonia agreed _____ with Adam.

6. **Roger:** I'm tired. Let's go home.

    Alicia: OK. Just five minutes more.

    Roger wants _____.

7. **Alicia:** Sonia, can we give you a ride home?

    Sonia: Thanks, but I think I'll stay a little longer.

    Alicia offered _____.

    Sonia decided _____.

8. **Frank:** Good night. Please drive carefully.

    Roger: Don't worry. I will.

    Roger promised _____.

4. A Letter

Sonia wrote a letter to her friend about Frank's party, but there are six mistakes in using the gerund and infinitive. Find and correct them.

Dear Lisa,

  I expected ~~hearing~~ *to hear* from you by now. I hope you're OK. I'm busy but happy. Last night I went to a party at one of my classmate's homes. I was really nervous. You know how I usually avoid to go to parties because I have trouble remembering people's names. Well, last night things were different. Before the party, I read a book about improving your memory, and I practiced doing some of the memory exercises. They really helped. As a result, I stopped to worry about what people would think of me, and I tried to pay attention to what people were saying. And guess what? I had a good time!

  I'm even planning going dancing with this guy from my class.

  Why don't you consider to visit me? I really miss seeing you.

  Please write. I always enjoy to hear from you.

        Sonia

5. In Other Words

Sonia and Adam are on their first date. They agree on everything. Read one person's opinion and write the other's. If the first person used the gerund, use the infinitive. If the first person used the infinitive, use the gerund.

1. **Sonia:** It's fun to meet new people.

   Adam: I agree. _____ Meeting new people is fun. _____

2. **Sonia:** Remembering names is hard, though.

   Adam: I know. _____ It's hard to remember names. _____

3. **Adam:** It's difficult to make new friends.

   Sonia: That's true. _____

4. **Sonia:** It's important to relax.

   Adam: You're right. _____

5. **Adam:** Dancing is fun.

   Sonia: I agree. _____

6. **Sonia:** It's important to tell the truth.

   Adam: Yes. _____

7. **Sonia:** It's nice to get to know someone like you.

   Adam: I feel the same way. _____

8. **Adam:** Being with you is wonderful.

   Sonia: Thanks. _____, too.

COMMUNICATION PRACTICE

6. Practice Listening

The school newspaper is interviewing Sonia about her opinions on dating. Read the list of activities. Listen to the interview. Then listen again and check the things Sonia does and doesn't do when she is first getting to know someone.

	Things Sonia does	Things Sonia doesn't do
1. go for walks	✓	☐
2. go dancing	☐	☐
3. go bowling	☐	☐
4. go to the movies	☐	☐
5. have pizza out	☐	☐
6. make dinner at home	☐	☐
7. have a picnic	☐	☐

7. Social Situation Survey

How do you feel and act in new social situations? Complete these sentences. Use the gerund or the infinitive. Then discuss your answers with a partner.

When I'm in a new social situation, I

1. enjoy _____
2. always expect _____
3. never hesitate _____
4. dislike _____
5. don't mind _____
6. am afraid of _____
7. sometimes feel like _____
8. avoid _____
9. often regret _____
10. keep _____
11. always try _____
12. believe it's important _____
13. feel nervous about _____

8. Test Your Memory

Look at this picture for two minutes. Try to remember each person's name and what each person said. Then close your book. Work with a partner. How much can the two of you remember? Write down the information and then check your answers with your book.

Example:
A: Ann enjoys dancing.
B: I don't think that's right. Ann enjoys jogging.

9. Stop Forgetting

Work in small groups. Reread the article on page 220. Discuss these questions:

1. Do you have trouble remembering people's names?

2. Do you follow any of the experts' memory tips?

3. What other things do you have trouble remembering?

4. What tricks do you use to remember things?

    Example:
    A: I sometimes forget to pay my rent.
    B: Oh, I always make a note on my calendar when the rent is due.

I. *Complete the interview with the gerund or infinitive forms of the verbs in parentheses.*

Interviewer: You're one of the best baseball players today, Cliff. Who

taught you _____*to play*_____?
1. (play)

Cliff: I learned _____ a ball with my dad. We
2. (hit)

used to play together for hours on weekends.

Interviewer: What was the most important thing he taught you?

Cliff: Dad believed in _____ fun. He always
3. (have)

forgot about _____ when he played.
4. (win)

By _____ with him, I learned the same
5. (play)

attitude.

Interviewer: When did you decide _____ a
6. (become)

professional?

Cliff: Too early—in elementary school. That was a mistake. I

was too young _____ that decision.
7. (make)

Interviewer: Why?

Cliff: My schoolwork suffered. I thought a lot about

_____ a pro ball player, and I didn't
8. (become)

think much about _____ homework.
9. (do)

Interviewer: Did anything happen to change your mind about

school?

Cliff: Yes, I planned _____ to City High
10. (go)

School, which had a great team. Then I found out that

my grades were probably too low for the school

_____ me.
11. (accept)

Interviewer: But you did graduate from City High School.

Cliff: Yes, I did. My parents urged me _____
12. (study)

harder. I followed their advice and I've never stopped

_____.
13. (study)

II. *Choose the best response to each sentence.*

1. Is Tom home yet?

   a. No. He stopped buying dinner.

   (b.) No. He stopped to buy dinner.

2. I just found your keys. They were in your coat pocket!

   a. I don't remember putting them in my pocket.

   b. I don't remember to put them in my pocket.

3. You didn't vote this year. Why not?

   a. We're young enough to vote.

   b. We're too young to vote.

4. Why did you buy a Datalator?

   a. By organizing my appointments.

   b. To organize my appointments.

5. How did you finish everything so fast?

   a. By planning my time.

   b. To plan my time.

6. Why are all your grades so low?

   a. I stopped studying.

   b. I stopped to study.

7. Women make good military officers.

   a. They work hard enough to get the job done.

   b. They work too hard to get the job done.

8. I'm used to eating a big breakfast.

   a. Why did you stop?

   b. Me, too. It gives me a lot of energy.

III. *Each sentence has one error with gerunds or infinitives. Find and correct the error.*

1. It's difficult <u>to</u> study in a foreign country, so students need to prepare for the experience.

2. Students look forward to experiencing another country, but they worry about not to make a good impression on their hosts.

3. They're afraid of not understanding the culture, and they don't want to making mistakes.

4. There are books that can advise them against wear the wrong clothing and making the wrong gestures.

5. However, it's natural to have some problems; no one can get used to live in a new culture immediately.

6. Therefore, no one gets away from feeling some culture shock; it's important realize this fact.

IV. *Complete the conversation. Use the prepositions in the box and the gerund form of the verbs in parentheses.*

for	to	in	without	by	about

A: Carla, your English is just great. How did you learn so quickly?

B: _____By using_____ some special strategies.

_____1. (Use)_____

A: Like what?

B: First, I got used _____ my time. I scheduled time _____

_____2. (plan)_____ _____3. (watch)_____
television and writing letters in English to my pen pal, for example.

A: How did you practice speaking?

B: Well, at first I was very nervous _____ English. I had to learn to talk

_____4. (speak)_____
_____ about mistakes. I used deep breathing exercises and music to calm

_____5. (worry)_____
down.

A: What else helped you relax?

B: Jokes. I got interested _____ jokes in English. That way I always had

_____6. (learn)_____
something to say, and I also learned a lot about American culture.

V. *Complete each conversation with the correct phrase in parentheses.*

1. **A:** Let's go jogging.

   B: I don't know. You always run _____too fast_____ for me to keep up with you.

(too fast/fast enough)
   A: OK. Let's go swimming, then.

2. **A:** Why did I get an F on this paper?

   B: Your handwriting was _____ for me to read.

(n't messy enough/too messy)
   A: Then how did you know the answers were wrong?

3. **A:** Have you tried the coffee?

   B: I will in a minute. It's _____ to drink yet.

(too cool/not cool enough)
4. **A:** This steak is _____ to eat.

(too tough/ n't tough enough)
   B: Send it back and ask for something else.

5. **A:** John didn't make the soccer team.

   B: Why not? He's a good player.

   A: But he doesn't play _____ to win.

(too aggressively/aggressively enough)
6. **A:** What did the forecaster say about thunderstorms?

   B: I'm not sure. The radio wasn't _____ for me to hear.

(loud enough/too loud)

VI. *Complete the paragraph with the words in the box. Use each word once.*

it's	eat	to	follow	~~you~~
stop	eating	stopping	smoking	following

Your doctor has warned _____you_____ to stop smoking. Your friends are urging you
1.

_____ quit. Even your dry cleaner suggests _____. (He said you
2.   3.

burned holes in your suit jacket.) You've finally decided to _____ their advice.
4.

_____ not easy to give up a habit like smoking, but _____ these three
5.   6.

suggestions will help:

    a. _____ drinking coffee and tea completely. Drink water instead. Caffeine causes
           7.
       people to want a cigarette.

    b. When you want a cigarette, just put off _____ for five minutes at a time. Your
                            8.
       urge to smoke will pass soon.

    c. Avoid _____ big meals for a few weeks. Try not to _____
             9.   10.
       much meat or very spicy foods.

If you follow these suggestions, it shouldn't be too hard to give up this unhealthy habit.

VII. *Complete the conversation by writing the words and phrases in parentheses in the correct order.*

A: Why are so many people starting home-based businesses?

B: In offices, work hours are often _____too long for people_____ to spend time with their families.
                                    1. (people/too long/for)

A: Do business owners really work fewer hours?

B: No, they work more. But they can arrange their time. Their hours _____
                                                                     2. (enough/for them/are flexible)
    to have family time too.

A: What do you warn new business owners about?

B: I _____ their privacy. Remember, the business phone is always going to
            3. (them/to think about/advise)
    ring in the middle of the family dinner.

A: Anything else?

B: _____ the loneliness of working alone, especially when you're used to a
            4. (important/It's/to know about)
    big office.

A: What kind of home businesses are people starting?

B: Well, as I said, a lot of people _____ family responsibilities anymore.
                                   5. (enough/don't have/time for)
    Many home-based businesses supply services like shopping and planning parties.

A: You mean, someone will pay me for shopping?

B: Sure. In fact, I _____ planning your own shopping business. My class for
                 6. (you/to start/encourage)
    new business owners starts next week.

VII

Modals and Related Verbs and Expressions

INTRODUCTION

In spite of difficulties, Kristi Yamaguchi won an Olympic gold medal for figure skating in 1992. Read and listen to the article about her.

Today, tiny Kristi Yamaguchi is one of the giants of figure skating. However, Yamaguchi had to overcome several difficulties before she **was able to succeed**. She was born with a serious foot problem and wore special shoes until she was six years old. She is also very small, and she **cannot do** some of the jumps that stronger skaters **can do.** How **was** she **able to win** the 1992 gold medal? "She has guts," was one skater's answer.

Yamaguchi fell in love with skating in 1976, at age four. She **couldn't skate** then because of her foot problem, but she **was able to start** lessons when she was six. As a

child, she worked with her coach for long hours and practiced every day with her partner, Rudi Galindo.

Kristi and Rudi were small and graceful, and they **could skate** beautifully together. "We were both little jumpers," says Yamaguchi. By 1989, they **were able to compete** against adults and **win** the U.S. national championships.

In 1990 Yamaguchi decided to skate alone. Her skating improved rapidly after that. Recently she **has been able to give** almost perfect performances. Yamaguchi's talent and hard work brought her success in 1992 and the Olympic gold medal for women's figure skating.

ABILITY: *CAN* AND *COULD**

STATEMENTS			
SUBJECT	**CAN/COULD (NOT)**	**BASE FORM OF VERB**	
I You He She We You They	**can (not)**	**skate**	now.
	could (not)		last year.

CONTRACTIONS		
cannot OR can not	=	can't
could not	=	couldn't

*Can and *could* are modals. Modals have only one form. They do not have *-s* in the third-person singular.

YES/NO QUESTIONS		
CAN/COULD	**SUBJECT**	**BASE FORM OF VERB**
Can	I you he she we you they	**skate?**
Could		

SHORT ANSWERS		
AFFIRMATIVE		
Yes,	you I he she	**can.**
	you we they	**could.**

SHORT ANSWERS		
NEGATIVE		
No,	you I he she	**can't.**
	you we they	**couldn't.**

WH- QUESTIONS			
WH- WORD	**CAN/COULD**	**SUBJECT**	**BASE FORM OF VERB**
How well	**can** **could**	she you	**skate?**

ABILITY: *BE ABLE TO*

STATEMENTS			
SUBJECT	**BE**	**(NOT) ABLE TO**	**BASE FORM OF VERB**
I	am	(not) able to	practice.
You	are		
He She	is		
We You They	are		

YES/NO QUESTIONS			
BE	**SUBJECT**	**ABLE TO**	**BASE FORM OF VERB**
Is	she	able to	practice?

SHORT ANSWERS		
AFFIRMATIVE		
Yes,	she	is.

SHORT ANSWERS		
NEGATIVE		
No,	she	isn't.

WH- QUESTIONS				
WH- WORD	**BE**	**SUBJECT**	**ABLE TO**	**BASE FORM OF VERB**
When	is	she	able to	practice?

Grammar Notes

1. Use *can* to describe an ability in the present.

Josh **can swim**, but he **can't skate**.

2. You can also use *be able to* to describe an ability in the present or future.

I**'m able to park** a car, but I**'m not able to drive** in traffic yet.
They**'ll be able to visit** us next year, but they **won't be able to stay** long.

Note: *Can* is used much more frequently than *be able to* in the present tense.

3. Use either *could* or *was/were able to* to describe a <u>general ability</u> in the past.

Kristi's grandfather **could speak** Japanese and English.
Kristi and Rudi **were able to practice** together every day.

4. You must use *was/were able to* to describe a <u>special achievement</u> or a <u>single event</u> in the past.

Finally, she **was able to win** her first race. NOT ~~She could win her first race~~.

5. You can use either *couldn't* or *wasn't/weren't able to* for any negative sentence describing past ability.

General ability:

He **couldn't speak** Chinese.   OR   He **wasn't able to speak** Chinese.

Special achievement:

They **couldn't win** the race.   OR   They **weren't able to win** the race.

6. For forms and tenses other than the present or past, you must use *be able to*.

Jean **wants to be able to play** soccer next year. (infinitive form)
He **hasn't been able to practice** for a long time. (present perfect)

Note: Use *can* and *could* to say that something is possible, to make guesses and polite requests, to make suggestions, and to ask for and give permission. See Units 28, 29, 31, 35, and 36 for these uses of *can* and *could*.

FOCUSED PRACTICE

1. Discover the Grammar

⊙⊙ *Read and listen to the conversation between Rita Pratt and her driving instructor. Underline the words and phrases that describe ability. Then complete the Student Progress Report.*

Tim: That was a good lesson, Rita. You used turn signals the whole time. And you <u>were able to make</u> that left turn in heavy traffic.

Rita: Thanks, Tim. But I'm a little worried. I keep trying, but I haven't been able to park the car properly. And I still can't back up in a straight line.

Tim: Hey, don't feel bad about that. When you started lessons last week, you could start the car, and you could steer it—and that was all. You couldn't even make right turns. This week you can drive in traffic, and you can even make difficult left turns. You've made a lot of progress in two weeks.

Rita: That's true. But can I learn how to park in time for my road test?

Tim: Sure you can.

Rita: Really? I want to be able to drive to the mountains for a camping trip in July.

Tim: You can take the test sooner than that. In fact, I was able to schedule your road test for May 20.

Rita: That's next week! I won't be able to park by next week!

Tim: Sure you will.

LANE Driving School
Student Progress Report
Skills: Check (✔) the week

Student's Name ____Rita Pratt____   Date of Road Test _____

	Week of		
Student can	May 2	May 9	_____
• start car			
• steer car			
• use signals			
• make right turn			
• make left turn		✔	
• drive in traffic			
• park			
• back up			

2. Now I Can

Complete the paragraphs with can, can't, could, *and* couldn't.

1. Steven An has made a lot of progress in English. Last semester he ___couldn't___ order a meal in a

a.
   restaurant or talk on the telephone. His friends helped him do everything. Now he _____

b.
   speak English in a lot of situations.

2. For a long time, Jim and Marie _____ agree on a family sport. Jim loves tennis. Marie has just

a.
   started taking lessons, but she still _____ play. Marie _____ swim, but Jim hates the

b. c.
   water. Five years ago, they took up dancing. After a few lessons, they _____ tango beautifully

d.
   together. This year, they're going to compete in Buenos Aires. I think they _____ win.

e.

3. A few years ago I _____ jog five miles easily, but now I _____ run very far at all.

a. b.
   Yesterday I _____ even run to the corner to catch my bus. I think I'll start exercising again.

c.
   I'm a little tired now, but I _____ start tomorrow.

d.

4. Once Julia's car had a flat tire on the highway. She _____ change the tire, and she waited a

a.
   long time for help. It was a terrible experience. After that, she took a course in car repair. Now she
   _____ change a flat tire and take care of her own car.

b.

3. At the Skating Rink

Complete each conversation with the correct form of be able to *and the verb
in parentheses.*

1. **A:** I heard your sister wanted to take lessons. ____Was____ she ____able to start____?

a. (start)
   B: Yes, she was. She started last month.

   A: How's she doing?

   B: Very well. She doesn't fall down much anymore, but she still _____ backwards.

b. (skate)

2. **A:** _____ you _____ Russian as a child, Mrs. Suraikin?

a. (speak)
   B: Yes, I was. We spoke it at home, so I _____ it fluently.

b. (speak)
   A: _____ your children _____ Russian too?

c. (speak)
   B: No, unfortunately my children never learned Russian. They only speak English.

3. **A:** I _____ my math assignment for yesterday. I practiced for a competition all

a. (finish)
   week, and I was just too tired to do homework.

   B: When _____ you _____ it?

b. (do)

(continued on next page)

A: Probably by next week.

4. **A:** I heard there was a fire in your building yesterday. Was anyone hurt?

    B: No, the firefighters _____ everyone out of the building.

(get)

5. **A:** I hurt my ankle last Saturday. I _____ since then.

a. (not practice)

    B: That's too bad. _____ you _____ next week?

b. (practice)

    A: I hope so. I'll call you on Monday. Maybe we _____ on Tuesday.

c. (get together)

4. Achievement

Read this student's paragraph about a famous skater. There are five mistakes. Find and correct them with can, could, *and* be able to.

     Scott Hamilton was a sickly kid who couldn't ~~played~~ ^{play} sports, but he became the best skater of his time. The first time Scott put on skates, he couldn't to stand up because he was weak from many years of sickness. However, after he skated for a year, his doctor announced, "He's healthy!" Scott was a talented skater, and he was able to improve quickly. When he was thirteen, he could win the Junior U.S. Championship. Soon after that, he almost quit skating because his parents can't afford to pay for his lessons anymore. However, a rich family offered to help, so Scott was able continue skating. Scott skated like an athlete, not like a dancer. He changed the style of men's figure skating. In 1984 he won the big prize—the Olympic gold medal.

COMMUNICATION PRACTICE

5. Practice Listening

🔲🔲 *Rita is telling her brother Roy about her camping trip. Listen and circle true* (T) *or false* (F) *for each statement.*

1. Rita drove to the mountains.   Ⓣ   F
2. Rita and John found the campgrounds easily.   T   F
3. They didn't put up their tent because it was dark.   T   F
4. They didn't make a campfire because it rained.   T   F
5. John and Rita decided to leave after two days.   T   F
6. Rita didn't swim, but John did.   T   F
7. Rita will show Roy pictures next week.   T   F

6. Can You Drive?

Work with a partner. Imagine you are planning a trip by car across the United States next summer. You want to camp on the way. Look at the list of skills and tell each other what you can and can't do. Add to the list.

Example:
    A: Can you drive a car?
    B: Yes, but I can't read a map in English.

drive a car
read a map in English
ask for directions in English
follow directions in English
check the oil in your car
change a flat tire
make a campfire
cook over a campfire
order food in a restaurant
buy stamps in a post office
make a long-distance telephone call

_____

_____

7. What Can You Do Now?

What can you do now that you couldn't do two years ago? What will you be able to do next year? Make a list and then discuss your list with a partner.

Example:
Two years ago I couldn't use a computer at all. This year I can type on a computer. Next year I'll be able to use it on my job.

Permission: May, Could, Can, Do you mind if . . . ?

INTRODUCTION

◼◼ *Read and listen to this excerpt from a TOEFL® preparation booklet.*

SOME FREQUENTLY ASKED QUESTIONS ABOUT THE TOEFL TEST

• **Can I take** the TOEFL test more than once?

Yes. **You can take** the TOEFL test as many times as you want.

• **May I register** for the test on the same day as the test?

No, **you may not.** You must register before the test.

• I don't have a checking account. **Could I send** cash for my registration fee?

No, we do not accept cash. **You may send** a money order, however.

• My students are going to take the test for the first time. They don't want schools to see bad test scores. **Can they cancel** their scores after the test?

Yes, they can. If the students feel that they did not do well, **they can cancel** their scores at the end of the test. In that case, we won't send the scores to any of the schools listed.

FORM

TEST BOOK NUMBER

NAME

SEAT NUMBER

SIGNATURE

REGISTRATION NUMBER

SECTION 1
1. Ⓐ Ⓑ Ⓒ Ⓓ
2. Ⓐ Ⓑ Ⓒ Ⓓ
3. Ⓐ Ⓑ Ⓒ Ⓓ
4. Ⓐ Ⓑ Ⓒ Ⓓ
5. Ⓐ Ⓑ Ⓒ Ⓓ
6. Ⓐ Ⓑ Ⓒ Ⓓ
7. Ⓐ Ⓑ Ⓒ Ⓓ
8. Ⓐ Ⓑ Ⓒ Ⓓ

SECTION 2
1. Ⓐ Ⓑ Ⓒ Ⓓ
2. Ⓐ Ⓑ Ⓒ Ⓓ
3. Ⓐ Ⓑ Ⓒ Ⓓ
4. Ⓐ Ⓑ Ⓒ Ⓓ
5. Ⓐ Ⓑ Ⓒ Ⓓ
6. Ⓐ Ⓑ Ⓒ Ⓓ
7. Ⓐ Ⓑ Ⓒ Ⓓ
8. Ⓐ Ⓑ Ⓒ Ⓓ

SECTION 3
1. Ⓐ Ⓑ Ⓒ Ⓓ
2. Ⓐ Ⓑ Ⓒ Ⓓ
3. Ⓐ Ⓑ Ⓒ Ⓓ
4. Ⓐ Ⓑ Ⓒ Ⓓ
5. Ⓐ Ⓑ Ⓒ Ⓓ
6. Ⓐ Ⓑ Ⓒ Ⓓ
7. Ⓐ Ⓑ Ⓒ Ⓓ
8. Ⓐ Ⓑ Ⓒ Ⓓ

PERMISSION: *MAY, COULD, CAN, DO YOU MIND IF . . . ?*

YES/NO QUESTIONS			
MAY/COULD/CAN*	SUBJECT	BASE FORM OF VERB	
May Could Can	I he she we they	start	now?

May, *could*, and *can* are modals. Modals have only one form.
They do not have *-s* in the third-person singular.

SHORT ANSWERS			
AFFIRMATIVE			
Sure. Certainly. Of course. Why not?	Yes,	you he she they	can. may.

SHORT ANSWERS		
NEGATIVE		
No,	you he she they	can't. may not.

DO YOU MIND IF	SUBJECT	VERB
Do you mind if	I we they	start?
	he she it	starts?

SHORT ANSWERS
Not at all. Go right ahead.

STATEMENTS			
SUBJECT	MAY/CAN (NOT)	BASE FORM OF VERB	
You He They	may (not) can (not)	start	now.

CONTRACTIONS
cannot OR can not = can't

Note: *May not* is not contracted.

Grammar Notes

1. Use *may, could,* and *can* to ask permission.

> **May** I **call** you next Friday?
> **Could** we **use** our dictionaries?
> **Can** he **come** to class with me next week?

Some people feel that *may* is more formal than *can* and *could.* You can use *may* when you ask formal permission to do something.

> **May** I **leave** the room?

Be careful! Requests for permission always refer to the present or the future. When you use *could* to ask for permission, it is not past tense.

> A: **Could** I register for the examination **tomorrow?**
> B: Certainly. The office will be open at 9:00 A.M.

2. We often say *please* when we ask permission.

> Could I ask a question, **please**?
> May I **please** ask a question?

3. Use *Do you mind if* to ask for permission when it is possible your action will inconvenience someone or make someone uncomfortable.

> A: **Do you mind if** I clean up tomorrow?
> B: Yes, actually, I do mind. I hate to see a mess in the kitchen in the morning.

Be careful! Note that a negative answer to the question *Do you mind if* gives permission to do something. It means *"It's OK. I don't mind."*

> A: **Do you mind if** my brother comes to class with me?
> B: **Not at all**. (Your brother may come with you.)

4. Use *may* or *can* to answer requests for permission. Don't use *could* in answers.

> A: Could I borrow this pencil?
> B: Yes, of course you **can**.

> NOT
> ~~Yes, you could.~~
> ~~No, you couldn't.~~

We also frequently use the following expressions instead of modals to answer requests for permission.

> A: Could I close the window?
> B: Certainly.
>   Go ahead.
>   Sure.
>   No, please don't. It's hot in here.

5. When people refuse permission, they usually do so indirectly. They soften the refusal with an apology and an explanation.

> Student: Can I please have five more minutes to answer this question?
> Teacher: I'm sorry, but the time is up.

6. Sometimes, when the rules are very clear, someone will refuse permission without an explanation.

> Driver: Can I park here?
> Police Officer: No, you can't.

Note: *May, can,* and *could* are also used to express possibility. See Unit 35.

Can and *could* are also used to talk about ability and to make requests. See Units 27 and 29.

FOCUSED PRACTICE

1. Discover the Grammar

Write the letter of the correct response to each request for permission.

a. No, he can't. He has to complete an accident report first.

b. Not at all. There's plenty of time.

c. Sure they can. There's plenty of room.

d. Yes, you may. The test starts in ten minutes.

e. I'm sorry, he's not in. Can I take a message?

f. Certainly. Here they are.

1. _d._

2. ____

3. ____

4. ____

5. ____

6. ____

2. Giving the Go-Ahead

*Mr. Hamad is supervising a TOEFL® test. Complete each conversation with
the word in parentheses and the correct pronouns.*

1. (can)

Mr. Hamad: It's 9:00. _____*You can*_____ come into the room now. Please show me your tickets as
  a.

   you come in.

Sofia: My brother isn't taking the test. _____ come in with me?
  b.

Mr. Hamad: No, I'm sorry, _____. Only people with tickets are permitted in the exam
  c.

   room.

2. (may)

Mr. Hamad: I'm going to hand out the tests now. Write your name on the front in pencil, but don't

   start the test yet. Remember, _____ start the test until I tell you.
  a.

Ahmed: I'm sorry I'm late. _____ come in?
_{b.}

Mr. Hamad: Yes, _____. We haven't started the test yet.
_{c.}

3. (could)

Rosa: _____ use a pen to write my name?
_{a.}

Mr. Hamad: No, you have to use a pencil.

Rosa: Jamie, _____ borrow this pencil please? I only brought a pen.
_{b.}

Jamie: Sure, take it. I brought a few.

4. (can)

Mr. Hamad: OK. We're ready to start. Open your test booklets and read the instructions.

Jean: Excuse me. We're late because our train broke down. _____ still come in?
_{a.}

Mr. Hamad: I'm sorry, _____. We've already started the test.
_{b. (not)}

3. Taking the Test

Read the directions to this section of a test similar to part of the TOEFL®.
Then complete the test questions.

<u>Directions</u>: These conversations take place on a train. Each conversation has four underlined words or phrases. They are marked (A), (B), (C), and (D). Find the underlined word or phrase that is incorrect. Fill in the space that corresponds to the letter of the incorrect word or phrase.

Example:

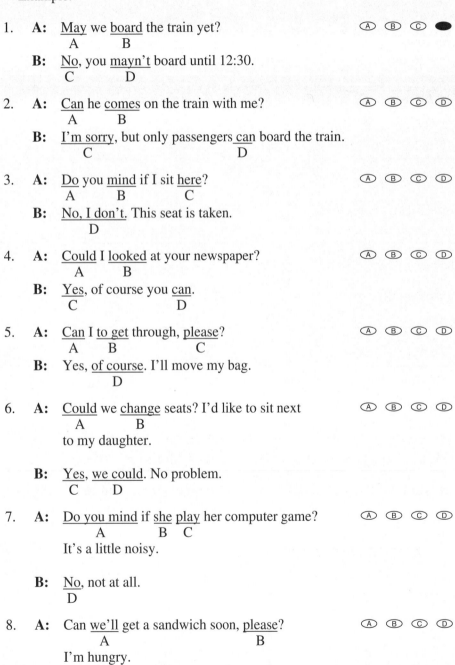

1. **A:** <u>May</u> we <u>board</u> the train yet?
        A   B
     B: <u>No</u>, you <u>mayn't</u> board until 12:30.
         C   D
Ⓐ Ⓑ Ⓒ ●

2. **A:** <u>Can</u> he <u>comes</u> on the train with me?
        A   B
     B: <u>I'm sorry</u>, but only passengers <u>can</u> board the train.
         C   D
Ⓐ Ⓑ Ⓒ Ⓓ

3. **A:** <u>Do</u> you <u>mind</u> if I sit <u>here</u>?
        A   B   C
     B: <u>No, I don't</u>. This seat is taken.
         D
Ⓐ Ⓑ Ⓒ Ⓓ

4. **A:** <u>Could</u> I <u>looked</u> at your newspaper?
         A   B
     B: <u>Yes</u>, of course you <u>can</u>.
         C   D
Ⓐ Ⓑ Ⓒ Ⓓ

5. **A:** <u>Can</u> I <u>to get</u> through, <u>please</u>?
        A   B   C
     B: Yes, <u>of course</u>. I'll move my bag.
            D
Ⓐ Ⓑ Ⓒ Ⓓ

6. **A:** <u>Could</u> we <u>change</u> seats? I'd like to sit next
        A   B
     to my daughter.

     B: <u>Yes</u>, <u>we could</u>. No problem.
         C   D
Ⓐ Ⓑ Ⓒ Ⓓ

7. **A:** <u>Do you mind</u> if <u>she</u> <u>play</u> her computer game?
           A   B C
     It's a little noisy.

     B: <u>No</u>, not at all.
         D
Ⓐ Ⓑ Ⓒ Ⓓ

8. **A:** Can <u>we'll</u> get a sandwich soon, <u>please</u>?
          A   B
     I'm hungry.

     B: <u>Sure</u> we <u>can</u>. Let's go find the club car.
         C   D
Ⓐ Ⓑ Ⓒ Ⓓ

4. Celebrating

Lucy got high TOEFL® scores. She's going to celebrate by attending a concert with some friends. Write questions to ask for permission. Use the words in parentheses.

1. Lucy's friend Carl came to pick her up for the concert. He wants his friend Bob to come along.

   Carl: I have an extra ticket. <u>Do you mind if Bob comes along?</u>
   (Do you mind if)

   Lucy: Not at all.

2. Carl decides to call Bob and invite him. He wants to use Lucy's phone.

   Carl: Great. I'll call him right now. _____
   (Could)

   Lucy: Sure. It's in the kitchen.

3. Carl, Bob, and Lucy want to park in front of the stadium. Lucy asks a police officer.

   Lucy: Excuse me, officer. We're going to the concert.

   _____
   (Can)

   Officer: No, you can't. It's a tow-away zone.

4. The usher at the concert wants to see their tickets.

   Usher: _____
   (May/please)

   Carl: Certainly. Here they are.

5. Lucy, Bob, and Carl want to move up a few rows. Bob asks an usher.

   Bob: All those seats are empty. _____
   (Could/please)

   Usher: Sure. Go right ahead.

6. Bob and Carl want to tape the concert. Lucy asks the usher first.

   Lucy: My friends brought their tape recorder.

   _____
   (Can)

   Usher: No, they can't. No one is allowed to record the concert or take pictures.

7. Lucy hates the music, and she wants to leave. Bob and Carl don't seem to like it either.

   Lucy: This music is giving me a headache.

   _____
   (Do you mind if)

   Bob: I don't mind.

   Carl: Me neither. Let's *all* leave.

COMMUNICATION PRACTICE

5. Practice Listening

🔘🔘 *Listen and write the number of each conversation. Then listen again and decide if permission was given or refused. Check the appropriate column.*

		permission given	permission refused
a. ____	child/parent	☐	☐
b. ____	travel agent/customer	☐	☐
c. _1_	police officer/driver	✔	☐
d. ____	boy/girlfriend's mother	☐	☐
e. ____	employee/employer	☐	☐

6. Asking Permission

Work in small groups. Read the following situations and decide what to say.
Think of as many things to say as possible.

1. You're visiting some good friends. The weather is very cold, but they don't seem to mind. Their windows are open, and the heat is off. You're freezing.

   Examples:
   Do you mind if I close the windows?
   May I borrow that sweater?
   Can you turn on the heat?
   Could I make some hot tea?

2. Your teacher is explaining something to the class, and you're getting completely confused. The teacher is very friendly, and he has office hours several times a week. He also spends a lot of time talking to students after class.

3. You have a small apartment. Two friends are coming to visit your town for a week, and they want to stay with you. What can you say to your roommate?

4. You're at a concert with some friends. You like the performer very much. You have your tape recorder and your camera with you. Sometimes this performer talks to fans and signs concert programs after the concert.

7. Role Play

Work in pairs. Read the following situations. Take turns being Student A and Student B.

Student A

1. You were absent from class yesterday. B, your classmate, always takes good notes.

Example:
A: May I copy your notes from class yesterday?
B: Sure. Here they are.
A: And could you tell me the assignment?
B: It's pages 20 through 25 in the textbook.

2. You're at work. You have a terrible headache. B is your boss.

3. You're a teenager. You and your friend want to travel to another city to see a concert. You want to borrow your family's car. Your friend has a licence and wants to drive.

4. B has invited you to a small party. At the last minute, your two cousins show up. They have nothing to do the night of the party.

Student B

1. A is in your class. You are always willing to help your classmates.

2. A is your employee. A has a lot of work to do for you today.

3. A is your son/daughter. You like this friend, and you have no objection to lending him or her the car. However, you want the friend to be careful.

4. Your party is at a restaurant, and you have already arranged for a certain number of people. Besides, this is supposed to be a small party for a few of your close friends.

U N I T

29

Requests:
*Will, Would,
Could, Can,
Would you
mind . . . ?*

INTRODUCTION

 *Marcia Jones is an administrative assistant. She works for Joan Sanchez. Read and listen to the recorded messages that Marcia received today and the messages she left for other people.*

At 8:00 A.M. Joan Sanchez, Marcia's boss, called and left a message for Marcia.

* This is Joan, Marcia. I'll be out of town until Tuesday. **Would** you please **photocopy** the monthly sales report for me? Thanks.

At 9:15 Marcia called Ann Chen in the Photocopy Department and left a message.

* Ann, this is Marcia Jones in Sales. I'm sending you our sales report. **Could** you **make** one copy? Oh, and **would you mind delivering** it to me when you're finished? It's a rush. Thanks.

At 12:30 Marcia's mother called her.

* Hi, Marcia. It's Mom. I'm sorry to bother you, but my car just broke down. **Can** you **drive** me to the doctor after work today? Thanks, honey.

At 2:45 Marcia's boyfriend called her.

* Marcia, this is Mike calling. I have good news. I passed all my exams. **Will** you **pick up** something special at the bakery? I'd like to invite some friends. See you later.

At 4:30 Ann Chen from the Photocopy Department called Marcia.

* Ms. Jones, this is Ann in the copy center. Your sales report is finished. I know you requested copies for today. I'm sorry, but I can't deliver them right now. I'm the only one here today. **Could** you **send** someone to pick them up?

REQUESTS: *WILL, WOULD, COULD, CAN, WOULD YOU MIND . . . ?*

QUESTIONS			
WILL/WOULD COULD/CAN*	**SUBJECT**	**BASE FORM OF VERB**	
Will Would Could Can	you	mail	this letter for me?
		drive	me to the doctor?
		pick up	some groceries?

SHORT ANSWERS	
AFFIRMATIVE	
Sure Certainly Of course	(I **will**). (I **can**).

SHORT ANSWERS
NEGATIVE
I'm sorry, but I **can't**.

*Will, would, could, and *can* are modals. Modals do not have *-s* in the third-person singular.*

WOULD YOU MIND	**GERUND**	
Would you mind	mailing	this letter for me?
	driving	me to the doctor?
	picking up	some groceries?

No, not at all. I'd be glad to.

Grammar Notes

1. Use *will, can, would,* and *could* to ask someone to do something. We often use *can* and *will* for informal requests. We use *could* and *would* to soften requests and make them sound less demanding.

   Marcia's sister: **Can** you **turn on** the TV?
   Marcia's co-worker: **Could** you **answer** my phone for me, Marcia?

2. Use *please* to make the request more polite. Note the word order in these sentences:

   Could you **please** close the door?
   Could you close the door, **please?**

3. We also use *Would you mind* + the gerund to make polite requests.

   Note that a negative answer means that you will do what the person requests.

   A: **Would you mind waiting** for a few minutes? Mr. Caras is still in a meeting.
   B: **Not at all.** (OK. I'll do it.)

4. People usually expect us to say *yes* to polite requests. When we cannot say *yes*, we usually apologize and give a reason.

   A: **Could** you **take** this to Susan Lane's office for me?
   B: **I'm sorry, I can't**. I'm expecting an important phone call.

   Be careful! Do not use *could* or *would* in response to polite requests.

   A: I'm cold. **Would** you **shut** the window, please?
   B: Certainly. NOT ~~Yes, I would.~~

FOCUSED PRACTICE

1. Discover the Grammar

▶◀ *Marcia has a new co-worker. Read and listen to their conversations.*
Underline all the polite requests.

1. **Marcia:** Hi. You must be the new secretary. I'm Marcia Jones. Let me know if you need anything.

   Lorna: Thanks, Marcia. <u>Could you show</u> me the coat closet?

   Marcia: Certainly. It's right over here.

2. **Lorna:** Marcia, would you explain these instructions for the fax machine? I don't understand them.

   Marcia: Sure. Just put your letter in here and dial the number.

3. **Marcia:** I'm leaving for lunch. Would you like to come?

   Lorna: Thanks, but I can't right now. I'm really busy.

   Marcia: Do you want a sandwich from the coffee shop?

   Lorna: That would be great. Can you get me a tuna sandwich and a small orange soda?

   Marcia: Sure. Will you answer my phone until I get back?

   Lorna: Certainly.

4. **Marcia:** Lorna, would you mind making a pot of coffee? Some clients are coming in a few minutes, and I make terrible coffee.

   Lorna: I'm sorry, but I can't do it now. I've got to finish this letter before 2:00.

   Marcia: That's OK. Thanks anyway.

5. **Marcia:** I'm going home now. Don't forget to turn off the printer before you leave.

   Lorna: I won't.

   Marcia: By the way, I'm not coming to work tomorrow. Could you give this report to Joan Sanchez for me?

   Lorna: Sure.

2. Asking for Favors

Mike's roommate, Jeff, is having problems today. Check the appropriate response to each request.

1. Mike, would you please drive me to class today? My car won't start.

   a. _____ Yes, I would.   b. **✓** I'd be glad to.

2. Would you mind lending me five dollars? I'm getting paid tomorrow.

   a. _____ Not at all.   b. _____ Yes.

3. Mike, can you take these books back to the library for me? I'm running late this morning.

        a. _____ I'm late for class, too. Sorry.   b. _____ No. I can't.

4. Could you lock the door on your way out? My hands are full.

        a. _____ Yes. I could.   b. _____ Sure.

5. Can you turn the radio down? I need to study for my math quiz this morning.

        a. _____ Certainly.   b. _____ Not at all.

6. Will you pick up some milk on the way home this afternoon?

        a. _____ No, I won't.   b. _____ I'm sorry, I can't. I'll be at work until 8:00.

3. Would You Mind?

Look at the sentences in the box. Choose one for each picture.

> Buy some cereal.
> Call back later.
> Close the window.
> ~~File these reports.~~
> Shut the door.
> Wait for a few minutes

File these reports.
_____
a.

_____
b.

_____
c.

_____
d.

_____
e.

_____
f.

(continued on next page)

*Now complete the following polite requests. Use the words in parentheses
and the information from the pictures.*

1. _____Can you please close the window?_____ It's freezing in here.
   (Can)

2. _____ I've finished reading them.
   (Will)

3. _____ Mr. Rivera is still in a meeting.
   (Would you mind)

4. _____ on the way home? We don't have
   (Can)
   any left.

5. _____ in fifteen minutes? Miss Sanchez is
   (Could)
   talking on another telephone right now.

6. _____ I can't think with all that noise in
   (Would)
   the hall.

COMMUNICATION PRACTICE

4. Practice Listening

🔊 *Joan Sanchez has planned a busy weekend. Listen to the conversation.
Then listen again and check the things that belong on her schedule.*

a. __✓__ take Luis to the dentist   e. _____ go to the movies

b. _____ take kids to the library   f. _____ walk Mom's dog

c. _____ babysit for Joan's daughter   g. _____ pick up the car at the garage

d. _____ go to a party   h. _____ go to the gym with Pat

5. I'd Be Glad to

Work with a group. Make out your own schedule for the weekend. Then ask group members to help you out. Use polite requests.

SATURDAY OCTOBER 18	SUNDAY OCTOBER 19
Morning	Morning
Afternoon	Afternoon
Evening	Evening

Example:

A: Can you drive me to the mall Saturday morning?

B: Sorry, I can't. I'm working Saturday morning.

OR

Sure, I'd be glad to.

Advice: Should, Ought to, Had better

INTRODUCTION

🔊 *Read and listen to this page from an advertisement for Capital Training Institute.*

CAPITAL
Training Institute

Here are the answers to questions our students often ask:

Q: What are the best jobs these days?

A: For the next ten years, the best opportunities will be in service jobs. High school graduates **ought to think** about fields like health care and restaurant services. There will be a lot of jobs for nurses and restaurant managers.

Q: How **should** I **prepare** for a service job?

A: You will need a high school education for any good job. That means you**'d better not quit** high school. In fact, you **should plan** to get more education after you graduate.

Q: I can't go to college. Will I still find a job?

A: Many jobs don't require a college education. For example, secretaries and travel agents often move up to better positions. But be careful—you **shouldn't take** a job unless it will offer you a good future. At Capital, you can get the skills you need for a job with a future.

Q: I want to start my own business. **Should** I **get** a job first?

A: Definitely. You**'d better get** some experience before you start your own business. Appliance repairers and truck drivers often start their own companies after a few years on the job.

ADVICE: *SHOULD, OUGHT TO, HAD BETTER**

STATEMENTS			
SUBJECT	***SHOULD/OUGHT TO/ HAD BETTER***	**BASE FORM OF VERB**	
I You He She We You They	**should (not)** **ought to** **had better (not)**	**look for** **quit**	a job. school.

CONTRACTIONS
should not = shouldn't had better = 'd better

*Should and *ought to* are modals. *Had better* is similar to a modal.
These forms do not have *-s* in the third-person singular.

YES/NO QUESTIONS			
SHOULD	**SUBJECT**	**BASE FORM OF VERB**	
Should	I he she we they	**quit**	school?
		look for	a job?

SHORT ANSWERS		
AFFIRMATIVE		
Yes,	you he she you they	**should.**

SHORT ANSWERS		
NEGATIVE		
No,	you he she you they	**shouldn't.**

WH- QUESTIONS				
WH- WORD	***SHOULD***	**SUBJECT**	**BASE FORM OF VERB**	
How When Where	**should**	I he she we they	**prepare**	for a job?

Grammar Notes

1. Use *should* and *ought to* to say that something is advisable.

> Fred and Tara **should answer** that want ad soon.
> They **shouldn't wait.**

We do not usually use the negative of *ought to* in American English. We use *shouldn't* instead.

Note: *Ought to* is often pronounced /ɔṭə/ in informal speech.

2. Use *had better* for urgent advice—when you believe that something bad will happen if the person does not follow the advice.

> Kids, you**'d better leave** now, or you'll miss the school bus.

Be careful! *Had better* always refers to the present or the future, never to the past (even though it uses the word *had*). The negative of *had better* is *had better not*. NOT ~~had not better~~.

3. Use *should* for questions. We do not usually use *ought to* or *had better* for questions.

> **Should** I **go** to secretarial school?
> When **should** I **apply**?

4. It is usually considered impolite to give advice to people of equal or higher status (such as friends or teachers) unless they ask for it. However, it is polite to give advice to these people when they ask for it.

> **Should** I **shake** hands with the interviewer?
> Yes, you **should.**

When we give unasked-for advice, we often soften it with *maybe, perhaps*, or *I think*.

> Myra, **maybe** you **ought to call** Capital Training Institute.

Note: Sometimes we use *must* or *have to* to give very strong advice. This kind of advice is similar to talking about necessity or obligation. See Unit 33.

FOCUSED PRACTICE

1. Discover the Grammar

Two students are looking at the bulletin board at Capital Training Institute. Read their conversations and underline the words and phrases that give advice. Then complete each conversation with the number of the correct job notice.

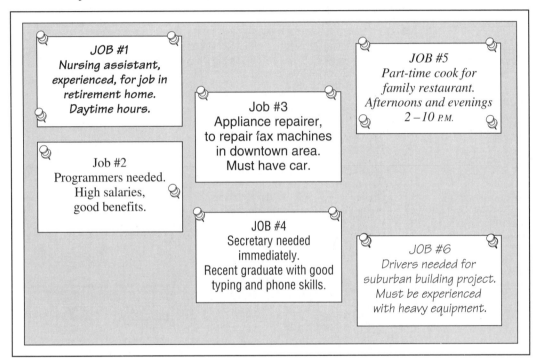

JOB #1
Nursing assistant, experienced, for job in retirement home. Daytime hours.

Job #2
Programmers needed. High salaries, good benefits.

Job #3
Appliance repairer, to repair fax machines in downtown area. Must have car.

JOB #4
Secretary needed immediately. Recent graduate with good typing and phone skills.

JOB #5
Part-time cook for family restaurant. Afternoons and evenings 2 – 10 P.M.

JOB #6
Drivers needed for suburban building project. Must be experienced with heavy equipment.

1. **A:** Jake just finished a job for CTX builders. He's looking for work.

   B: He <u>should</u> call about number __6__. He's got a lot of experience now.

2. **A:** I wanted a part-time job this semester. I think I'll apply for number _____.

   B: Maybe you shouldn't apply for that one. You have night classes, remember?

3. **A:** Pam quit her job at City Hospital because she couldn't work at night.

   B: She ought to apply for number _____. Older people really like her.

4. **A:** The company offered Cindy number _____.

   B: Well, she'd better not take it. She hates to drive in the city.

5. **A:** Kate and Denny are always complaining about their salaries.

   B: Programmers can make good money. They should call and find out about number _____.

6. **A:** Tom's finishing his secretarial course this week.

   B: Really? We'd better tell him about number _____. They need someone right away.

2. Am I Wrong?

Read the letters to an advice columnist. Then choose the correct words in parentheses to complete the columnist's advice.

1. **Q:** Two companies have offered my husband a job. He likes Company A very much. He dislikes Company B, but they have offered him more money. I say money is the most important thing. Am I wrong?

   A: Yes, you are. Your husband won't do a good job at Company B because he dislikes the company. He _____'d better_____
   ('d better/shouldn't)
   take the job with Company A.

2. **Q:** I've been a nurse for ten years. The hospital in our town has closed, and I haven't been able to find a new job. I want to change careers. Would that be a good idea?

   A: That would be a big mistake. You will have no experience in your new career. You
   _____
   (ought to/'d better not)
   change careers now.

3. **Q:** It's the holiday season, and my daughter has just graduated from secretarial school. I think this is a good time to look for jobs, but she wants to wait until after the holidays. Who's right?

   A: You are. During the holidays, she will have very little competition for jobs. She _____
   _____
   ('d better/shouldn't)
   wait until after the holidays.

4. **Q:** I want to change jobs. I can't take a vacation right now, so I don't have time to go on interviews. What can I do?

   A: Employers often interview before 9:00. It's a good time because there are few interruptions. You _____
   (ought to/shouldn't)
   ask for interviews before 9:00.

5. **Q:** I have been a cook for ten years, and I make a high salary. The restaurant is going to close soon, and I need a new job quickly. Maybe I should ask for less money.

   A: That's not a good idea. Employers will not know you are a first-class cook. You _____
   _____
   ('d better/shouldn't)
   ask for a lower salary.

6. **Q:** I teach class for travel agents, and my students are getting ready for job interviews. They want to discuss salary very early in the interview. What should I tell them?

   A: That's the best way to ruin an interview. They _____ wait.
   (shouldn't/'d better)

3. Friendly Advice

Read the conversations. Write advice with maybe, perhaps, *or* I think. *Use the words in parentheses.*

1. **A:** I'm tired. I studied all weekend for my exam.

   B: _____Maybe you'd better get some rest._____ The exam is tomorrow morning.
   (maybe/'d better get some rest)

2. **A:** I'm hungry. I haven't eaten since breakfast.

   B: _____ The snack bar is open now.
   (I think/ought to have a sandwich)

3. **A:** I have a headache, but I just took two aspirins an hour ago.

   B: _____ Lie down instead.
   (Perhaps/'d better not take any more)

4. **A:** My brother hasn't made any progress in English this semester.

   B: _____ TV really helps my English.
   (Maybe/should watch more TV)

5. **A:** I'm not earning enough money as a waitress.

B: _____ Then you could find a better job.
    (I think/should learn some new skills)

6. **A:** I broke my glasses, and I don't have another pair.

B: _____ I'll give you a ride.
    (Maybe/shouldn't drive to work)

4. Customs

Kim Yee has just started working in the United States. His boss has invited him to dinner at his home, and Kim is asking his English teacher, Scott, some questions. Complete their conversation with should, ought to, *or* had better *and the words and phrases in parentheses.*

Kim: _____How should I dress?_____ In a suit?
          1. (How/dress?)

Scott: You don't have to. I think _____, but you can wear casual
                                       2. (look/neat)

clothes.

Kim: _____
          3. (What time/arrive?)

Scott: It's really important to be on time. They're expecting you at 7:00, so

_____. It's OK to be a little late, but don't make your new boss
4. (arrive after 7:15)

wait too long for you!

Kim: _____
          5. (bring a gift?)

Scott: That's a good idea. But get something small. _____ It would
                                                        6. (buy an expensive gift)

embarrass him.

Kim: _____
          7. (What/buy?)

Scott: I think _____.
                   8. (get some flowers)

COMMUNICATION PRACTICE

5. Practice Listening

A teacher at Capital Institute is giving his students advice about taking their final exam. Listen. Then listen again and check the sentences that agree with his advice.

1. __✓__ Sleep well the night before the test.

2. _____ Stay up late and study the night before the test.

3. _____ Sleep late and skip breakfast.

4. _____ Leave plenty of time to get to school.

5. _____ Start answering questions right away.

6. _____ Read the exam completely before you start.

7. _____ Do the difficult sections first.

8. _____ Be sure to finish the test.

6. What Should I Do?

Work with a partner. Imagine that your partner has been offered a job in a country that you know very well. Give some advice about customs there. Then switch roles. Use the topics that follow and some of your own.

- Calling your boss by his or her first name
- Shaking hands when you first meet someone
- Calling a co-worker by a nickname
- Bringing a gift to your host or hostess
- Asking for a second helping of food when you are a guest
- Crossing the street before the light turns green

Add your own topics.

- _____
- _____

Examples:
You'd better not call your boss by her first name.
You should shake hands when you first meet someone.

7. Problem Solving

Work in small groups. Take turns telling each other about problems you are having. They can be real problems or invented problems, or you can choose from the examples below. Let the others in the group give advice.

Examples:

Problem: I'm having trouble making friends.

Advice: You should come to the students' lounge. You ought to spend more time with the rest of us . . .

Other problems: I don't think I'm earning enough money. I don't have enough free time.

Suggestions:
Let's, How
about...?,
Why
don't...?,
Could, Why
not...?

INTRODUCTION

Read and listen to this excerpt from a school newspaper.

the Griffin

Vol 5: 775   February 17

Let's Travel!

A lot of international students in the United States want to travel—but it's too expensive, or they don't know where to go. Some students don't have travel partners, and they don't want to travel alone.

Are you spending your vacation in the dorm for any of these reasons? If so, **why don't** you **try** staying at youth hostels when you travel? Hosteling is cheap, and it's fun. Best of all, you'll meet friendly people from all over the world.

Do you like cities? **Why not be** a guest at the historic Clay Hotel in Miami?

(Gangsters used to meet there.) Or you **could spend** the night at a former fire station in San Diego. Both these hostels cost under 15 dollars a night.

Maybe you prefer the outdoors. **How about a ranch** in Rocky Mountain National Park or a lighthouse on Cape Cod?

Wherever you go, you'll meet talkative travelers, share stories with them, and learn about North America.

SUGGESTIONS

LET'S (NOT)	BASE FORM OF VERB	
Let's (not)	take	the train.
	stay	in a castle.

HOW ABOUT	GERUND/NOUN	
How about	taking	the train?
	the train?	

(MAYBE)	SUBJECT	COULD*	BASE FORM OF VERB	
(Maybe)	I you he she we they	could	travel	with a group.

Could is a modal. Modals have only one form. They do not have *-s* in the third-person singular.

WHY	DON'T/ DOESN'T	SUBJECT	BASE FORM OF VERB	
Why	don't	I we you they	go	to San Diego?
	doesn't	he she		

WHY NOT	BASE FORM OF VERB	
Why not	go	to San Diego?

Grammar Notes

1. Use *Let's, How about, (Maybe) . . . could, Why don't/doesn't,* and *Why not* to make suggestions. We usually use these expressions when we are speaking in informal situations. We do not usually write them or use them in formal situations.

> A: **Let's take** a trip this summer.
> B: **How about going** to San Francisco?
> A: **Maybe** we **could drive** there.
> B: **Why don't** we **ask** Luke to go with us?
> A: Good idea. **Why not leave** right after final exams?

Be careful! When someone uses *Why not* and *Why don't/doesn't* to make a suggestion, these expressions are not information questions. The speaker does not expect to receive information from the listener. Compare:

> Suggestion: A: **Why don't** you **visit** Jill in New York?
> B: That's a good idea.

> Information question: A: **Why don't** you **eat** meat?
> B: Because I don't like it.

2. *Let's* always includes the speaker. It means *Here's a suggestion for you and me.*

> **Let's go** to Miami. We need a vacation. (I suggest that we go to Miami.)

3. Note the different forms to use with these expressions.

Base form of the verb

> Let's **take** the train.
> Maybe we could **take** the train.
> Why not **take** the train?
> Why don't we **take** the train to New York?
> Why doesn't she **take** the train to New York?

Gerund or a noun

> How about **taking** the train?
> How about **the train?**

Note: Making suggestions is sometimes similar to giving advice. See Unit 30 on advice.

4. Notice the punctuation at the end of each kind of suggestion.

Statements	Questions
Let's go to a concert.	**How about** going to a concert?
Maybe we **could** go to a concert.	**How about** a concert?
	Why don't we go to a concert?
	Why not go to a concert?

FOCUSED PRACTICE

1. Discover the Grammar

🔲🔲 *Jane Lazaro and Laila Hassan are visiting San Diego. Read and listen to their conversation. Underline the suggestions.*

Jane: What do you want to do today?

Laila: Why don't we go to the zoo? I hear it's fantastic.

Jane: I know, but I really want to go shopping soon. I need to get some gifts for my family.

Laila: Then let's go to Old Town. There are a lot of shops there.

Jane: OK. Maybe we could go to the zoo tomorrow.

Laila: That's fine with me. It's hard to believe we've been here a week. You know, we haven't even gone to the harbor yet.

Jane: Why not go there for dinner tonight? We could take the trolley from Old Town.

Laila: That sounds like fun. But let's not go to an expensive restaurant.

Jane: Here's a good one in the guidebook—Grand Cafe. It's cheap, and it's right on the water.

Now read the conversation again and check the places in the guidebook they will visit.

PLACES TO GO IN SAN DIEGO

✓ • **The San Diego Zoo.** Over 3,000 animals live in this famous zoo. Take the bus tour or see it all from the air in the Skyfari Tramway.

• **Old Town.** Experience Early California in these adobe buildings and lovely plazas. Shop for handicrafts in a Mexican street market.

• **Mission Bay Aquatic Beach.** 4,600 acres of fun. Free beaches, plus campgrounds, fishing areas, golf courses, and much more. Get a map from the Visitor Center.

• **Sea World.** The star is Shamu, the killer whale, but you will also love the penguins. Laser shows and fireworks on summer nights. Musicians and jugglers add to the fun.

• **San Diego Harbor.** Stroll through the parks, fish from the piers, or just watch the boats from a waterside restaurant. Visitors should see San Diego from the water; ferries and water taxis will take you there.

PLACES TO EAT

(Dinner for two: A = under $20
B = $25–$50   C = $50+)

• **Grand Cafe** (A) Seaport Village   Outdoor dining right on the water; moderate prices, good food.

• **Alberto's Star of the Sea**   (C) 1234 Harbor Dr. Elegant; coat and tie.

• **Casa de Bandano**   (B) Congress St.   Mexican food; evening entertainment.

2. Making Plans

Complete the travelers' conversations. Choose the appropriate expression in parentheses.

1. **A:** I feel like having seafood for dinner, but we went to Alberto's for seafood last night.

   B: _____Why not_____ go again tonight? The food's good, and it has a great view of the harbor.
   (Why not/Let's not)

2. **A:** I'm really tired. _____ resting before we go out?
   (Let's/How about)

   B: That's a good idea. I'm tired too.

3. **A:** Marie wants to buy some Native American crafts.

   B: _____ she look in Old Town? She'll find a lot of crafts shops there.
   (Why doesn't/Why don't)

4. **A:** I want to explore San Diego Bay.

   B: _____ rent bikes tomorrow? There are bike paths all around the Bay.
   (Let's not/Why don't we)

5. **A:** A group of foreign students just checked into the hostel.

   B: _____ ask them to join us for dinner.
   (How about/Maybe we could)

6. **A:** I don't want to go home tomorrow. I'm having a really good time here.

   B: So am I. _____ leave tomorrow.
   (Let's/Let's not)

3. Let's . . .

Use the phrases in the box, and write a suggestion for each conversation. Add pronouns and change the verb as necessary. Punctuate each suggestion correctly.

share a cab	go to the beach
buy another one	take a trip together
try that new pizza place	~~buy tickets~~

1. **A:** There's a BOYZ II MEN concert at the stadium next weekend.

   B: You work near the stadium. Why don't ___you buy tickets?___

2. **A:** It's going to be hot tomorrow.

   B: We have the day off.

   How about _____

3. **A:** Toasters are on sale. Maybe we could buy one for your brother's wedding.

   B: We bought toasters for the last three weddings.

   Let's not _____

4. **A:** I don't know what to do on spring vacation. I'm sick of staying in the dorm.

   B: Me, too. Maybe _____

Grammar Notes

1. Use *prefer*, *would prefer*, and *would rather* to talk about things or activities that you like better than other things or activities.

> Most of the time, we **prefer to eat out.**
> I**'d rather eat out** tonight.
> I**'d prefer Chinese food.**

Note: We often use *prefer* to express a general preference and *would prefer* or *would rather* to talk about a preference in a particular situation.

2. *Prefer* and *would prefer* may be followed by a noun, a gerund, or an infinitive.

>   noun   noun
> I usually prefer **magazines**, but right now I'd prefer a **newspaper**.
>   gerund
> Beth prefers **reading** magazines.
>   infinitive   infinitive
> Beth's husband prefers not **to read** magazines. He prefers **to read** newspapers.

3. A comparison with *to* may also follow *prefer/would prefer* + noun or *prefer/would prefer* + gerund.

> I prefer **newspapers to magazines**.
> Beth would prefer **reading magazines to reading newspapers**.

4. *Would rather* can only be followed by the base form of a verb.

> A: Would you rather **eat out** or **cook** dinner at home tonight?
> B: I'd rather **eat out**.

5. A comparison with *than* may also follow *would rather*.

> I'd rather **eat out than cook**. = I like eating out better than cooking.

6. We often use *I'd rather not* to refuse an offer, suggestion, or invitation.

> A: Would you like some dessert?
> B: I**'d rather not.** I've had enough to eat.

Note: The negative of **I'd rather** is **I'd rather not,** NOT ~~I wouldn't rather~~.

Be careful! We do not use *will* to talk about preferences.

> I'd rather be in your class next semester. NOT ~~I will rather be in your class next semester~~.

FOCUSED PRACTICE

1. Discover the Grammar

◘◘ *Arlene and Jim are looking for a place to rent. Read and listen to the conversation. Underline the phrases that express preference.*

Arlene: My husband and I are looking for a place to rent.

Realtor: A house or an apartment?

Arlene: We 'd really <u>prefer a house</u>, but it depends on the rent. I'm a student, and we'd rather not spend more than about $600 a month right now.

Realtor: Have you decided on a location? We have some nice places in the West End.

Arlene: Actually, we'd prefer to live on the North Side. It's closer to the university.

Realtor: Do you want a one-bedroom or a two-bedroom place?

Arlene: We'd rather have two bedrooms.

Realtor: OK. I think I can find something for you on the North Side. Do you have a car? It might be hard to find parking there.

Arlene: No, we prefer walking to driving in the city. But we want to be near a bus stop.

Realtor: I have a small house near the University for $550. I can show it to you today.

Arlene: That would be great. Oh, by the way, we have a cat. Is that OK?

Realtor: To tell the truth, the landlord would prefer not to rent to people with pets. What would you like to do? Do you still want to see the house?

Arlene: No, I'd rather not bother. We don't have much time to find a place. What else do you have on the North Side?

Now mark Arlene and Jim's preferences.

Renter Preferences

Name: _____ Arlene and Jim Lewis _____

Area: (North Side) South Side East End West End

Type: House Apartment

Size: _____ Bedrooms Maximum rent: _____

Transportation: _____ Car _____ Bus _____ Walk

Keep pets: _____ Yes _____ No

COMMUNICATION PRACTICE

5. Practice Listening

🎧 *Arlene is ordering in a restaurant. Listen to her conversation with the waiter. Then listen again and circle the items on the menu that Arlene wants.*

FISH DINNER
Comes with your choice of
Soup (tomato or onion)
and salad
rice or potato
coffee, tea, soda (diet or regular)
apple pie or ice cream

STEAK DINNER
Comes with
salad and baked potato
coffee, tea, or
soda (diet or regular)
apple pie

6. What's on TV?

Work in small groups. Look at the TV schedule and try to agree on something to watch at 8:00 P.M. Use would rather *or* would prefer *to talk about your preferences.*

	8:00
❷	**Baseball** The Mets vs. the Dodgers. Third game in a five-game series.
❹	**Science Watch.** Are we alone in the universe?
❽	**My Life with Henry.** Henry meets an old girlfriend.
⑫	World News.
(CNN)	Washington Report.
㉟	**Movie★** (1987) *The Monster of Monroe Street.* Man turns into a monster and terrorizes neighborhood. Frightening.
㊷	**Movie★★★★** (1988) *Who's There?* Comedy about computer programmer. Light and entertaining.
㊾	**Movie★★★** (1955) *It's My Life.* Black-and-white drama about the lives and relationships of four friends. Serious and moving.

Example: **A:** Let's watch the ball game at 8:00.
B: I don't really like baseball. I'd prefer to watch "My Life with Henry."

7. If I Had My Way

Read the choices below. In pairs, discuss your preferences. Give reasons for your choices.

1. live in the city/live in the country

2. work in an office/work at home

3. be married/be single

4. be a man/be a woman

   Example:
   A: I'd rather live in the city than in the country. There's a lot more to do.
   B: Really? I'd prefer the country. It's quieter.

Now ask your partner about some other choices.

Would you rather . . . ?

8. Bumper Stickers

Bumper stickers like these are fashionable right now.

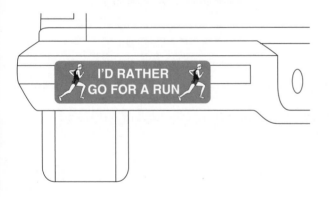

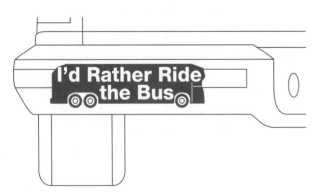

Design your own bumper sticker with would rather. *Explain it to a classmate.*

9. Choices

Complete the shopper's questionnaire on page 272. Discuss your answers with a partner. Give reasons for your choices.

Example:
A: I'd rather buy my own clothes. That way I get things that I really like.
B: Not me. I prefer not to shop for clothes. I think it's a waste of time.

10. Rank Order

Look at the list of some favorite leisure-time activities. Rank them in the order of your own preferences. (1= most favorite, 12 = least favorite)

Favorite
Leisure-Time Activities

_____ Watch television	_____ Watch sports
_____ Go to the movies	_____ Play sports
_____ Listen to popular music	_____ Read books
_____ Travel	_____ Read newspapers or magazines
_____ Cook	_____ Play cards
_____ Eat in restaurants	_____ Do crafts (woodworking, sewing, etc.)

Ask some classmates about their preferences. Have a class discussion. Is there any difference between men's and women's preferences?

Examples:
Would you rather listen to music than cook?
Would you prefer playing sports to watching sports?
Do you prefer books or magazines?
In my survey, men prefer watching sports to playing sports.

INTRODUCTION

▼

Read and listen to this excerpt from the introduction to a driver's manual.

Becoming a Driver

In our society, people are always on the move, and most people **have to drive** to get from one place to another. With so many people on the roads, it is necessary for everyone to know how to drive safely. That's why you—and all other drivers—**must pass** a test to get a driver's license before you drive.

It takes time and practice to become a safe driver. You **will have to learn** how to drive safely in fog, snow, and other dangerous weather conditions. You **will** also **have to learn** how to drive in different traffic situations. In the city, for example, you **have to be** careful about traffic at cross-streets. On expressways, you **don't have to deal** with cross-traffic, but you **must know** how to change lanes and pass other cars.

Finally, you **have to learn** the driving laws. Many of these are common sense. For example, according to the law, you **must wear** your seat belt when you drive. And, of course, you **must not drive** under the influence of alcohol.

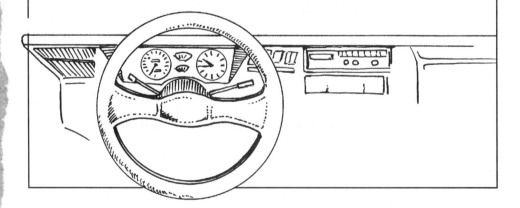

Grammar Notes

1. Use *have to*, *have got to*, and *must* to express necessity. Note these differences among the three expressions:

    a. *Have to* is the most common expression in everyday use.

      Everyone **has to pass** a road test before getting a driver's license.

    Have to is usually pronounced /hæftə/ in informal speech.

    b. *Have got to* is usually only used in spoken English and informal writing. When it is used orally, it often expresses strong feelings on the part of the speaker.

      We**'ve got to stop** for lunch soon. I'm starving.

    Got to is usually pronounced /gɑɾə/ in informal speech.

    c. *Must* is used to express obligation in writing, including official forms, signs, and notices.

      You **must stop** completely at a stop sign.

    Americans do not usually use *must* when speaking to or about another adult. Sometimes people use *must* to tell a child there is no choice in a situation.

      You **must wear** your seat belt.

2. *Must* and *have got to* refer only to the present or the future.

      Everyone **must take** an eye test in order to get a driver's license.
      I**'ve got to get** glasses soon because I didn't pass the eye test.

    Use the correct form of *have to* for all other tenses.

      Sheila **has had to drive** to work for two years. (present perfect)
      She**'ll have to renew** her license next year. (future)
      After his traffic accident, Sal **had to take** a driver-improvement class. (past tense)

3. Use *have to* for most questions.

      Does Paul **have to drive?** He always goes too fast.
      When **will** he **have to leave?**
      Did he **have to drive** all night?

    We almost never use *must* or *have got to* in questions.

4. Be careful! *Must* and *have (got) to* have similar meanings. However, the meanings of *must not* and *don't/doesn't have to* are very different.

    a. *Must not* is used to express **prohibition.**

      You **must not drive** without a license. It's against the law.

    b. *Don't/doesn't have to* expresses that something is **not necessary.** It means that there is a choice.

      You **don't have to drive** tomorrow. I can do it.

5. We often use *can't* instead of *must not* to express prohibition in spoken English.

      You **can't turn** left here. It's a one-way street.

Note: *Must* and *have (got) to* are also used to make assumptions. See Unit 36.

FOCUSED PRACTICE

1. Discover the Grammar

Read Bob Randall's telephone conversation with a clerk from the California Department of Motor Vehicles. Underline the words in the conversation that express necessity, lack of necessity, or prohibition.

Clerk: Department of Motor Vehicles. May I help you?

Bob: I'm moving to California soon, and I have some questions. My Illinois license is good for five years. <u>Will I have to get</u> a California driver's license when I move?

Clerk: Yes, <u>you will.</u> It's the law—California residents must have a California driver's license.

Bob: When will I have to get my California license?

Clerk: You can't use your old license longer than ten days after you become a resident. So, come in and apply for your California license right after you get here.

Bob: Do I have to take any tests?

Clerk: Since you already have an Illinois license, you probably won't have to take the road test here in California. But you will have to take the written test.

Bob: How about the eye test?

Clerk: Oh, everyone's got to take the eye test.

Bob: OK. Thanks a lot. You've been very helpful.

Now check the appropriate box for each statement.

	Necessary	Not Necessary	Prohibited
1. get a California driver's license	✔	☐	☐
2. use the Illinois license for longer than ten days	☐	☐	☐
3. take the written test	☐	☐	☐
4. take the road test	☐	☐	☐
5. take the eye test	☐	☐	☐

2. Following the Rules

Complete these rules from a driver's handbook. Use must *or* must not.

1. You _____must not_____ drive on a public road
   without a license or permit.

2. Bicycle riders _____ ride on
   freeways. Cars drive fast on freeways, and bicycles
   can cause accidents.

3. A parent or guardian _____ sign the
   driver's license application of anyone under
   eighteen years old.

4. You _____ speed up when another
   driver is trying to pass you.

5. You _____ pay $10 when you apply
   for a license.

6. You _____ take an eye test.

7. All drivers _____ be able to read and
   understand the simple English in highway traffic
   and direction signs.

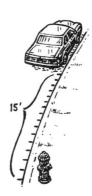

8. You _____ park within fifteen feet of
   a fire hydrant. Fire trucks must be able to reach the
   fire hydrant in case of a fire.

9. The driver and front-seat passenger
   _____ wear seat belts. Seat belts
   save lives.

10. You _____ signal before you turn.

3. Getting Ready

The Randalls have checked off the things they've already done to get ready to move to California. Read the lists and write sentences about what the Randalls have to do and don't have to do.

Bob
✓ clean car
buy gas
check the oil

Ann
buy a road map
✓ call the moving company again
get the kids' school records
✓ buy film

Jim and Sue
✓ pack clothes and toys for the trip
say goodbye to friends
buy gifts for teachers

Bob doesn't have to clean the car.

He has to buy gas.

_____

_____

_____

_____

_____

_____

_____

_____

4. Car Games

Bob's family is driving to their new home in California. Complete the conversations with short answers or the correct form of have to, have got to, *or* can't *and the verb in parentheses.*

1. Use *have to* or *can't*

   Bob: What time _____do_____ we ___have to leave___?

a. (leave)

   Ann: We _____ later than 9:00. We _____ at the Holiday Motel in

b. (start)   c. (check in)
   Centerville by 5:00.

2. Use *have to*

   Bob: _____ we _____ for lunch? We're running late already.

a. (stop)

   Ann: Yes, _____. The kids are starving, and so am I.

b.

3. Use *have to*

   Bob: Wow—what a crowd! We _____ never _____ for a table at

a. (wait)
   McBurger's before.

   Ann: I know. There are a lot of people on the road today.

4. Use *have to*

   Sue: Mom, _____ you _____? I want you to sit back here with us.

a. (drive)

   Ann: Yes, _____. It's a long trip, and your father drove all morning.

b.

5. Use *have got to* or *can't*

   Ann: Hey kids, here's a good car game. Each player chooses a kind of car. You get a point for

   every one you see.

   Jim: Toyota! There's one! And there's another!

   Sue: Hey! That's not fair! He _____ me a turn too.

a. (give)

   Ann: You _____ like that in the car, kids. I _____ attention to the

b. (shout)   c. (pay)
   road, and you're making so much noise that I can't.

6. Use *have got to*

   Ann: We _____ gas soon. There's only a quarter tank left.

a. (buy)

   Bob: There'll be a rest stop in about ten miles.

7. Use *have to*

   Jim: Where did you go, Dad?

   Bob: I went to look for a telephone. I _____ the motel to tell them we were going

a. (call)
   to be late.

5. *Must not* or *Don't have to*

Read the signs from the Holiday Motel and complete each statement, using must, must not, *or* don't have to.

1. You __must not__ play ball in the swimming pool.

2. You _____ wear shoes in this bar.

3. You _____ run near the pool.

4. You _____ leave yet. It's only eight o'clock.

5. Children under twelve _____ swim without an adult.

6. You _____ use tokens. It takes quarters too.

COMMUNICATION PRACTICE

6. Practice Listening

🔊 *Listen to the conversation. Then listen again and write the number of each conversation next to the appropriate sign.*

a. _____

b. _____

c. _____

d. __1__

e. _____

f. _____

7. Reading the Signs

Work in pairs. Where do you find these signs? Discuss what they mean. What do you have to do? What are you not allowed to do?

1.

Example:
You can find this in a restaurant, doctor's office, or school. It means you can't smoke.

2.

3.

4.

5.

QUIET
Please

6.

7.

8.

9.

8. Invent a Sign

Draw your own sign to illustrate something people have to do or must not do. Show it to a classmate. See if he or she can guess the meaning. Decide where the sign belongs.

9. Taking Care of Business

Make a list of your most important tasks for this week. Check off the things you've already done. Tell a partner what you have to do and what you don't have to do. Report to a group.

Examples:
I don't have to do English homework. I've already done it.
Hamed has to wash the car. He doesn't have to go shopping because he went on Monday.

Expectations: Be supposed to

INTRODUCTION

Read and listen to this etiquette column from the newspaper.

Dear Ms. Etiquette,

What **is** the maid of honor **supposed to do** in a wedding ceremony? My best friend is getting married soon. She has invited me to be her maid of honor. I am new in this country, and I'm not sure what my friend expects of me.

Dear Reader,

You should be very proud. In the past, the bride's sister **was supposed to serve** as her maid of honor, and the groom's brother **was supposed to be** his best man. Today, however, the bride and groom can ask anyone they want. Your friend's invitation means that she values your friendship very highly.

The maid of honor is the bride's assistant, and the best man is the groom's. Before the wedding, these two **are supposed to help** the couple prepare for the ceremony. You might help the bride send the wedding invitations, for example. The day of the wedding, the best man **is supposed to drive** the groom to the ceremony. During the ceremony, the maid of honor holds the bride's flowers. After the wedding, the maid of honor and the best man are both **supposed to sign** the marriage certificate as witnesses.

"When we got there, we found a crowd of bikers admiring the view," laughed Beth Strickland.

When Bill kissed his bride, the audience burst into loud applause and rang their bicycle bells. "We weren't supposed to have fifty wedding guests, but we love biking, and we're not sorry," Bill said.

When they packed to leave the island the next day, Beth left her wedding bouquet at the hotel. She remembered it minutes before the ferry was supposed to leave. Bill jumped on his bike, recovered the flowers, and made it back to the ferry before it departed.

"We bikers are supposed to stay fast and fit," he said. "Now I know why."

Read the article again. Circle true (T) *or false* (F) *for each statement.*

1. The Stricklands planned a big wedding.	T		(F)
2. The weather forecaster predicted rain.	T		F
3. The Stricklands invited fifty wedding guests.	T		F
4. The ferry followed a schedule.	T		F
5. People believe that bikers are in good shape.	T		F

2. Getting Ready

Complete the conversations with the verb in parentheses and a form of be supposed to.

1. **A:** Gary called while you were out.

   B: _____Am_____ I __supposed to call__ him back?

a. (call)

   A: No, he'll call you later in the afternoon.

2. **A:** The dress store called, too. They delivered your wedding dress to your office.

   _____ they _____ that?

a. (do)

   B: No, they weren't! They _____ it here. That's why I stayed home today.

b. (deliver)

3. **A:** Let's get in line. The rehearsal _____ in a few minutes.

a. (start)

   B: We're bridesmaids. Where _____ we _____?

b. (stand)

   A: Right here, behind Netta.

4. **A:** Hi. Where's Netta?

   B: Go home! You _____ here!

a. (be)

   A: Why not?

   B: The groom _____ the bride the day of the wedding until the ceremony.

b. (see)

   It's bad luck.

(continued on next page)

5. **A:** Sophie, could I borrow your handkerchief, please?

B: Sure, but why?

A: I _____ something old, something new, something borrowed, and
a. (wear)
something blue. I don't have anything borrowed.

B: It _____ this afternoon. Maybe I should lend you my umbrella instead.
b. (rain)

3. Responsibilities

Read Sophie's letter to a friend. There are four mistakes with be supposed to.
Find and correct them.

> May 6, 1994
>
> Dear Kasha,
>
>   I have some wonderful news. My friend Netta
> is getting married soon, and she's asked me
> to be her maid of honor. She and Gary want a big
>   *are*
> wedding—they ∧ supposed to have about two
> hundred guests. I have a lot of responsibilities.
> I will be supposed to give Netta a shower before
> the wedding. (That's a party where everyone brings
> presents for the bride.) I be also supposed to help
> her choose the bridesmaids' dresses. The best
> man's name is Jim. He'll help Gary get ready. I
> haven't met him yet, but he's supposed to be
> very nice.
>
>   I'd better say goodbye now, or I'll be late for the
> rehearsal. I supposed to leave five minutes ago.
>
>   Love,
>   Sophie

COMMUNICATION PRACTICE

4. Practice Listening

🎧 *It's the day of the wedding. Listen to the conversations. Then listen again and circle the correct words.*

1. Netta *is/isn't* supposed to be at the church by 2:00.

2. The photographer *is/isn't* supposed to take pictures during the ceremony.

3. Members of the bride's family *are/aren't* supposed to sit on the right.

4. The maid of honor *is/isn't* supposed to walk behind the bride.

   Guests *are/aren't* supposed to say "congratulations" to the groom.

5. Guests *are/aren't* supposed to throw rice at the bride and groom.

5. Customs

Work in small groups. Discuss these important events. What are people in your culture supposed to do and say at these times? Are people expected to give certain gifts? Report to the class.

a wedding

an important birthday

a graduation ceremony

an engagement to be married

an anniversary

a birth

a funeral

> **Example:**
> Red is supposed to bring good luck, so in my country the bride
> is supposed to wear a red wedding dress.

Future Possibility: May, Might, Could

INTRODUCTION

🔊 *Read and listen to this TV weather report.*

The cold front that has been affecting much of the country is moving toward our area. Temperatures **may drop** as much as thirty degrees by tomorrow morning, and we **might** even **see** some snow flurries later on in the day. By evening, winds **could reach** 40 mph. So bundle up—it's going to be really cold out there!

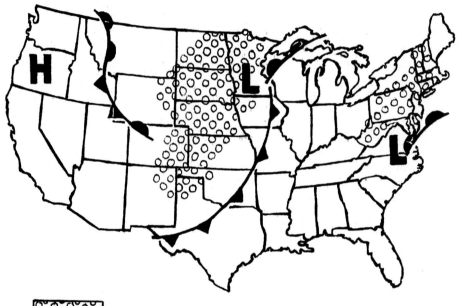

  SNOW

FUTURE POSSIBILITY: *MAY, MIGHT, COULD*

STATEMENTS			
SUBJECT	***MAY/MIGHT/COULD*** *	**BASE FORM OF VERB**	
I You He She It We You They	**may** (not) **might** (not) **could**	**get**	cold.

*May, might, and *could* are modals. Modals have only one form.
They do not have *-s* in the third-person singular.

QUESTIONS
Are you going to drive to work in the snow?

SHORT ANSWERS		
I We	**might** (not).	
	may (not).	
	could.	

Grammar Notes

1. Use *may, might,* and *could* to talk about future possibility.

> It **could rain** tomorrow.
> It **may be** windy later.
> It **might get** cold.

Be careful! Notice the difference between *may be* and *maybe*. Both express possibility. *May be* is a modal + verb. It is always two words.

> He **may be** late today.

Maybe is not a modal. It is an adverb. It is always one word, and it comes at the beginning of the sentence.

> **Maybe** he'll take the train. NOT ~~He'll maybe take the train.~~

2. Use *may not* and *might not* to express the possibility that something will not happen.

> There are a lot of clouds, but it **might not rain**.

Be careful! Use *couldn't* to express the idea that something is **impossible.**

> A: Why don't you ask John for a ride?
> B: I **couldn't do** that. He's too busy.

3. We usually do not begin questions about possibility with *may, might,* or *could.* Instead we use *will* or *be going to* and phrases such as *Do you think . . . ?* or *Is it possible that . . . ?* However, we often use *may, might,* or *could* in short answers to these questions.

> Do you think it'll rain tomorrow?   It **may.**
> Do you think she has a copy of today's paper?   She **might.**
> Will he drive to work in the rain?   He **might not.**
> Is it possible that they'll close the office?   They **could.**
> When do you think it's going to start raining? It **might start** by 9:00.

In the examples above, you can also use the modal alone in short answers. However, we often include *be* in short answers to questions with *be* as the main verb.

> Do you think we'**ll be** late for work? We **might be.**

FOCUSED PRACTICE

1. Discover the Grammar

Alice is a college student who works part-time. Read and listen to the conversation. Underline the words that express future possibility.

Alice: Are you going to drive to work tomorrow?

Bill: I <u>might</u>. Why?

Alice: I just heard the weather report. It may snow tonight.

Bill: Then I might take the 7:30 train instead. I have a 9:00 meeting, and I don't want to miss it. Do you have a class tomorrow morning?

Alice: No, but I'm going to go to the library to work on my paper. Maybe I'll take the train with you.

Bill: We could have lunch together after you go to the library.

Alice: Oh, I'm sorry. I have a class at noon every day this week.

Bill: Cut class tomorrow. One day won't make any difference.

Alice: I couldn't do that. I'll meet you at six at the train station, OK? I'm going to take the 6:30 train home.

Bill: I might not catch the 6:30 train. My boss said something about working late tomorrow. I'll call you and let you know what I'm doing.

Read the conversation again. Check the appropriate box for each activity.

Bill's schedule	certain	possible	impossible
shovel snow from front steps		✓	
take 7:30 A.M. train			
9:00 A.M. meeting			
meet Alice for lunch			
call Alice			
work until 8:00 P.M.			

Alice's schedule	certain	possible	impossible
ride train with Bill			
go to library—work on paper			
go to class			
lunch with Bill			
6:00 P.M.—meet Bill at station			
take 6:30 train home			

2. Making Plans

Alice is graduating from college with a degree in Early Childhood Education. Complete this paragraph from her diary. Choose the appropriate words in parentheses.

I just got the notice from my school. I <u>'m going to</u> graduate in June, but I still don't have
1. (might not / 'm going to)

plans. Some day-care centers hire students before they graduate, so I _____ apply for
2. (could / couldn't)

a job now. On the other hand, I _____ apply to a graduate school and get my master's
3. (might / might not)

degree.

I'm just not sure, though—these past two years have been hard, and I _____ be
4. (may / may not)

ready to study for two more years. At least I *am* sure about my career. I _____ work
5. ('m going to / might)

with children—that's certain. I made an appointment to discuss my plans with my teacher, Mrs.

Humphrey, tomorrow. I _____ talk this over with her. She _____ have
6. (maybe / may)   7. (won't / might)

an idea.

3. *I Might*

Look at Alice's schedule for Monday. She put question marks next to the items she wasn't sure about. Write seven sentences about Alice's plans for Monday. Use may *or* might *(for things that are possible) and* be going to *(for things that are certain).*

<u>MONDAY</u>

call Bill at 9:00

buy some notebooks before class?

go to meeting with Mrs. Humphrey at 11:00

have coffee with Sue after class?

go to work at 1:00

go shopping after work?

take 7:00 train?

Alice is going to call Bill at 9:00.

_____

_____

_____

_____

_____

_____

4.   Storm Warning

For each question, write a short answer with could *or* couldn't. *Use* be *when necessary.*

1. Do you think the roads will be dangerous? It's snowing really hard.

   _____ They could be. _____ It's a big storm.

2. Will the schools stay open?

   Oh, no. _____ It's too dangerous for school buses in a storm like this.

3. Will it be very windy?

   _____ The winds are very strong already.

4. Will it get very cold?

   _____ The temperature in Centerville is below zero.

5. Is it possible that the storm will be over by Monday?

   _____ It's moving pretty quickly now.

6. Do you think it will be warmer on Tuesday?

   _____ It's stopped snowing in Centerville already.

COMMUNICATION PRACTICE

5.   Practice Listening

▣▣ *Listen to the weather forecast. Then listen again and check* Certain *or* Possible *for each forecast.*

	Certain	Possible
Friday		
Sunny	☐	☑
Low fifties	☐	☐
Saturday		
Sunny	☐	☐
60°	☐	☐
Windy	☐	☐
Sunday		
Cold	☐	☐
Windy	☐	☐
Snow	☐	☐

6. Possibilities

Look at these student profiles from a school newspaper. Work with a group.
Talk about what these students might do in the future. Use the information
in the box or your own ideas.

Name: Alice Lane
Major: Early Childhood
Education
Activities: Caribbean Students'
Association, School Newspaper
Likes: adventure, new people
Dislikes: snow, boring routines
Plans and Dreams: "I plan to
teach in a preschool. I dream
about traveling around the world."

Name: Nick Vanek
Major: Information Systems
Activities: Computer Club,
Runners' Club
Likes: learning something new
Dislikes: crowded places
Plans and Dreams: "I plan
to go to a four-year college.
I dream about becoming an
inventor."

Future Possibilities

Occupations	Hobbies	Achievements
• computer programmer	• disco dancing	• fly on space shuttle
• teacher	• skiing	• teach in Alaska
• manager, day-care center	• creative writing	• develop a computer program for making word puzzles

Example:
Alice is on the school newspaper. She might do creative writing as a hobby.
Nick hates crowded places. He couldn't work on the space shuttle.

7. Ambitions

Now write your own profile. Work with a partner and discuss your own
future possibilities. Be ambitious and think big!

Name: _____

School Major or Job: _____

Activities or Hobbies: _____

Likes: _____ **Dislikes:** _____

Plans and Dreams: _____

_____

INTRODUCTION

Assumptions: May, Might, Could, Must, Have to, Have got to, Can't

In Conan Doyle's stories, Sherlock Holmes and his friend, Dr. Watson, solved many crimes together. Read and listen to The Red-Headed League, *the story of one of their adventures.*

When Dr. Watson arrived, Sherlock Holmes was with a visitor.

"Dr. Watson, this is Mr. Jabez Wilson," said Holmes. Watson shook hands with a fat, red-haired man.

"Mr. Wilson **must write** a lot," Dr. Watson said.

Holmes chuckled. "You **could be** right. But why do you think so?"

"His right shirt cuff looks very old and worn. And he has a small hole in the left elbow of his jacket. He probably rests his left elbow on the desk when he writes."

Wilson looked amazed. "Dr. Watson is correct," he told Holmes. "Your methods **may be** useful after all."

"Please tell Dr. Watson your story," said Holmes.

"I have a small shop," began the red-haired man. "I don't have many customers, so I was very interested in this advertisement. My clerk, Vincent, showed it to me." He handed Watson a wrinkled piece of newspaper.

An American millionaire started the Red-Headed League to help red-headed men.

The League now has one position open. The salary is £4 per week for four hours of work every day.

The job is to copy the encyclopedia in our offices.

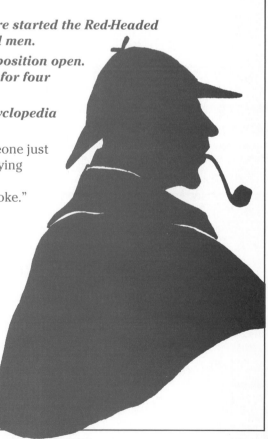

"They **couldn't pay** someone just for having red hair and copying the encyclopedia," Watson laughed. "This **has to be** a joke."

"It **might not be**," said Holmes. "Listen to the rest of the story."

"I got the job, and I worked at the League for two months. I copied *Apple, Animals,* and *Archery*, and I rubbed this hole in my sleeve. Then this morning I found a note on the door." Wilson gave Holmes the note. . . .

307

ASSUMPTIONS: MAY, MIGHT, COULD, MUST, HAVE TO, HAVE GOT TO, CAN'T

	AFFIRMATIVE STATEMENTS		
SUBJECT	MAY/MIGHT/ COULD/MUST*	BASE FORM OF VERB	
I You He She We You They	may might could must	be write work	right. a lot. at the Red-Headed League.
It		be	a joke.

*May, might, could, and must are modals. Modals have only one form.
They do not have -s in the third-person singular.

SUBJECT	HAVE (GOT) TO	BASE FORM OF VERB	
I You We They	have (got) to	be write work	right. a lot. at the Red-Headed League.
He She	has (got) to		
It		be	a joke.

	NEGATIVE STATEMENTS			
SUBJECT	MAY/MIGHT/ CAN/COULD/MUST	NOT	BASE FORM OF VERB	
I You He She We They	may might can could must	not	be write work	right. a lot. at the Red-Headed League.
It			be	a joke.

CONTRACTIONS		
cannot or can not	=	can't
could not	=	couldn't

Note: We usually do not contract may not, might not, and must not when we make assumptions.

QUESTIONS
Does he work there?

SHORT ANSWERS	
SUBJECT	**MODAL**
He	**may (not).** **might (not).** **could (not).** **can't.** **must (not).** **has (got) to.**

YES/NO QUESTIONS: *CAN* AND *COULD*			
CAN/COULD	**SUBJECT**	**BASE FORM OF VERB**	
Can **Could**	he	**be**	a criminal?

SHORT ANSWERS WITH *BE*		
SUBJECT	**MODAL**	***BE***
He	**may (not)** **might (not)** **could (n't)** **can't** **must (not)** **has (got) to**	**be.**

WH- QUESTIONS			
WH- **WORD**	*CAN/COULD*	**SUBJECT**	**BASE FORM OF VERB**
Who What	**can** **could**	it they	**be?** **want?**

Grammar Notes

1. We often make assumptions, or "best guesses," about present situations based on information that we have.
   A logical guess based on facts is a conclusion. Use *must, have to,* and *have got to* to state conclusions based on facts.

Fact	Conclusion
Wilson only has one clerk.	His shop **must be** quite small.
Wilson's shop has few customers.	Wilson **must not earn** much money.
The Red-Haired League pays men because they have red hair.	It **has to be** a joke.

   Note: *Have got to* is used informally:

   It**'s got to be** a joke.

   Have to is usually pronounced /hæftə/

   and *got to* is usually pronounced /gɑtə/ in informal speech.

2. When we are less certain, we express possibilities. Use *may, might,* and *could* to express possibilities about a situation.

Fact	Possibility
Wilson has a hole in his sleeve.	He **may write** a lot.
Wilson needs a job.	His shop **might not do** much business.
Mr. Holmes is very interested in crime.	He **could be** a detective.

3. *Can't* and *couldn't* often express a feeling of disbelief or impossibility.

   Vincent **couldn't be** dishonest! I've trusted him for months.

4. We do not usually use *may* or *might* in questions about possibility. We use *can* and *could.*

   Could Vincent **be** a criminal?
   Someone's coming. Who **can** it **be?**

5. In short answers, you can use the modal alone or *have (got) to.*

Does Ann live near here?	She **could.** I run into her a lot.
Does she still work at Wilson's?	She **may not.** I saw a new clerk there.

   Be careful! Use *be* in short answers to questions that include *be.*

Is Ron working in the city now?	I'm not sure. He **might be**.
Is he still with City Bank?	He **has to be**. He goes there every day.

   Note: *Must, have to,* and *have got to* are also used to express necessity. See Unit 33.
   May, might, and *could* are also used to express future possibilities. See Unit 35.
   May, can, and *could* are also used to express permission. See Unit 28.

FOCUSED PRACTICE

1. Discover the Grammar

Read the next part of The Red-Headed League. *Underline the phrases that state conclusions and express possibilities.*

Sherlock Holmes studied the note:

The Red-Headed League does not exist anymore.

"This <u>could be</u> serious," Holmes told Wilson. "What can you tell us about your clerk Vincent?"

"Vincent couldn't be dishonest," replied Wilson. "In fact, he took this job for half-pay because he wanted to learn the business. His only fault is photography."

"Photography?" Holmes and Watson asked together.

"Yes," replied Wilson. "He's always running down to the basement to work with his cameras."

Wilson left soon after that.

"Wilson's clerk might be the key to this mystery," Holmes told Watson. "Let's go see him." An hour later, Holmes and Watson walked into Wilson's shop. The clerk was a man of about thirty, with a scar on his forehead. Holmes asked him for directions. Then he and Watson left the shop.

"My dear Watson," Holmes began. "It's very unusual for a thirty-year-old man to work for half-pay. This clerk has to have a very special reason for working here."

"Something to do with the Red-Headed League?" Watson asked.

"Yes. Perhaps the clerk placed that ad in the newspaper. He may want to be alone in the shop. Did you look at his legs?"

"No, I didn't."

"He has holes in his trouser knees, and his knees are very wrinkled and dirty. He must spend his time digging a tunnel from Wilson's basement. But where?"

Holmes hit the ground sharply with his walking stick. "The ground isn't hollow, so the tunnel must not be here in front of the shop. Let's walk to the street in back of Wilson's shop."

◖◗ *Read and listen to the second part of the story again. What does Holmes believe about each of the statements that follow? Check* Possibility *or* Conclusion *for each statement.*

	Possibility	Conclusion
1. Something serious is happening.	✔	☐
2. The clerk is the key to the mystery.	☐	☐
3. The clerk has a special reason for working in Wilson's shop.	☐	☐
4. He put the ad in the newspaper because he wants to be alone in the shop.	☐	☐
5. He's digging a tunnel from Wilson's basement.	☐	☐
6. The tunnel isn't in front of the shop.	☐	☐

2.   A Picture Is Worth a Thousand Words

Look at the picture. Think about it in connection to the story, The Red-Headed
League. *Make assumptions and circle the appropriate words.*

1. It *must*/*could* be nighttime.
2. Number 27 *might/can't* be a bank.
3. Those boxes *couldn't/must* be very heavy.
4. There *must not/could* be gold in them.
5. The manager *might not/must* want people to know about this delivery.
6. He *couldn't/may* worry about robbers.
7. He *might/must not* want to store the boxes in the basement.
8. The buildings *may/must* be near Wilson's shop.

3. Drawing Conclusions

Look at the poster and the map of Wilson's neighborhood. Use the evidence and the words in parentheses to write sentences with must *and* must not.

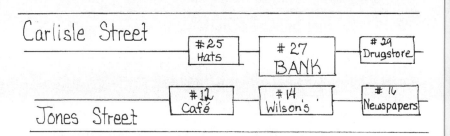

1. Wilson's clerk is the man on the poster.

   <u>He must be a criminal.</u>
   (He/be a criminal)

2. The man on the poster is named John Clay.

   _____
   (Vincent/be the clerk's real name)

3. He's committed a lot of crimes, but the police haven't caught him.

   _____
   (He/be very careful)

4. The address of the bank and the address in the picture for exercise 2 are the same.

   _____
   (Number 27 Carlisle Street/be City Bank)

5. The hat shop and the drugstore don't make much money.

   _____
   (Vincent's tunnel/lead to those shops)

6. There's a lot of money in the bank, and it's very close to Wilson's shop.

   _____
   (Vincent's tunnel/lead to the bank)

4. It's Got to Be

Ann and Marie are buying hats. Read the dialogue and rewrite the underlined sentences another way. Use have got to *or* can't *and the word in parentheses.*

Ann: Look at this hat, Marie. What do you think?

Marie: Oh, come on. <u>That's got to be a joke.</u>

You can't be serious.
————————————————————————
1. (serious)

Anyway, it's much too expensive. Look at the price tag.

Ann: $100! <u>That can't be right.</u>

————————————————————————
2. (wrong)

Marie: I know. <u>It can't cost more than $50.</u>

————————————————————————
3. (less)

Anyway, let's talk about it over lunch. I'm getting hungry.

Ann: It's too early for lunch. <u>It has to be before 11:00.</u>

————————————————————————
4. (after)

Marie: Look at my watch. It's already 12:30.

Ann: Then let's go to Cafe Au Lait. It's on Jones Street. <u>It can't be far.</u>

————————————————————————
5. (nearby)

Marie: Let's go home after lunch. I don't feel well.

Ann: Oh come on. <u>You're fine.</u> You must be hungry.

————————————————————————
6. (sick)

5. Speculations

Write a short answer to each question. Use might *or* must *and include* be *where necessary.*

A: That's a terrible cough. I think you're getting the flu. What do you think?

B: You're right. I ___must be___. I have fever and a sore throat, too.
         1.

A: This bottle of cough medicine is empty. Do we need some more?

B: We _____. I'm not sure. Check the shelf in the bathroom.
         2.

A: There isn't any cough medicine here. Are we all out of it?

B: We _____. That was the last bottle. Never mind. I can drink tea and honey.
         3.

A: I'll go get you some cough medicine. Does that nighttime cough medicine work?

B: It _____. It's worth a try.
      4.

A: I forgot to cash a check today. Do you have any money?

B: I _____. Look in my wallet. It's on the table downstairs.

5.

A: I found it. Does Drake's Drugstore stay open after nine?

B: It _____. Their advertisement says "Open 'til eleven."

6.

6. Maybe It's the Cat

Mr. and Mrs. Wilson are trying to get to sleep. Write questions and answers with could/couldn't be *and* can/can't be.

1. (could be)

Mrs. Wilson: Shh! I heard someone at the door.

It's 9:30. Who _____*could*_____ it _____*be*_____?

a.

Mr. Wilson: It _____*could be*_____ a late customer.

b.

Mrs. Wilson: No, it _____. The shop has been closed for hours. Maybe it's the cat.

c.

2. (can be)

Mr. Wilson: It _____. I put the cat out before we went to bed.

a.

Mrs. Wilson: _____ it _____ Vincent?

b.

He's always down in the basement with his cameras.

Mr. Wilson: No, Vincent went out an hour ago. He _____ back this early.

c.

3. (could be)

Mrs. Wilson: What _____ it _____ then?

a.

Mr. Wilson: That door rattles whenever the wind blows. It _____ the wind.

b.

Mrs. Wilson: That must be it. Let's go to sleep.

COMMUNICATION PRACTICE

7. Practice Listening

That night, Holmes, Dr. Watson, and a police captain met in front of City Bank. Listen to their conversation. Then listen again and check Possibility *or* Conclusion *for each statement below.*

	Possibility	Conclusion
1. It's 10:00.	☐	✔
2. They have a long wait.	☐	☐
3. There are 2,000 gold coins in one box.	☐	☐
4. John Clay knows about the gold.	☐	☐
5. Clay's tunnel is finished.	☐	☐
6. The tunnel is under the bank floor.	☐	☐
7. John Clay is dangerous.	☐	☐
8. Clay is waiting for Wilson to go to sleep.	☐	☐
9. There's someone in the tunnel.	☐	☐
10. The man is John Clay.	☐	☐

8. Tell-Tale Signs

Look at the pictures. State a conclusion or a possibility about the owner of each item. Compare your answers with your classmates'.

1.

Example:
He must be a very good student.
He could be the best in the class.
He may study hard.

2.

3.

4.

5.

9. Possible Explanations

Read the following situations. In pairs, discuss possible explanations for each situation. Then come to a conclusion. Discuss your explanations with the rest of the class. Use your imagination!

1. You've been calling your sister on the phone for three days. No one has answered.

   Example:
   A: She might be at the library. She always studies hard for her exams.
   B: I don't think so. She's already finished her exams.
   A: You could have the wrong number.
   B: This is the number I always call. I think she's been on vacation this week.
   A: Then she must be away.

2. You are on the street. You have asked a woman three times for the time. She hasn't answered you.

3. You go to dinner with a good friend. Your friend hardly says a word all evening.

4. You went on a picnic in the park. You ate strawberries and cheese. Now you are sneezing and your eyes are watering.

5. You're at a party, and no one is talking to you.

10. What Could It Be?

Look at this picture. In small groups, discuss what it possibly represents.
Then check the Answer Key.

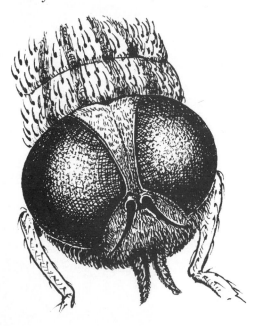

Examples:
It could be a picture of a Martian.
It might be a caterpillar with sunglasses.

I. *Circle the letter of the appropriate response to each question.*

1. Could you drive me to work tomorrow?
   a. Sure. I leave at seven-thirty.
   b. I could last year, but I can't anymore.

2. Could you speak English last year?
   a. I'd be glad to.
   b. Yes, I could.

3. Can you swim?
   a. Yes, I can. I'd be glad to.
   b. Yes, I can. I really enjoy it.

4. Do you think Fred has the report?
   a. Yes, he may. It's OK with me.
   b. He might. Let's ask him.

5. Will the weather improve tomorrow?
   a. It might be.
   b. It might.

6. May I ask a question?
   a. Yes, you may. What is it?
   b. You may. I'm not sure.

7. Do you have to practice every day?
   a. Yes, I have.
   b. Yes, I do.

8. Why don't we go to the beach today?
   a. Good idea.
   b. Because the car broke down.

9. Do we have any more orange juice?
   a. We might have.
   b. We might.

II. *Complete the conversation with the correct words or phrases in parentheses.*

A: This apartment is depressing me.

B: _____Why not_____ redecorate? We have some free time.
   1. (Why not/Must we)

A: OK. Where _____ we start?
   2. (should/were able to)

B: Maybe we _____ start with the hall. It's easy to put up
   wallpaper.   3. (could/couldn't)

A: How much wallpaper do we need?

B: We _____ measure the walls and find out.
   4. ('d better/mustn't)

A: This wallpaper is pretty. _____ start putting it up.
   5. (Let's/We must)

B: We _____ clean the walls first.
   6. ('ve got to/can)

A: OK. The walls are clean. _____ putting up the wallpaper now?
   7. (How about/Can we)

319

B: Well, first we _____ paint the walls with this stuff.
8. (have to/shouldn't)

A: You said it was easy to put up wallpaper.

B: We have to do it right, or the paper _____ fall off.
9. (might/might not)

A: On second thought, the apartment isn't really that bad. Maybe we _____ redecorate after all.
10. (don't have to/mustn't)

III. *There are nine errors in this interview. Find and correct them.*

A: Many people take personality tests before they get married. Does this mean that people with different personalities shouldn't t̶o̶ get married?

B: No, not at all. In fact, people with very different personalities can had very good relationships.

A: Why do people take the tests then?

B: With the test results, couples able to learn about possible trouble areas in their relationships.

A: Can you give us an example?

B: Let's say a couple is looking for an apartment. The woman prefers to move into a modern apartment. She'd not rather spend time fixing up a place. Her boyfriend would rather to fix up a charming old place. One is a thinker, very analytical. The other is a dreamer.

A: People like that must have tremendous problems.

B: But they also have tremendous possibilities. In this relationship, the thinker mights become more imaginative. The dreamer will can become more analytical.

A: When people are very different, what should they avoid doing?

B: They must not to try to change their partners. This will destroy the relationship. Instead, they ought to appreciating their differences.

IV. *Bob and Rita have a commuter marriage. Complete Bob's fax to Rita by choosing the correct word in parentheses.*

Dear Rita,

I _____wasn't able to_____ call tonight because our meeting just ended. It's midnight and you
1. (wasn't able to/didn't have to)
_____ be asleep already. I'm sending you this fax instead. I have good news
2. (dont' have to/must)
and bad news. The bad news first—I _____ get to Boston this weekend—
3. (won't be able to/mustn't)
more meetings. _____ come here instead? The cherry trees are in bloom,
4. (Do you mind/Why don't you)
and Washington _____ be the most beautiful city in the world right now. I
5. (has got to/couldn't)
_____ stay in the office on Saturday, but we _____
6. ('ll be able to/have to)   7. (might/shouldn't)
be able to spend time together on Sunday. Anyway, I _____ see you after
8. ('ll be able to/'m supposed to)
work. The good news is that the company _____ transfer me to Boston in six
9. (couldn't/is supposed to)
months. Maybe we _____ live like this much longer.
10. (won't have to/should)
I'll call you in the morning.

Love,

Gary

V. *Complete the conversation with* don't have to *or* 'd better not.

1. **A:** This library book is overdue.

   B: I'll take it back. I'm going that way.

   A: Thanks. Now I _____*don't have to*_____ go out today.

2. **A:** Have some more coffee.

   B: Thanks, but I _____ have any more, or I won't sleep.

3. **A:** Mom's birthday is next week.

   B: We _____ forget to buy a card today.

4. **A:** Look at that line!

   B: I'm glad I bought our tickets early. Now we _____ wait.

5. **A:** The sky is getting awfully dark.

   B: We _____ stay here. I don't want to be outside in a thunderstorm.

6. **A:** Hurry up. We're late.

   B: What's the hurry? Today's Saturday. You _____ go to school today.

VI. *Write a sentence about each situation. Use the negative or affirmative form of the modal and the phrase in parentheses.*

1. John has a lot of headaches. At school, he can't see the board unless he sits in the front row.

   _____*He might need glasses.*_____
   (might/need glasses)

2. You're looking at some jewelry. It's very beautiful and it's made of gold.

   _____
   (must/be expensive)

3. You've called your friend at work several times today. He doesn't answer, and he hasn't returned your messages.

   _____
   (must/be at work today)

4. You've invited some friends for dinner, and you've served curry. Everyone except your friend Sue has had two servings. Sue hasn't even finished one.

   _____
   (might/like curry)

5. Carl's roommate has just left for a trip to Hong Kong. You've seen him off at the airport. A few minutes after you get back home, the doorbell rings.

   _____
   (could/be Carl's roommate)

6. Your sister often forgets important appointments. You want her to come to your graduation. You've sent her an invitation, but you haven't called to remind her to come. You're worried.

   _____
   (may/remember to come)

(continued on next page)

7. You just bought a painting for ten dollars at a garage sale. Your friend Tim knows a lot about art. He says that the painting looks like a Whistler. At first you laugh, but then you look at some Whistler paintings in a book.

_____
(could/be very valuable)

8. There are two airports in your city. You go to one airport to pick up a friend, but he isn't there.

_____
(might/be at the other airport)

VII. *Complete the conversation with the correct forms of the verbs in parentheses.*

A: I'm calling from Radex Technology. Our computers are down. _____Could_____ you

_____send_____ a service person?
  1. (could/send)

B: _____ you _____ someone today? Our technicians are all
                                   2. (have to/have)

busy. I _____ Sally tomorrow.
       3. (be able to/send)

A: My boss _____ something now. _____ she
              4. (have got to/finish)

_____ this afternoon?
5. (be able to/come)

B: I'm sorry, she won't. I'll send her first thing in the morning.

A: _____ I _____ to your supervisor? We just
                            6. (may/talk)

_____ that long.
7. (can/wait)

C: This is Mrs. Chen. _____ I _____ you?
                                               8. (may/help)

A: Yes. I'm calling from Radex Technology. You really _____ someone out here
                                                          9. (must/send)

today.

C: I'll see what I can do. _____ I _____ you back in ten minutes?
                                                    10. (can/call)

VIII

Nouns and Articles

INTRODUCTION

▼

◉◉ *Read and listen to part of an article about Columbus.*

Columbus sailed from **Spain** in **September 1492,** looking for **gold** and **spices. Native Americans** greeted him wearing **jewelry** made of **popcorn** and offering **gifts** of **corn. Columbus** found **little gold** on that **trip,** but he collected **many plants,** including **corn,** to bring back to **Spain**.

Columbus didn't know it, but the **corn** was much more valuable than **gold. Farmers** from **Europe** to **Asia** accepted it immediately. They grew it on cold **mountainsides** and in tropical **forests.** Today it feeds millions of **people** all over the **world**.

On his second **trip, Columbus** brought back **a few cacao beans** to make **chocolate. Europeans** and **Asians** loved this new **drink,** and soon they were paying **a great deal of money** for the **beans. Cacao beans** became so valuable in **Central America** that they were used as **cash** for two hundred **years**.

Tomatoes and **potatoes** took **some time** to become popular. Eventually, however, they became the **basis** of **a lot of** popular **foods.** It's hard to imagine **life** without **popcorn, pizza,** french fried **potatoes,** or **chocolate.** Thanks to **Native American cultures,** we don't have to.

NOUNS AND QUANTIFIERS

PROPER NOUNS
Columbus sailed from **Spain**. He spent **September** and **October** at sea. He came to **Central America**.

COMMON NOUNS
Explorers sailed all over the **world**. They spent **months** at **sea**. He found a new **continent**.

COUNT NOUNS
Her **necklace** was beautiful. Their **necklaces** were beautiful. Columbus found **many** new **plants**. He found **a few spices**. Europeans used **a lot of spices**.

NON-COUNT NOUNS
Their **jewelry** was beautiful. He didn't find **much silver**. He found **a little gold**. They drank **a lot of tea**.

Grammar Notes

1. <u>Proper nouns</u> are the names of particular people, places, or things. They are usually unique (there is only one). These are some categories and examples of proper nouns:

People	Columbus, Queen Isabella, Native Americans
Places	Asia, Spain, Central America, Europe
Months	September, October
Days	Monday, Tuesday
Holidays	Christmas, Passover, Ramadan
Languages and Nationalities	Chinese, English, Portuguese, Spanish
Seasons	the spring, the summer, the fall, the winter

Capitalize the first letter of most proper nouns. We do not usually use an article (*a/an* or *the*) with a proper noun. See Unit 38 for more information about articles.

Note: Seasons are usually not spelled with a capital letter, and they are often preceded by *the*.

   Columbus arrived in **the fall**.

2. <u>Common nouns</u> refer to people, places, and things. However, they are not the names of particular individuals. For example, *woman* is a common noun, but *Queen Isabella* is a proper noun. These are some categories and examples of common nouns:

people	explorer, sailor, farmer
places	mountainside, forest, city, country, continent
things	beans, chocolate, corn, gifts, money

(continued on next page)

3. Common nouns can be either **count** or **non-count.** Count nouns (also called countable nouns) are things that you can count separately. They can be singular or plural. For example, you can say *a ship* or *three ships*. You can use *a/an* or *the* before count nouns.

    a ship   **the** ship   **three** ships

Non-count nouns (also called uncountable or mass nouns) are things that you cannot count separately. For example, in English you can say *gold*, but you usually cannot say *a gold* or *two golds*. Non-count nouns usually have no plural forms. We usually do not use *a/an* with non-count nouns.

    chocolate   gold   beauty   English

When a non-count noun is the subject of a sentence, its verb must be singular. Pronouns that refer to non-count nouns must also be singular.

    Corn is more valuable than gold. **It feeds** millions of people.

Non-count nouns often fall into the following categories:

Abstract words	courage, education, loneliness, music, time
Activities	cooking, exploring, farming, reading, sailing
Fields of study	astronomy, geography, history, mathematics
Foods	corn, chocolate, fish, pasta, rice, meat
Gases	air, helium, oxygen, smoke, steam
Liquids	water, lemonade, milk, gasoline
Materials	cotton, plastic, nylon, silk
Particles	dust, sand, sugar, salt
Natural phenomena	cold, electricity, weather, rain, thunder

Be careful! Some common non-count nouns do not fit into the above categories. You must memorize nouns such as the following:

advice	garbage	mail
information	homework	money
equipment	jewelry	news
furniture	luggage	work

    This handmade **jewelry** is beautiful.
    The news is on from 6:00 to 7:00 in the evening.

4. You can use the quantifiers *some, enough,* and *a lot of* with both count and non-count nouns.

Count	Non-count
There are **some hamburgers** left.	There's **some pizza** left.
There are **enough hamburgers** for everyone.	There's **enough pizza** for everyone.
There are **a lot of hamburgers**.	There's **a lot of pizza**.

5. You can use *a few, several,* and *many* with count nouns in affirmative sentences. You can use *a little* and *a great deal of* with non-count nouns in affirmative sentences.

Count	Non-count
They wore **a few** bracelets.	They wore **a little** jewelry.
Many farmers grow corn.	The United States exports **a great deal of** corn.
Columbus made **several trips** across the Atlantic.	

Note: When *many* is used with nouns that are not the subject of a sentence, it is more formal than *a lot of*. Sometimes writers use *much* in affirmative sentences with non-count nouns. This is very formal.

He found **many** new foods.	(formal)
He found **a lot of** new foods.	(less formal)
He brought **much wealth** back to Europe.	(very formal)

6. You can use *many* with count nouns and *much* with non-count nouns in negative sentences and in questions. This is appropriate for both formal and informal English.

We don't have **many tomatoes** left.	
We don't have **much meat** either.	
How **many hours** will this take?	
How **much time** do you need?	

7. Be careful! Do not confuse *a few* and *a little* with *few* and *little*. *Few* and *little* usually mean *not enough*.

We have **a little time** left to shop. (not a lot of time, but enough)	
We have **little time** left to shop. (probably not enough time)	

FOCUSED PRACTICE

1. Discover the Grammar

Tina Arbeit sailed around the world alone on a small boat. Read the interview with her. Underline the nouns.

Interviewer: It took a lot of <u>courage</u> to make this journey. Why did you decide to sail around the world alone?

Tina: I needed a goal. I didn't want any more formal education, but I didn't know what else to do. I got my boat, *Katya*, for my nineteenth birthday, and I knew right away that I wanted to do this.

Interviewer: When did you start?

Tina: I left New York on May 15, two and a half years ago, and I headed for Panama.

Interviewer: How far did you travel?

Tina: 30,000 miles.

Interviewer: *Katya* looks small. How much were you able to take with you?

Tina: I didn't have much money, so I didn't bring many things. I used the stars to navigate, not electronic equipment.

(continued on next page)

Interviewer: What did you eat?

Tina: I bought food in different ports. I loved going to markets and learning about local cooking. And I collected water when it rained.

Interviewer: How did you spend your time when you were sailing?

Tina: At first I listened to the news a lot, but after a while I preferred music. And I did a lot of reading.

Interviewer: What was difficult for you?

Tina: The loneliness. I had my cat, Typhoon, but I missed my family.

Interviewer: What was the best part of the trip?

Tina: The sight of this harbor. I'm so glad to be back for Thanksgiving.

Write each noun in the correct column.

Proper Nouns

Katya		

Common Nouns

Count Nouns	Non-count Nouns
journey	courage

2. Making Plans

Alice and Fred are planning a hiking trip. Complete their conversation with the correct form of the word in parentheses.

Fred: There 's _____ 1. (be) still a lot of _____ 2. (work) to do this evening. We have to plan the food for the trip.

Alice: I've been reading this book about camping. There _____ 3. (be) some good _____ 4. (advice) about food in it.

Fred: What does it say?

Alice: We should bring a lot of _____ 5. (bean) and _____ 6. (rice).

Fred: I bet _____ 7. (potato) _____ 8. (be) good on camping trips too.

Alice: Fresh _____ 9. (vegetable) _____ 10. (be) too heavy to carry. Maybe we can get some when we pass through a town.

Fred: _____ 11. (be) the _____ 12. (equipment) ready? We should go over the checklist.

Alice: I did that. We need some _____ 13. (battery) for the radio.

Fred: Why do we need a radio? I thought we were running away from civilization.

Alice: But the _____ 14. (news) never _____ 15. (stop). I still want to know what's happening.

Fred: That's OK with me. By the way, do we have enough warm _____ 16. (clothing)? It gets chilly in the mountains.

Alice: That's true. And the _____ 17. (cold) really _____ 18. (bother) me at night.

Fred: But we have warm sleeping _____ 19. (bag).

Alice: And I have you!

3. Happy Campers

Complete these excerpts from a book about family camping. For each paragraph, use the quantifiers in parentheses.

1. (a little/a few)

Try to get _____a little_____ exercise before a
a.
long camping trip. It will help you feel better on the trip.

_____ good stretching exercises every
b.
day will help. _____ walking or
c.
swimming is also useful.

2. (many/a great deal of)

You will need _____ information for
a.
a long trip. Your public library has _____
b.
books about family camping. The National Park Service can
also supply _____ advice.
c.

3. (a/some, much/many)

Making a fire is _____ skill, but it's
a.
easy to learn. You won't need _____
b.
practice before you can build a roaring campfire. Start with

_____ paper and leaves. Place the
c.
wood on top of these, and leave spaces for air. Don't use

_____ big pieces of wood. Put two or
d.
three over the sticks, and keep the rest to the side.

4. (How much/How many)

Plan your food in advance. _____
a.
sandwiches are you going to make? _____
b.
bread will you need? Are you planning popcorn and pancakes?

_____ butter should you bring for these
c.
treats? _____ eggs will you need? Make
d.
sure you have enough of everything before you leave.

5. (few/a few, little/a little, a lot of)

On our family's first camping trip, we had

_____ equipment and almost no
a.
experience, but we still had _____ fun.
b.
It was a blast. We swam, we hiked, and we made new friends.

Of course, we had _____ problems, but
c.
not many. Anyway, _____ inconve-
d.
nience didn't interfere with our fun.

Today more than 60 million people in the United States

enjoy camping. In fact, _____ campsites
e.
are available in the summer without a reservation.

4. Keeping Records

Tina kept a diary of her trip. There are many errors with nouns and with verb and pronoun agreement. Find and correct them.

>   C
> October 27. I have been on the ~~c~~Canary Islands for three days now. I'll start home when the weathers are better. I was so surprised when I picked up my mails today. My family sent some birthday presents to me. My Birthday is the 31st. I won't open any gifts until then.
>
> october 29. I think the weather is getting worse. I heard thunders today, but there wasn't many rain. Typhoon and I stayed in bed. I started reading a novel, brave New World.
>
> october 30. I left the Canary Islands today—just like columbus. There's a strong wind and plenty of sunshine now. I went 250 miles.
>
> October 31. I'm 21 today. To celebrate, I drank little coffee for breakfast and I opened my presents. I got some perfume and some pretty silver jewelries.
>
> November 1. The electricities are very low. I'd better save them until I get near New York. I'll need the radio then. It rained today, so I collected a few waters for cooking.

COMMUNICATION PRACTICE

5. Practice Listening

Alice and Fred are planning to make cookies for their trip. Listen to them talk about the recipe. Then listen again and check the ingredients that they have enough of. Listen a third time and make a shopping list of things that they need to buy.

Ingredients	Shopping List
2 cups of butter	butter
✓ 3 cups of brown sugar	
2 cups of oatmeal (uncooked)	
4 cups of flour	
1 cup of cornflakes	
8 eggs	
1 cup of raisins	
2 cups of chocolate chips	

6. Desert Island

Work with a group. Imagine that you are about to be shipwrecked near a deserted tropical island. You have room in your lifeboat for all the members of your group plus five of the things on the list that follows. Decide what to take and give your reasons. Compare your choices with other groups'.

sugar	fishing equipment	telescope
flour	portable TV set	compass
pasta	radio	maps of the area
beans	batteries	a book, *Navigating by the Stars*
chocolate	axe	a book, *Tropical Plants You Can Eat*
fresh water	cooking pot	fireworks

Example:
I think we should bring a lot of beans. We might not find any food on the island.

7. Lists

Work with a group. Plan a party for your class. Make a list of food and other things you will need for the party. When you finish, compare your list with other groups'.

Example:
A: Let's have some music.
B: Good idea. I can bring a cassette player.

Read and listen to this advertisement for a new video game.

Space Defender
A New Game From Intendo!

An evil **magician** from **a universe** beyond ours is trying to conquer **the Earth. The magician** is Zado, and he has four helpers—they are all monsters, and they all have magic powers like Zado's. Fortunately you are also **a magician,** and can destroy Zado and his team. Here's how **the game** works.

You are **a Space Defender,** and it is your job to save **the Earth** from Zado. At **the start,** you have **some gold** and **some weapons,** but you are alone. You must train fighters to defeat **the magician.** When the fighters win **a battle,** you can use **the gold** to buy magic tools and medicine. Your team becomes stronger each time it wins.

Music is **a powerful force** in Space Defender—it tells you when Zado is near, and it signals your new magic power.

Hurry and defend your planet. Be **the first kid** on your block to save **the world!**

ARTICLES: DEFINITE AND INDEFINITE

INDEFINITE ARTICLE *(A/AN)*
Let's play **a video game**. Super Mario Brothers is **a good game**. It's **an adventure**.

DEFINITE ARTICLE *(THE)*
The best game is Space Defender. I played it at **the video store**.

NO ARTICLE
We won **gold** and **weapons**. **Video games** are very popular.

Grammar Notes

1. A noun is <u>definite</u> (specific) when you and your listener both know which person, place, or thing you mean. Use the definite article, *the*, with nouns that are specific for you and your listener. You can use *the* with most nouns, count and non-count, singular and plural.

    A: I bought **the video game** yesterday.
    B: Great! You've been talking about it for a long time. Is it fun?

    (B knows which video game A means. They've spoken about it before.)

    A: **The new games** are great.
    B: I think so too. I'm glad we bought them.

    (B knows which games A means. They have talked about them before.)

    A: I bought **the medicine**.
    B: Good. Why don't you take some right away?

    (A and B both know which medicine A means. They have already spoken about it.)

2. Use *the* when a person, place, or thing is unique—there's only one.

    There's a hole in **the ozone layer**.
    The moon is about 250,000 miles from **the Earth**.

3. Use *the* when the context makes it clear which person, place, or thing you mean.

    A: What do you do?
    B: I'm **the pilot**.

    (A and B work on a plane with only one pilot. A is a new crew member.)

    A: **The music** was great.
    B: I enjoyed it too.

    (A and B are coming out of a concert.)

Often, a phrase or an adjective such as *right, wrong, first, best,* or *only* identifies which one.

> "Donkey Kong" was **the first video game** with a story.
> Ben pushed **the wrong button** and lost the game.

4. A noun is <u>indefinite</u> (not specific) when either you or your listener do not have a particular person, place, or thing in mind. Use the indefinite article *a/an* with singular count nouns that are not specific.

> A: Let's buy **a video game**.
> B: Good idea.

(A and B are not talking about a specific game.)

Use *a* before consonant sounds and *an* before vowel sounds.

> **a** magician
> **an** evil magician

It is the sound, not the letter, that determines whether to use *a* or *an*.

> **an honest** Space Defender   honest = /ˈɑnəst/
> **a universe** beyond ours   universe = /yuʷnəvɜrs/

5. Use *some* or no article with plural count nouns and with non-count nouns that are not specific.

> **plural count noun, not specific**
>
> **New games** are coming out all the time.

(The speaker doesn't mention which games.)

> **non-count noun, not specific**
>
> A: Sorry I took so long. I had to buy **(some) medicine**.
> B: Oh. Are you sick?

(B doesn't know what kind of medicine A bought.)

6. A noun is often indefinite the first time a speaker mentions it. It is usually definite after the first mention.

> **An evil magician** is trying to conquer the Earth. **The magician** is very powerful, but so are you. You have **some gold**. Use **the gold** to buy **medicine**.
> **The medicine** makes you stronger.

7. Use *a/an* for singular count nouns when you classify (say what something or someone is).

> A: What do you do for a living?
> B: I'm **a pilot**. And you?
> A: I'm **a doctor**.

8. Use no article for plural count nouns and for non-count nouns when you classify.

> A: What are those?
> B: They're **magic tools**. We can buy them and get stronger.
> A: What's that?
> B: It's **gold**. I just won it.

(continued on next page)

Be careful! Do not use *some* when you classify.

> A: Look at those sharks!
> B: Those aren't **sharks**. They're **dolphins**. NOT ~~They're some dolphins~~.

9. Use no article with plural count nouns and non-count nouns to make general statements. *Some* in general statements means *some, but not all.*

> Sue loves **video games**. (video games in general)
> **Music** is relaxing. (music in general)
> I like **some video games**, but a lot of them are really boring.

1. Discover the Grammar

Read the conversations. Circle the letter of the statement that best describes each conversation.

1. **Fred:** I'm bored

   Cora: Let's rent a video game.

   Fred: OK.
   - a. Fred knows which game Cora is going to rent.
   - (b.) Fred and Cora aren't talking about a particular game.

2. **Cora:** Mom, where's the new video game?

   Mom: Sorry, I haven't seen it.
   - a. Mom knows that Cora rented a new game.
   - b. Mom doesn't know that Cora rented a new game.

3. **Fred:** I'll bet it's in the hall. You always drop your things there.

   Cora: I'll go look.
   - a. There are several halls in Fred and Cora's house.
   - b. There is only one hall in Fred and Cora's house.

4. **Fred:** Was I right?

   Cora: You weren't even close. It was on a chair in the kitchen.
   - a. There is only one chair in the kitchen.
   - b. There are several chairs in the kitchen.

5. **Fred:** Wow! Look at that! The graphics are awesome.

   Cora: So is the music.
   - a. All video games have good pictures and music.
   - b. The game Cora rented has good pictures and music.

6. **Cora:** This was fun. But why don't we rent a sports game next time?

   Fred: Good idea. I love sports games.
   - a. Fred is talking about sports games in general.
   - b. Fred is talking about a particular sports game.

2. Fun and Games

Complete the conversations with a, an, *or* the.

1. **A:** _____A_____ car just pulled up. Are you expecting someone?

   B: No, I'm not. I wonder who it is.

2. **A:** Can we use _____ car?

   B: OK, but bring it back by 11:00 o'clock.

3. **A:** Let's turn off _____ game system before we leave.

   B: We don't have to. We can just leave it on Pause.

4. **A:** Do you have _____ game system?

   B: Yes, I do. I just bought a Mega Genesis.

5. **A:** Do you see the video store? I was sure it was on Main Street.

   B: I think it's on _____ side street, but I'm not sure which one.

   A: I'll try this one.

6. **A:** There it is.

   B: You can park right across _____ street.

7. **A:** Can I help you?

   B: Do you have any new games?

   A: _____ newest games are in the front of the store.

8. **A:** We'd better go. We've been here for _____ hour.

   B: That was _____ fastest hour I've ever spent.

   A: I know. Let's take the Marco Brothers game, OK?

9. **A:** Excuse me. I'd like to rent this game.

   B: Just bring it to _____ cashier. She's right over there.

10. **A:** My cousin just got _____ summer job.

    B: What does he do?

    A: He's a cashier at _____ amusement park.

    B: Really? Which one?

    A: Blare Gardens.

11. **A:** Whew! _____ sun got really hot. It must be almost noon.

    B: We were supposed to be home by 11:00. Let's hurry.

3. Scary Rides

Complete the sentences with the *where necessary. Use* the *for specific statements. Don't use any article for general statements.*

A: I'm going to Blare Gardens next weekend. You work there. What's it like?

B: That depends. Do you like _____—_____ scary rides?
1.

A: A lot.

B: Then you're going to love _____ rides at Blare Gardens.
2.

A: What's _____ most exciting ride there?
3.

B: The Python. I've seen people actually shaking before they got on it.

A: Sounds like fun. By the way, how's _____ food? I hate _____ hot dogs.
4.   5.

B: Then you might have a little problem. They sell _____ hot dogs and _____
6.   7.

pizza, and that's about it. But do you like _____ music?
8.

A: I love it. I listen to _____ country music all the time. Why?
9.

B: _____ music at Blare Gardens is great. They have _____ best country music
10.   11.

groups in the state.

A: What exactly do you do there? Maybe we'll see you.

B: You won't recognize me. I wear a Scooby Doo costume and guide people around _____
12.

park.

4. Person, Place, or Thing?

This is a quiz game. Each item has three clues. Complete the clues with a/an *or* the *where necessary. Some nouns do not need an article. Then write the answers for each item. Use* a/an *or* the *where necessary for the answers.*

Answers

whales   Tarzan   Australia
Cleopatra   Great Wall of China   roller coaster

Clues

1. He's _____*a*_____ person in _____ story.
a.   b.

In _____ story, he lives in _____ tree with his wife, Jane, and his son, Boy.
c.   d.

He hates _____ cities.
e.

Answer: He's _____

2. It's _____ longest structure in the world.
   a.
   _____ emperor built it.
   b.
   It's so big that _____ astronauts can see it from space.
   c.
   Answer: It's _____

3. It's _____ smallest continent.
   a.
   There are _____ kangaroos and other interesting animals there.
   b.
   Europeans found _____ gold there in 1851.
   c.
   It's _____

4. You can find one in _____ amusement park.
   a.
   It scares _____ people, but they still love it.
   b.
   _____ tallest one is in Japan.
   c.
   It's _____

5. She was _____ intelligent and beautiful woman.
   a.
   She was_____ most famous queen of Egypt.
   b.
   She ruled _____ country with her brother.
   c.
   She was _____

6. They are _____ biggest animals that have ever lived.
   a.
   Some of them sing _____ songs.
   b.
   They have _____ fins, but they aren't _____ fish.
   c.   d.
   They're _____

5. Fairy Tales

Read the article about video games. There are nine errors with a, an, *and* the. *Find and correct them.*

                                 The plumber

Once there was a plumber named Mario. ~~Plumber~~ had beautiful girlfriend. One day, a ape fell in love with the girlfriend and kidnapped her. The plumber chased ape to rescue his girlfriend.

This simple tale became "Donkey Kong," a first video game with a story. It was invented by Sigeru Matsimoto, a artist with Nintendo, Inc. Matsimoto loved the video games, but he wanted to make them more interesting. He liked fairy tales, so he invented story similar to a famous fairy tale. Story was an immediate success, and Nintendo followed it with The Mario Brothers. The rest is video history.

COMMUNICATION PRACTICE

6. Practice Listening

●● *Listen to the conversations. Then listen again and circle the correct article.*

1. **A:** Let's go to (an)/the amusement park this weekend.
   B: That's a great idea. I haven't ridden a roller coaster in ages.

2. **A:** Is Mark *a/the* manager at Blare Gardens now?
   B: Yes, he is.

3. **A:** Have you played *a/the* video game yet?
   B: No, I haven't. I'm going to right now.

4. **A:** It's 6:00. Let's pick up *a/the* pizza.
   B: OK. Do you want me to go?

5. **A:** What's that?
   B: It's *a/the* new ride. Do you want to try it?

6. **A:** Look! A shark!
   B: That's not a shark, silly. It's *a/the* dolphin from the water show.

Read your completed conversations. Circle the letter of the statement that best describes each conversation.

1. a. A has a specific amusement park in mind.
   (b.) A isn't thinking of a particular amusement park.

2. a. There is only one manager at Blare Gardens.
   b. There are several managers at Blare Gardens.

3. a. A and B are in a video arcade. There are a lot of video games.
   b. A and B are at home. They have a new video game.

4. a. A and B have already ordered a pizza. Now it's time to pick it up.
   b. A and B haven't ordered a pizza. A is hungry and wants to order one.

5. a. There are several new rides. This is one of them.
   b. This is the only new ride. A and B have both heard about it.

6. a. There are several dolphins in the water show. This is one of them.
   b. There's only one dolphin in the show, and this is it.

7. Quiz Show

Work with a group. Choose five interesting or famous things. Write three clues for each thing. Then join another group. Give your clues and ask the other group to guess what each thing is. Look at exercise 4 for ideas.

Example:
   A: It protects you from the sun. It gets thinner when you turn on the air conditioner. There's a hole in it.
   B: Is it the ozone layer?
   A: Yes, it is.

8. Story Time

Work with a partner. Identify the people, places, and things in the pictures. Use the nouns in the box to label the first picture. Use a/an *or the* the *where necessary.*

tower	~~magic wand~~	gold	superhero	moon
wall	sword	magician	ground	bottle
laser gun	~~silver coins~~	warrior	stars	

Example:
A: What's that?
B: It's a magic wand.
A: And those?
B: I think they're silver coins.

wand

coins

After you label the first picture, invent a story about the two pictures. Write your story and then tell it to the class.

P A R T

VIII

Review or SelfTest

▼

I. *Complete each conversation with the correct form of the words in parentheses.*

1. **A:** We got _____a lot of mail_____ today.
   <u>a. (many / a lot of) (mail / mails)</u>
   B: How _____ came?
   <u>b. (much / many) (letter / letters)</u>

2. **A:** Are you still majoring in mathematics?
   B: No, _____ interest me much
   <u>a. (it / they) (doesn't / don't)</u>
   anymore.

3. **A:** There _____ some new
   <u>a. ('s / are)</u>
   _____ in the office.
   <u>b. (equipment / equipments)</u>
   B: I know. I saw _____ new _____.
   <u>c. (several / a great deal of)</u>   <u>d. (computer / computers)</u>

4. **A:** Do you enjoy camping?
   B: _____ OK, but I prefer staying in hotels.
   <u>a. (It's / They're)</u>

5. **A:** I put _____ in the tomato sauce.
   <u>a. (too much / too many) (salt / salts)</u>
   B: No, you didn't. _____ just
   <u>b. (It / They) (tastes / taste)</u>
   fine to me.

6. **A:** Did you watch the six o'clock news?
   B: No. I missed _____ today.
   <u>a. (it / them)</u>

7. **A:** I brought _____ luggage on this trip.
   <u>a. (a lot of / a)</u>
   B: How _____ do you have?
   <u>b. (much / many) (bag / bags)</u>

8. **A:** Jones is a very unpopular mayor. Many people are voting
   against him. He has _____ friends in politics.
   <u>a. (few / a few)</u>
   B: You're right. He won't get _____ support.
   <u>b. (much / many)</u>

9. **A:** I love Nancy Griffith's music.
   B: I like _____ too.
   <u>a. (it / them)</u>

II. *Complete the conversations with* a *or* the.

1. **A:** Did anyone feed _____the_____ cat today?
   B: I did. Why?
   A: He's still hungry.

2. **A:** Look at my picture.
   B: It's lovely. What kind of cat is that?
   A: It's not _____ cat. It's _____ dog.

3. **A:** Shut _____ door. It just blew open.
   B: OK.

4. **A:** It was cold last night.

   B: I know. _____ ground is still frozen.

5. **A:** How's _____ weather in San Francisco?

   B: Sunny. How's New York?

6. **A:** Who's that woman in the blue uniform?

   B: She must be _____ captain of this ship.

7. **A:** What does Martha do?

   B: She's _____ navigator. She works for World Cargo.

8. **A:** We need _____ new car.

   B: I know. But we'll have to wait.

9. **A:** I need _____ car today.

   B: OK. Can you drop me off at work?

III. *Each sentence has one mistake with an article or a noun. Find and correct the error.*

1. Many popular flavorings come from Native Ⱥmerican cultures.

2. For example, chili was unknown in an Asia or Europe a few hundred years ago.

3. Now it's the most popular spice in world.

4. It's hard to imagine Italian or Szechuan cookings without it.

5. A chocolate also comes from America.

6. For some American cultures, it was the medicine.

7. People mixed chocolate with Vanilla, another popular flavoring.

8. In the 1500s, only European kings and queens could afford an cup of chocolate.

9. Now People all over the world use chocolate, chili, and vanilla to flavor food.

IV. *Complete the conversation with the correct words or phrases in parentheses.*

A: Joe's birthday is tomorrow. Let's surprise him and give a party.

B: That's not _____ *much* _____ time.
    1. (much/many)

A: One day? That's _____. We still have candles and decorations left from the last
    2. (enough/too much)

   party.

B: Let's just make _____ hamburgers and fries. And I'll bake a cake.
    3. (a lot of/a great deal of)

   _____ chopped meat do we have?
    4. (How much/How many)

A: Only _____. And we only have _____ rolls.
    5. (a few/a little)   6. (a few/a little)

B: Put them on the list. I'll also need _____ eggs for the cake.
    7. (some/any)

(continued on next page)

A: _____?
8. (How many/How much)
B: Two. Is there _____ flour and sugar?
9. (any/many)
A: Not _____. I'll get more.
10. (much/many)
B: I think that's it.

A: Not quite. Joe's got _____ friends. We'd better start calling them.
11. (a lot of/much)
B: Why don't you go shopping? I'll call _____ people while you're gone.
12. (few/a few)

V. *Complete the sentences with* the *where necessary. Capitalize the first letter when you don't use* the.

1. _____—_____ ~~F~~friendship is very important to most people.

2. _____The_____ friendship of my classmates is very important to me.

3. Sue used _____ money in her bank account to pay her tuition.

4. _____ money isn't everything.

5. _____ travel can be educational.

6. _____ staying at home can be educational too.

7. _____ vegetables in our garden aren't ripe yet.

8. _____ vegetables contain a lot of vitamins.

9. _____ bicycles don't pollute the atmosphere the way cars do.

10. _____ bicycles in Sports Unlimited are on sale this week.

VI. *Complete the want ad with* a, an, *or* the.

EXECUTIVE ASSISTANT

_____The_____ president of this company is looking for _____ executive assistant.
1. / 2.
_____ assistant will work in _____ fast-paced office. No smokers, please—
3. / 4.
_____ office is smoke-free. _____ best person for this job will have a lot of
5. / 6.
energy and be able to work independently. _____ last day to apply is August 31.
7.

VII. *Complete the paragraphs with* a, an, the, *or* some.

1. Yesterday, I went to _____*the*_____ biggest video store downtown to rent _____
   a.   b.
   movies. I found _____ comedy and _____ adventure story. _____
                    c.   d.   e.
   comedy was very funny. I really enjoyed it. _____ adventure story wasn't that good.
                                               f.

2. We need to buy _____ office supplies fairly soon. We need _____ paper for the
                   a.   b.
   printer and _____ floppy disks. _____ paper is more important than
               c.   d.
   _____ disks, though. We'd better buy it this week.
   e.

3. I went to _____ party last weekend at my friend Tom's house. There were
              a.
   _____ interesting people at _____ party. _____ most interesting
   b.   c.   d.
   guest was _____ woman from Thailand. She showed me _____ pictures of her
             e.   f.
   home town. They were fascinating. Unfortunately, I don't remember _____ woman's
                                                                      g.
   name. I'll have to ask Tom.

1. Irregular Verbs

Base Form	Simple Past	Past Participle
arise	arose	arisen
awake	awoke	awoken
be	was/were	been
beat	beat	beaten
become	became	become
begin	began	begun
bend	bent	bent
bet	bet	bet
bite	bit	bitten
bleed	bled	bled
blow	blew	blown
break	broke	broken
bring	brought	brought
build	built	built
burn	burned/burnt	burned/burnt
burst	burst	burst
buy	bought	bought
catch	caught	caught
choose	chose	chosen
cling	clung	clung
come	came	come
cost	cost	cost
creep	crept	crept
cut	cut	cut
deal	dealt	dealt
dig	dug	dug
dive	dived/dove	dived
do	did	done
draw	drew	drawn
dream	dreamed/dreamt	dreamed/dreamt
drink	drank	drunk
drive	drove	driven
eat	ate	eaten
fall	fell	fallen
feed	fed	fed
feel	felt	felt
fight	fought	fought
find	found	found
fit	fit	fit
flee	fled	fled
fling	flung	flung
fly	flew	flown

(continued on next page)

Base Form	Simple Past	Past Participle
forbid	forbade/forbad	forbidden
forget	forgot	forgotten
forgive	forgave	forgiven
freeze	froze	frozen
get	got	gotten/got
give	gave	given
go	went	gone
grind	ground	ground
grow	grew	grown
hang	hung	hung
have	had	had
hear	heard	heard
hide	hid	hidden
hit	hit	hit
hold	held	held
hurt	hurt	hurt
keep	kept	kept
kneel	knelt	knelt
knit	knit/knitted	knit/knitted
know	knew	known
lay	laid	laid
lead	led	led
leap	leapt	leapt
leave	left	left
lend	lent	lent
let	let	let
lie (lie down)	lay	lain
light	lit/lighted	lit/lighted
lose	lost	lost
make	made	made
mean	meant	meant
meet	met	met
pay	paid	paid
prove	proved	proved/proven
put	put	put
quit	quit	quit
read /riʸd/	read /rɛd/	read /rɛd/
ride	rode	ridden
ring	rang	rung
rise	rose	risen
run	ran	run
say	said	said
see	saw	seen
seek	sought	sought
sell	sold	sold
send	sent	sent
set	set	set
sew	sewed	sewn/sewed
shake	shook	shaken
shave	shaved	shaved/shaven
shine	shone	shone
shoot	shot	shot

Base Form	Simple Past	Past Participle
show	showed	shown
shrink	shrank/shrunk	shrunk/shrunken
shut	shut	shut
sing	sang	sung
sink	sank	sunk
sit	sat	sat
sleep	slept	slept
slide	slid	slid
speak	spoke	spoken
speed	sped	sped
spend	spent	spent
spill	spilled/spilt	spilled/spilt
spin	spun	spun
spit	spat	spat
split	split	split
spread	spread	spread
spring	sprang	sprung
stand	stood	stood
steal	stole	stolen
stick	stuck	stuck
sting	stung	stung
stink	stank/stunk	stunk
strike	struck	struck
swear	swore	sworn
sweep	swept	swept
swim	swam	swum
swing	swung	swung
take	took	taken
teach	taught	taught
tear	tore	torn
tell	told	told
think	thought	thought
throw	threw	thrown
understand	understood	understood
upset	upset	upset
wake	woke	woken
wear	wore	worn
weave	wove	woven
weep	wept	wept
win	won	won
wind	wound	wound
withdraw	withdrew	withdrawn
wring	wrung	wrung
write	wrote	written

2. Common Non-action (Stative) Verbs

Emotions

admire
adore
appreciate
care
detest
dislike
doubt
envy
fear
hate
hope
like
love
regret
respect
trust

Mental States

agree
assume
believe
consider
disagree
disbelieve
estimate
expect
feel (believe)
find
guess
hesitate
hope
imagine
know
mean
presume
realize
recognize
remember
see (understand)
suppose
suspect
think (believe)
understand
wonder

Wants and Preferences

desire
need
prefer
want
wish

Perception and the Senses

feel
hear
notice
observe
perceive
see
smell
taste

Appearance

appear
be
feel
look
represent
resemble
seem
signify
smell
sound
taste

Possession

belong
have
own
possess

3. Irregular Comparisons of Adjectives and Adverbs

Adjective	Adverb	Comparative	Superlative
bad	badly	worse	worst
far	far	farther/further	farthest/furthest
good	well	better	best
little	little	less	least
many	—	more	most
much	much	more	most

4. Common Participial Adjectives

alarmed	alarming	fascinated	fascinating
amazed	amazing	frightened	frightening
amused	amusing	horrified	horrifying
annoyed	annoying	inspired	inspiring
astonished	astonishing	interested	interesting
bored	boring	irritated	irritating
confused	confusing	moved	moving
depressed	depressing	paralyzed	paralyzing
disappointed	disappointing	pleased	pleasing
disgusted	disgusting	relaxed	relaxing
distressed	distressing	satisfied	satisfying
disturbed	disturbing	shocked	shocking
embarrassed	embarrassing	surprised	surprising
entertained	entertaining	terrified	terrifying
excited	exciting	tired	tiring
exhausted	exhausting	touched	touching

5. Some Adjectives that Form the Comparative and Superlative in Two Ways

Adjective	Comparative	Superlative
common	commoner/more common	commonest/most common
cruel	crueler/more cruel	cruelest/most cruel
deadly	deadlier/more deadly	deadliest/most deadly
friendly	friendlier/more friendly	friendliest/most friendly
handsome	handsomer/more handsome	handsomest/most handsome
happy	happier/more happy	happiest/most happy
likely	likelier/more likely	likeliest/most likely
lively	livelier/more lively	liveliest/most lively
lonely	lonelier/more lonely	loneliest/most lonely
lovely	lovelier/more lovely	loveliest/most lovely
narrow	narrower/more narrow	narrowest/most narrow
pleasant	pleasanter/more pleasant	pleasantest/most pleasant
polite	politer/more polite	politest/most polite
quiet	quieter/more quiet	quietest/most quiet
shallow	shallower/more shallow	shallowest/most shallow
sincere	sincerer/more sincere	sincerest/most sincere
stupid	stupider/more stupid	stupidest/most stupid
true	truer/more true	truest/most true

6. Common Verbs Followed by the Gerund (Base Form of Verb + *-ing*)

acknowledge	endure	postpone
admit	enjoy	practice
appreciate	escape	prevent
avoid	explain	prohibit
can't help	feel like	quit
can't stand	finish	recall
celebrate	forgive	recommend
consider	give up (stop)	regret
delay	imagine	report
deny	justify	resent
detest	keep (continue)	resist
discontinue	mention	risk
dislike	mind (object to)	suggest
dispute	miss	understand

7. Common Verbs Followed by the Infinitive (*To* + Base Form of Verb)

afford	decide	pay
agree	deserve	prepare
appear	expect	pretend
ask	fail	promise
arrange	hope	refuse
attempt	hurry	request
begin	learn	seem
can't afford	manage	want
can't wait	mean	wish
choose	need	would like
consent	offer	

8. Common Verbs Followed by the Gerund or the Infinitive

begin	intend	remember*
can't stand	like	start
continue	love	stop*
forget*	prefer	try
hate		

*These verbs can be followed by either the gerund or the infinitive but there is a big difference in meaning.

9. Verbs Followed by Objects and the Infinitive

advise
allow
ask*
cause
choose*
convince
encourage
expect*
forbid
force

hire
invite
need*
order
pay*
permit
persuade
remind
require
teach

tell
urge
want*
warn
would like*

*These verbs can also be followed by the infinitive without an object (example: *ask to leave* or *ask someone to leave*).

10. Common Adjective + Preposition Expressions

be afraid of
be amazed at/by
be angry at
be ashamed of
be aware of
be awful at
be bad at
be bored with/by
be capable of
be careful of
be content with

be curious about
be excited about
be famous for
be fond of
be glad about
be good at
be happy about
be interested in
be pleased about
be ready for
be responsible for

be sad about
be safe from
be satisfied with
be sick of
be slow at
be sorry for/about
be surprised at/about/by
be terrible at
be tired of
be used to
be worried about

11. Common Verb + Preposition Combinations

advise against
apologize for
approve of
believe in
choose between
complain about

deal with
dream about/of
feel like
insist on
look forward to
object to

plan on
rely on
resort to
succeed in
think about

12. Spelling Rules for the Present Progressive

1. Add -ing to the base form of the verb.

   read   reading
   stand   standing

2. If a verb ends in a silent -e, drop the final -e and add -ing.

   leave   leaving
   take   taking

(continued on next page)

3. In a one-syllable word, if the last three letters are a consonant-vowel-consonant combination (CVC), double the last consonant before adding *-ing*.

```
CVC
↓↓↓
s i t              sitting
```

```
CVC
↓↓↓
r u n              running
```

However, do not double the last consonant in words that end in *w*, *x*, or *y*.

sew	sewing
fix	fixing
enjoy	enjoying

4. In words of two or more syllables that end in a consonant-vowel-consonant combination, double the last consonant only if the last syllable is stressed.

admít	admitting	(The last syllable is stressed)
whísper	whispering	(The last syllable is not stressed, so you don't double the *-r*.)

5. If a verb ends in *-ie*, change the *ie* to *y* before adding *-ing*.

die   dying

13. Spelling Rules for the Simple Present Tense: Third-Person Singular *(he, she, it)*

1. Add *-s* for most verbs.

work	works
buy	buys
ride	rides
return	returns

2. Add *-es* for words that end in *-ch*, *-s*, *-sh*, *-x*, or *-z*.

watch	watches
pass	passes
rush	rushes
relax	relaxes
buzz	buzzes

3. Change the *y* to *i* and add *-es* when the base form ends in a consonant + *y*.

study	studies
hurry	hurries
dry	dries

Do not change the *y* when the base form ends in a vowel + *y*. Add *-s*.

play	plays
enjoy	enjoys

4. A few verbs have irregular forms.

be	is
do	does
go	goes
have	has

14. Spelling Rules for the Simple Past Tense of Regular Verbs

1. If the verb ends in a consonant, add -ed.

   return   returned
   help   helped

2. If the verb ends in -e, add -d.

   live   lived
   create   created
   die   died

3. In one-syllable words, if the verb ends in a consonant-vowel-consonant combination (CVC), double the final consonant and add -ed.

   CVC
   ↓↓↓
   hop   hopped

   CVC
   ↓↓↓
   rub   rubbed

   However, do not double one-syllable words ending in -w, -x, or -y.

   bow   bowed
   mix   mixed
   play   played

4. In words of two or more syllables that end in a consonant-vowel-consonant combination, double the last consonant only if the last syllable is stressed.

   prefér   preferred   (The last syllable is stressed.)
   vísit   visited   (The last syllable is not stressed, so you don't double the t.)

5. If the verb ends in a consonant + y, change the y to i and add -ed.

   worry   worried
   carry   carried

6. If the verb ends in a vowel + y, add -ed. (Do not change the y to i.)

   play   played
   annoy   annoyed

   Exceptions: pay—paid, lay—laid, say—said

15. Spelling Rules for the Comparative *(-er)* and Superlative *(-est)* of Adjectives

1. Add *-er* to one-syllable adjectives to form the comparative. Add *-est* to one-syllable adjectives to form the superlative.

cheap	cheap*er*	cheap*est*
bright	bright*er*	bright*est*

2. If the adjective ends in *-e,* add *-r* or *-st.*

nice	nice*r*	nice*st*

3. If the adjective ends in a consonant + *y,* change *y* to *i* before you add *-er* or *-est.*

pretty	prett*ier*	prett*iest*

Exception:	shy	shy*er*	shy*est*

4. If the adjective ends in a consonant-vowel-consonant combination (CVC), double the final consonant before adding *-er* or *-est.*

```
CVC
↓↓↓
```
b i g	big*ger*	big*gest*

However, do not double the consonant in words ending in *-w* or *-y.*

slow	slow*er*	slow*est*
coy	coy*er*	coy*est*

16. Spelling Rules for Adverbs Ending in *-ly*

1. Add *-ly* to the corresponding adjective.

nice	nice*ly*
quiet	quiet*ly*
beautiful	beautifu*lly*

2. If the adjective ends in a consonant + *y,* change the *y* to *i* before adding *-ly.*

easy	eas*ily*

3. If the adjective ends in *-le,* drop the *e* and add *-y.*

possible	possibl*y*

However, do not drop the *e* for other adjectives ending in *-e.*

extreme	extreme*ly*

Exception:	true	tru*ly*

4. If the adjective ends in *-ic,* add *-ally.*

basic	basic*ally*
fantastic	fantastic*ally*

17. Pronunciation Table

These are the pronunciation symbols used in this text. Listen to the pronunciation of the key words.

VOWELS	
SYMBOL	KEY WORD
iʸ	beat
ɪ	bit
eʸ	bay
ɛ	bet
æ	bat
ɑ	box, car
ɔ	bought, horse
oʷ	bone
ʊ	book
uʷ	boot
ʌ	but
ə	banana, sister
aɪ	by
aʊ	bound
ɔɪ	boy
ɜr	burn
ɪər	beer
ɛər	bare
ʊər	tour

CONSONANTS	
SYMBOL	KEY WORD
p	pan
b	ban
t	tip
d	dip
k	cap
g	gap
tʃ	church
dʒ	judge
f	fan
v	van
θ	thing
ð	then
s	sip
z	zip
ʃ	ship
ʒ	measure
h	hot
m	sum
n	sun
ŋ	sung
w	wet
hw	what
l	lot
r	rot
y	yet

/t̬/ means that the /t/ sound is said as a voiced sound (like a quick English /d/).

From *Longman Dictionary of American English*, © 1983.

18. Pronunciation Rules for the Simple Present Tense: Third-Person Singular *(he/she/it)*

1. The third person singular in the simple present tense always ends in the letter *-s*. There are, however, three different pronunciations for the final sound of the third person singular.

/s/	/z/	/ɪz/
talks	loves	dances

2. The final sound is pronounced /s/ after the voiceless sounds /p/, /t/, /k/, and /f/.

top	tops
get	gets
take	takes
laugh	laughs

3. The final sound is pronounced /z/ after the voiced sounds /b/, /d/, /g/, /v/, /ð/, /m/, /n/, /ŋ/, /l/, and /r/.

describe	describes
spend	spends
hug	hugs
live	lives
bathe	bathes
seem	seems
remain	remains
sing	sings
tell	tells
lower	lowers

4. The final sound is pronounced /z/ after all vowel sounds.

agree	agrees
try	tries
stay	stays
know	knows

5. The final sound is pronounced /ɪz/ after the sounds /s/, /z/, /ʃ/, /ʒ/, /tʃ/, and /dʒ/. /ɪz/ adds a syllable to the verb.

relax	relaxes
freeze	freezes
rush	rushes
massage	massages
watch	watches
judge	judges

6. *Do* and *say* have a change in vowel sound.

say	/seʸ/	says	/sɛz/
do	/duʷ/	does	/dʌz/

19. Pronunciation Rules for the Simple Past Tense of Regular Verbs

1. The regular simple past always ends in the letter -d. There are, however, three different pronunciations for the final sound of the regular simple past.

/t/	/d/	/ɪd/
raced	lived	attended

2. The final sound is pronounced /t/ after the voiceless sounds /p/, /k/, /f/, /s/, /ʃ/, and /tʃ/.

hop	hopped
work	worked
laugh	laughed
address	addressed
publish	published
watch	watched

3. The final sound is pronounced /d/ after the voiced sounds /b/, /g/, /v/, /z/, /ʒ/, /dʒ/, /m/, /n/, /ŋ/, /l/, /r/, and /ð/.

rub	rubbed
hug	hugged
live	lived
surprise	surprised
massage	massaged
change	changed
rhyme	rhymed
return	returned
bang	banged
enroll	enrolled
appear	appeared
bathe	bathed

4. The final sound is pronounced /d/ after all vowel sounds.

agree	agreed
play	played
die	died
enjoy	enjoyed

5. The final sound is pronounced /ɪd/ after /t/ and /d/. /ɪd/ adds a syllable to the verb.

start	started
decide	decided

Index

Answer Key

Note: Where a short form or contracted form is given, the full or long form is also correct (unless the purpose of the exercise is to practice the short or contracted forms).

PART I Present

UNIT 1 Present Progressive

1.

Circled words: 'm (still) looking, 's really helping, are (you) doing, Are (you still) working, Are you going
Underlined words: 'm sitting, writing

2.

sun setting → sun is setting
it get → it's getting
I taking → I'm taking
Do you still working → Are you still working

3.

2. are, going
3. 's waiting
4. 'm working
5. aren't doing
6. 're, sitting
7. am *or* 'm sitting
8. am *or* 'm, thinking

4.

2. Are the babies sleeping?
3. How many nurses are helping you with the babies?
4. How are you preparing for your return home?
5. Are you planning to move?
6. Where are you living now?

5.

2. Baby 2 is reaching for objects. He isn't holding his head up, and he isn't rolling over.
3. Baby 3 is rolling over, and she is reaching for objects. She isn't holding her head up.
4. Babies 4 and 5 are holding their heads up, and they're rolling over. They aren't reaching for objects.

6.

1, 2, 5

7.–10.

Answers will vary.

UNIT 2 Simple Present Tense

1.

Underlined verbs: affects, affects, causes, agree, prescribe, lowers, claims, don't need, are, relax, lower, takes, tells
Circled adverbs: never, always, often, usually, always

2.

2. sits
3. watches
4. does
5. reads
6. hurries
7. stays
8. switches
9. cancels

3.

2. She's always in a hurry.
3. She never has time for breakfast.
4. She often skips dinner.
5. She rarely goes on vacation.
6. She's usually nervous.
7. She never relaxes.
8. She rarely sees her friends.

4.

3. Barbara doesn't speak very fast.
4. Barbara doesn't finish other people's sentences for them.
5. Barbara takes time to enjoy the moment.
6. Barbara doesn't worry a lot.
7. Barbara has enough time to finish things.
8. Barbara doesn't have health problems due to stress.
9. Barbara doesn't get angry easily.
10. Barbara goes on vacation every year.

5.

3. How long does he exercise?
   He exercises for half an hour.
4. Does he work on reports in the afternoon?
   No, he doesn't.
5. When does he see clients?
   He sees clients in the morning from 9:00 to 12:00.
6. Does he take a long lunch break?
   No, he doesn't.
7. What does he do from 12:30 to 5:00?
   He writes letters.
8. Where does he go at 5:30?
   He goes to night school. *or* He attends night school.
9. How long does his class last?
   It lasts an hour and a half.
10. When does he study?
    He studies at night from 8:00 to 9:00. *or* He studies after school from 8:00 to 9:00.

6.

2. always
3. never
4. sometimes
5. never
6. sometimes

7.

Answers will vary.

8.

1. b
2. a
3. c
4. b
5. a

9.-10.

Answers will vary.

UNIT 3 Contrast: Simple Present Tense and Present Progressive

1.

Circled verbs: doesn't want, 's listening, is moving, is taking, has, feels
Underlined verbs: takes

2.

2. is opening mail
3. meets
4. has lunch, is attending
5. is writing reports
6. writes reports
7. is returning
8. returns phone calls

3.

2. 'm listening
3. don't hear
4. sounds
5. is crying
6. is, coming
7. think
8. is coming
9. are visiting
10. go
11. Do, have
12. 's happening
13. take
14. leave
15. Do, think
16. think

4.

Length of today's commute: 45 minutes
2. True
3. False
4. True
5. True

5.

Possible answers:
She usually reads the paper, but today she's listening to music.
She usually wears a business suit, but today she's wearing jeans and a T-shirt.
She usually wears her hair up, but today she's wearing her hair down.
She's usually tense, but today she looks relaxed.

6.-7.

Answers will vary.

UNIT 4 Imperative

1.

2. c
3. b
4. d
5. a
6. e

2.

2. a driving instructor
3. a robber
4. a telephone operator
5. a receptionist
6. a boss
7. a husband or wife

3.

1. Fill the kettle with water.
2. Boil the water.
3. Put a teaspoon of coffee in the coffee cup.
4. Pour the boiling water into the cup.
5. Add milk or sugar, according to taste.
6. Stir the coffee.

4.

4, 6, 1, 2, 5, 3

5.-7.

Answers will vary.

PART I Review or SelfTest

I.

2. breathe 3. 's going 4. goes 5. rains 6. 's raining
7. 're dancing 8. dance 9. 's ringing 10. rings 11. are
sharing 12. share 13. rises, falls 14. 's rising, 's falling
15. is taking 16. takes, exercises

II.

2. Do you exercise? 3. When do you eat breakfast? 4. Do you
walk to school? 5. How long do you stay at school? 6. Do
you go back after lunch? 7. Do you ever have fun?

III.

2. a. 's b. doesn't seem 3. a. looks b. tastes c. 'm eating
4. a. 's driving b. don't hear 5. a. don't want b. know
6. a. is b. think 7. a. don't remember

IV.

2. He usually pays attention.   3. He rarely forgets his
homework.   4. Our car often doesn't start on cold
mornings.   5. It sometimes breaks down in traffic.
6. It's usually in the repair shop when we need it.

V.

2. rarely 3. often 4. never 5. always 6. sometimes
7. rarely 8. often

VI.

1. b. 'm brushing c. Is, getting d. 's looking for
2. a. smells b. Are, making c. are, eating
3. a. Do, know b. don't see
4. a. tastes b. 's c. 'm putting
5. a. 'm not b. have c. seems
6. a. feel *or* 'm feeling b. hear c. 're leaving

VII.

2. don't walk 3. lock 4. don't forget 5. Don't put
6. Put 7. Call 8. don't call 9. Have, enjoy

PART II Past

UNIT 5 Simple Past Tense

1.

did not know, saw, bit, ate, drank, hopped

2.

2. was 3. spent 4. didn't have 5. moved 6. appeared
7. returned 8. published 9. won 10. read 11. was 12. said

3.

2. Was he originally from the United States?
   Yes, he was.
3. What did he write?
   He wrote poetry.
4. Was he successful right away?
   No, he wasn't.
5. Where did he first become famous?
   He first became famous in England.
6. How many Pulitzer Prizes did he win?
   He won four (Pulitzer Prizes).
7. Did he like to speak in public?
   Yes, he did.
8. When did he die?
   He died in 1963.

4.

choosed ➔ chose
were ➔ was
didn't took ➔ didn't take
change ➔ changed
decide ➔ decided
Did . . . made ➔ Did . . . make

5.

2. d
3. e
4. a
5. c
6. b

6.-9.

Answers will vary.

UNIT 6 Used To

1.

used to live, used to go out, used to stay up, (used to) get up, used to get, used to love, used to mind

2.

2. used to have
3. used to dress
4 used to dance
5. used to wear

3.

2. used to wear
3. Did, use to sit
4. used to buy
5. Did, use to iron
6. Did, use to take
7. used to do
8. used to have

4.

2. Women didn't use to have permanent hair waves.
3. Crossword puzzles didn't use to appear in the newspapers.
4. People didn't use to change the time.
5. Women in the United States didn't use to vote.
6. Movies didn't use to have sound.

5.

Past: 3, 6
Now: 2, 4, 5, 7

6.-8.

Answers will vary.

UNIT 7 Past Progressive and Simple Past Tense

1.

2. b
3. b
4. a
5. b

2.

3. They were wearing sunglasses.
4. She wasn't smiling.
5. He wasn't holding a suitcase.
6. She was holding a suitcase.
7. They were taking the subway.
8. They weren't driving.

3.

3. was driving
4. was speaking
5. saw
6. stepped
7. was crossing
8. hit
9. didn't see
10. was talking
11. was eating
12. was crossing
13. noticed
14. tried
15. arrived
16. was bleeding

4.

2. Who exactly were you visiting?
3. Was she working at 7:00?
4. Was anyone else working with her?
5. What were you doing while she was working?
6. What were you doing when the lights went out?
7. What did you do when the lights went out?
8. Why were you running when the police saw you?

5.

3. When the crowd felt the earth move, they knew immediately it was an earthquake.
4. When the electric power went out, millions of people were watching the game on TV.
5. When the earth stopped moving, the police told the crowd to leave the stadium calmly.
6. When they got to their cars, they turned on their radios.
7. While they were driving home, they heard about a collapsed highway ahead.
8. When they heard the news of the collapsed highway, they got out of their cars.
9. When they finally got home, their neighbors were standing in the streets.
10. When they entered their homes, they discovered a lot of damage.

6.

Set 2

7.-10.

Answers will vary.

UNIT 8 Wh- Questions: Subject and Predicate

1.

2. a
3. d
4. b
5. e
6. c

2.

3. When does court begin?
4. How many witnesses testified?
5. Why did the jury find Adams guilty?
6. What happened?
7. How long did the trial last?
8. Who spoke to the jury?
9. How much did Adams pay his lawyer?
10. Who did the district attorney question?

3.

2. How did you get home?
3. Who gave you a ride?
4. What happened next?
5. Who did you see?
6. Who is Deborah Collins?
7. What did you do?
8. When did the police arrive?
9. How many police officers came?

4.

2. a
2. b
3. a
4. b
5. a
6. b
7. b
8. a

5.-6.

Answers will vary.

7.

Invention	Date	Inventor	Country
adding machine	1642	Pascal	France
car engine	1889	Daimler	Germany
bicycle	1885	Starley	England
electric battery	1800	Volta	Italy
tape recorder	1899	Poulsen	Denmark

PART II Review or SelfTest

I.

2. are having 3. bit 4. makes 5. spent 6. won 7. was
8. 'm reading

II.

2. didn't write 3. was 4. walked 5. took 6. went
7. didn't go 8. was 9. didn't take

III.

2. moved 3. did, live 4. spent 5. did, do 6. taught
7. Did, like 8. did, come 9. came

IV.

2. b 3. d 4. c 5. b 6. d 7. a 8. c

V.

2. wasn't driving 3. wasn't 4. happened? 5. hit 6. did, do
7. was trying 8. wasn't paying 9. Did, call 10. called

VI.

2. get → got
3. was arriving → arrived
4. He taking → He was taking
5. discussed → was discussing
6. I not paying → I wasn't paying

VII.

2. Was 3. was playing 4. were dancing 5. went
6. Did 7. had

PART III Future

UNIT 9 Future

1.

will be, are going to have, 'll start, 'll adjust, will (even) ask, (will even) tell, 'm speaking, begins, 'm going to talk, 'm going to show, will be, will, 'll be, will be

2.

2. They're going to have an accident.
3. He's going to fall in the hole.
4. It's going to rain.
5. They're going to get married.
6. He's going to be angry.
7. She's going to get wet.

3.

2. On Monday evening he's giving a lecture at Yale.
3. On Tuesday morning he's going to Washington at 8:00 A.M.
4. All day Wednesday he's working in the research lab.
5. On Thursday he's attending the annual Car Show.
6. On Friday morning he's talking on a radio show.

4.

2. will use
3. will, get
4. won't
5. 'll be *or* will be
6. 'll have *or* will have
7. 'll repair *or* will repair
8. will, be
9. will have
10. will look
11. 'll open *or* will open
12. 'll adjust *or* will adjust
13. 'll, control *or* will, control
14. Will, help
15. will
16. will, cost
17. won't be

5.

2. Professor Lin: How long does the trip to New Haven take?
   Information: It takes about two hours.
3. Professor Lin: So, what time does the 9:07 train arrive in New Haven?
   Information: It arrives (in New Haven) at 10:53 A.M.
4. Professor Lin: How often do morning trains depart for New Haven?
   Information: They depart eight times (a day).
5. Professor Lin: And what time does the last morning train leave New York?
   Information: It leaves (New York) at 11:07 A.M.

6.

2. a
3. b
4. a
5. b
6. b
7. b
8. b

7.

	Now	Future			Now	Future
2.	✔			5.		✔
3.	✔			6.		✔
4.		✔				

8.–11.

Answers will vary.

UNIT 10 ▼ Future Time Clauses

1.

2. a
3. b
4. a
5. b
6. b
7. b
8. b

2.

2. They are going to move to a larger apartment as soon as Jeff gets a raise.
3. After they move to a larger apartment, they're going to have a baby.
4. Sandy will get a part-time job after they have their first child.
5. By the time Sandy goes back to work full-time, their child will be two.
6. Sandy will work full-time while Jeff goes back to school.
7. Jeff will find another job when he graduates.

3.

2. won't have *or* am not going to have
3. graduate
4. 'm going to take *or* I'll take
5. learn
6. 'll look *or* 'm going to look
7. get
8. 'll try
9. are, going to do *or* will do
10. finish
11. Are, going to take
12. look

4.

a. 4
b. 2
c. 1
d. 5
e. 6
f. 3

5.–7.

Answers will vary.

PART III Review or SelfTest

I.

2. 'll need 3. won't continue 4. 'll stop 5. will stay 6. won't need 7. 'll have

II.

2. a 3. c 4. a 5. d

III.

are stay
I'm going to seeing
is going to attends
he will finish
I send you
I tell you

IV.

2. When are you leaving?
3. What flight are you taking?
4. When does it arrive?
5. Are you going to take a taxi to your hotel?
6. Do you want to share a taxi?

V.

1. 're going to 2. 'll be 3. 'll 4. 's going to 5. 'll have

VI.

2. get, 'll see 3. 'll stay, finish 4. graduates, 'll work
5. 'll read, eat 6. save, 'll buy

PART IV Present Perfect

UNIT 11 Present Perfect: For and Since

1.

2. b
3. a
4. a
5. a
6. a

2.

2. Yes, she has.
3. No, they haven't.
4. Yes, he has.
5. No, they haven't.
6. Yes, she has.
7. No, he hasn't.

3.

2. for
3. for
4. Since
5. Since
6. for

4.

2. How long have you had your MA degree?
   I've had my MA degree since 1989 *or* for five years.
3. Have you had any more training since you got your MA?
   Yes, I have.
4. How long have you been a physical education teacher?
   I've been a physical education teacher since 1989 *or* for five years.
5. How long have you been a sports trainer?
   I've been a sports trainer since 1987 *or* for seven years.
6. How long have you taken classes in self-defense?
   I've taken classes in self-defense for two months.
7. Have you won any awards since then?
   Yes, I have.
8. How long have you been a member of the NEA?
   I've been a member of the NEA since 1990 *or* for four years.

5.

2. 1980
3. 1992
4. two years
5. they got married

6.-7.

Answers will vary.

UNIT 12 Present Perfect: Already and Yet

1.

2. b
3. d
4. f
5. c
6. a

2.

2. Have, looked at, yet
3. 've already read
4. 've already seen
5. 've already eaten
6. haven't done yet
7. haven't taken, yet

3.

3. Mary has already gotten her 6-month DPT injection.
4. Mary hasn't received her 15–18-month polio immunization yet.
5. Mary has already been to the doctor for her MMR immunization.
6. Mary hasn't gotten a tetanus booster yet.
7. The doctor has already vaccinated Mary against the mumps.
8. Mary hasn't received her Hib vaccine yet

4.

4. *Annie Hall* 5. *Crocodile Dundee*

5.-6.

Answers will vary.

7.

	Already	Not Yet
3. a successful heart transplant (animal to human)		✔
4. a successful heart transplant (human to human)	✔	
5. a vaccine to prevent tooth decay		✔
6. a pillow that helps prevent snoring		✔
7. liquid sunglasses (in the form of eyedrops)	✔	
8. electric cars	✔	
9. flying cars		✔
10. light bulbs that can last 14 years	✔	

UNIT 13 Present Perfect: Indefinite Past

1.

2. F
3. T
4. F
5. F
6. F
7. T

2.

2. 've, taken
3. 've lived
4. Have, wanted
5. 've, wanted
6. have, traveled
7. 've lived

3.

3. Have we ever brought her breakfast in bed?
   No, we've never brought her breakfast in bed.
4. Have we ever bought her tickets for a show?
   No, we've never bought tickets for a show.
5. Has Mom ever taken a boat trip?
   Yes, she has.
6. Have we ever forgotten about Mother's Day?
   No, we've never forgotten about Mother's Day.
7. Has Mom ever complained about her present?
   No, she's never complained about her present.

4.

2. She's won the National Acting Award many times.
3. She hasn't had much rest lately.
4. She's seen this movie many times before.
5. She's just returned from a trip.
6. She's recently filmed her first TV talk show.

5.

2. Which shows have you been on?
   I've been on every talk show.
3. How many covers have you appeared on?
   I've appeared on the covers of ten major magazines.
4. Where have you traveled?
   I've traveled all over the world.
5. What famous people have you met?
   I've met *or* eaten dinner with the president of the United States and the queen of England.
6. How many continents have you visited?
   I've visited *or* been to five continents.

6.

b. Jamaica

7.

Answers will vary.

UNIT 14 Contrast: Present Perfect and Simple Past Tense

1.

2. a	5. b
3. b	6. b
4. a	7. a

2.

2. haven't stopped
3. 've only seen
4. came
5. didn't do
6. 've already had
7. drank

3.

2. How long have you had your job?
3. How long did you live in Detroit?
4. When did you get a job offer?
5. When did your company move?
6. How long have you lived apart?
7. How often did you see each other last month?
8. How often have you seen each other this month?

4.

2. In the '70s Joe was skinny. Since then he has grown heavy.
3. In the '70s Joe was a student. Since then he has become a successful businessman.
4. In the '70s Joe worked in a factory. Since then he has bought the business.
5. In the '70s Joe lived in England. Since then he has lived in Detroit and Chicago.

5.

2. I've had
3. Did you like
4. I've been
5. I've always wanted
6. have you been
7. haven't been
8. Have you seen

6.-8.

Answers will vary.

UNIT 15 Present Perfect Progressive

1.

2. b	5. a
3. a	6. a
4. b	

2.

2. 've been sleeping
3. 've been worrying
4. haven't been eating
5. 've been thinking
6. 've been looking
7. 've been reading
8. I've been asking

3.

2. They haven't been reading the newspaper.
3. They haven't been drinking coffee.
4. They've been drinking tea.
5. They haven't been smoking.
6. One woman's been crying *or* has been crying.
7. It's been raining.

4.

1. 3. 5.

5.-8.

Answers will vary.

UNIT 16 Contrast: Present Perfect and Present Perfect Progressive

1.

2. T
3. T
4. F
5. T
6. T
7. F
8. T

2.

2. has published
3. have already died
4. has given
5. has spoken
6. has created
7. have been studying
8. have been waiting
9. has lived *or* has been living
10. has worked *or* has been working

3.

2. have eaten
3. has killed
4. have been fighting *or* have fought
5. have decided
6. has been trying *or* has tried
7. has made *or* has been making
8. have died
9. have not been catching *or* haven't caught
10. have not been making *or* have not made
11. has become *or* has been becoming
12. has been trying *or* has tried

4.

2. How many times have you sprayed your corn fields this past month?
3. How long have you been permitting people to fish on your property?
4. How much water have you used for the animals this past year?
5. What pesticides have you applied to your crops?

5.

2. a
3. b
4. b
5. a
6. b

6.-7.

Answers will vary.

PART IV Review or SelfTest

I.

2. 've lost 3. 's, fallen 4. 've, paid 5. Have, written
6. haven't read 7. 've won 8. haven't told 9. Has, come

II.

2. Since, for 3. for 4. since 5. for 6. Since 7. since 8. for

III.

2. I've wanted 3. 's watched *or* 's been watching 4. 's, told
5. have, done *or* have, been doing 6. I've worked *or* 've been working 7. has, asked 8. have, had 9. 've read 10. 've been 11. 've, finished

IV.

2. moved 3. moved 4. have asked 5. haven't stopped
6. study 7. will fail 8. talk

V.

2. already 3. since 4. never 5. never 6. ever 7. for

VI.

2. a 3. c 4. a 5. c 6. a 7. c 8. a

VII.

2. since → for
3. have did → have done
4. has gained → have gained
5. have took → have taken
6. liked → has liked
7. has gave → has given
8. show → shown

VIII.

b. saw 2. a. drank b. haven't drunk c. 've been drinking
3. a. has written b. Did, write c. wrote 4. a. 've been cooking b. cooked c. 've cooked

PART V Adjectives and Adverbs

UNIT 17 Adjectives and Adverbs

1.

absolutely perfect,
apartment perfect,
serious students,
quiet neighborhood,
lovely apartment,
new building,
short walk,
express bus,
goes directly,
hardly makes,
walk peacefully,
wonderful parks,
rent affordable,
very affordable,
rent fast

2.

2. terribly disappointed
3. surprisingly easy
4. incredibly fast
5. very clearly
6. unusually loud

3.

2. large
3. happily
4. beautifully
5. nice
6. shy
7. hardly
8. good

4.

2. strictly
3. confidential
4. exceptional
5. interesting
6. carefully
7. easy
8. quickly
9. interesting
10. highly
11. well

5.

2. puzzled
3. puzzling
4. interesting
5. interested
6. fascinating
7. fascinated
8. disappointed
9. surprising

6.

2. F
3. T
4. T
5. F

7.-10.

Answers will vary.

UNIT 18 Adjectives: Equatives and Comparatives

1.

fluffier, more common, stickier, better than, n't as easy as,
The longer, the softer, worse than, less nutritious

2.

2. is not as expensive as
3. tastes as good as
4. doesn't taste as good as
5. doesn't smell as nice as
6. smells as good as

3.

2. hotter than
3. less expensive than
4. less spicy than
5. less salty than
6. milder than
7. healthier than
8. cheaper than

4.

expensive than ➔ more expensive than
more better ➔ better
convenienter ➔ more convenient
clean than ➔ cleaner than
nicer that ➔ nicer than

5.

2. the better, the higher
3. The smokier, the worse
4. The more crowded, the noisier
5. the saltier, the better
6. The bigger, the harder

6.

2. That's wrong. It's getting more and more expensive.
3. That's right. It's getting larger and larger.
4. That's wrong. It's getting longer and longer.
5. That's right. It's getting more and more expensive.

7.

	Ranger	Speedster
2. safe	☐	✔
3. comfortable	☐	✔
4. big	✔	☐
5. fuel efficient	✔	☐
6. fast	☐	✔

UNIT 19 Adjectives: Superlatives

1.

the smartest
the brightest
the funniest
the nicest
the most wonderful
the least mean
the greatest

2.

2. the happiest, of my life
3. the best, in the school
4. the coldest, of the year
5. the nicest, of all
6. the wisest, in our family

3.

2. The scarf is the most practical gift.
3. The book is the least expensive gift.
4. The scarf is the most expensive gift.
5. The book is the smallest gift.
6. The painting is the biggest gift.

8.

Answers will vary.

9.

2. bigger, Toronto
3. more popular, vanilla *or* less popular, chocolate
4. heavier, a tiger
5. more nutritious, brown rice *or* less nutritious, white rice
6. more fattening, cooked rice *or* less fattening, baked potato
7. more dangerous, the train *or* less dangerous, the bus

10.

2. h
3. g
4. f
5. c
6. a
7. d
8. b

11.

Answers will vary.

4.

2. What's the funniest thing you've ever done?
3. Who's the smartest person you've ever known?
4. What's the nicest place you've ever seen?
5. Where's the hottest place you've ever been?
6. What's the worst experience you've ever had?
7. What's the silliest thing you've ever said?
8. What's the longest book you've ever read?
9. What's the most valuable lesson you've ever learned?
10. What's the most difficult thing you've ever done?
11. What's the most enjoyable thing you've ever done?

5.

	Bracelet	Winter Coat	Picture Frame	Soap and Bubble Bath
1. least expensive	✔	☐	☐	☐
2. most practical	☐	✔	☐	☐
3. silliest	☐	☐	✔	☐
4. most romantic	☐	☐	✔	☐
5. sweetest	☐	☐	☐	✔

6.-8.

Answers will vary.

Adverbs: Equatives, Comparatives, Superlatives

1.

as well as
the most skillfully
the best
the farthest
the fastest
the harder he played, the better the Golds performed
more seriously...than
better and better

2.

2. stops as quickly as
3. doesn't stop as quickly as
4. shifts as easily as
5. doesn't shift as easily as
6. doesn't handle as well as
7. handles as well as

3.

2. better
3. faster
4. less
5. more rapidly
6. harder
7. more slowly than *or* slower than
8. more clearly
9. longer than
10. more quickly *or* quicker
11. as completely as
12. more carefully

4.

3. the slowest *or* the most slowly
4. slower than *or* more slowly
5. the farthest
6. faster than
7. higher than
8. the best
9. the worst

5.

4	Exuberant King
1	Get Packin'
5	Inspired Winner
3	Señor Speedy
2	Wild Whirl

6.-7.

Answers will vary.

PART V Review or SelfTest

I.

1. b. cozy c. Cheap d. perfect
2. a. incredibly b. new c. hardly d. terrific
3. a. GOOD b. beautiful c. well d. obedient e. quickly

II.

2. easier 3. more slowly *or* slower 4. more regularly
5. more quietly 6. worse 7. better 8. more expensive
9. harder 10. farther

III.

1. b. disgusted 2. a. exhausted b. exhausting 3. a. satisfying
b. satisfied 4. a. amazed b. amazing 5. a. embarrassed
b. embarrassing 6. a. confusing b. confused

IV.

2. faster, more confused 3. later, sillier 4. harder, more
fluently 5. more often, bigger 6. louder, faster 7. more
profusely, worse

V.

1. b. most c. the d. of e. best
2. a. big b. than c. many d. much e. exciting f. sooner

VI.

a busiest time → the busiest time
the nervous I got → the more nervous I got
biggest deal → the biggest deal
more frequently he called → the more frequently he called
as expensive the last time → as expensive as the last time

UNIT 21 Gerunds: Subject and Object

1.

swimming,
participating, Jogging,
(go) jogging, running,
joining, competing

2.

2. Eating
3. increasing
4. doing, swimming
5. walking, running
6. going

3.

2. quit smoking *or* has quit smoking
3. go swimming
4. denied smoking *or* denies smoking
5. admits *or* admitted being
6. avoids eating
7. mind exercising
8. are considering taking

4.

OK to do: 4. 6. 7.
Not OK to do: 1. 2. 3. 5.

5.-7.

Answers will vary.

PART VI Gerunds and Infinitives

UNIT 22 Gerunds after Prepositions

1.

for dealing, are tired of hearing,
are not used to working,
believe in giving, think about
speaking, look forward to hearing

2.

2. for having
3. about getting
4. at learning, about not doing
5. about going, about driving
6. on coming
7. to staying, relaxing
8. of reading, going
9. about cooking
10. against going, instead of spending

3.

2. have
3. have
4. being
5. going
6. doing, studying
7. earn, spend, spending
8. living

4.

2. In some cases, students just complain instead of making suggestions for improvements.
3. Students get annoyed with teachers for coming late to class.
4. You can improve your grades by studying regularly.
5. We can make changes by telling the administration about our concerns.
6. The administration can help by listening to our concerns.

5.

2. F
3. F
4. T
5. F
6. F

6.-7.

Answers will vary.

U N I T 23 Infinitives after Certain Verbs

1.

wants me to tell, need to talk, refuses to understand, 'd like to have, want to be, ask her to think, force her to understand, decided to talk

2.

2. would like to forget
3. refuses to do
4. forces me to be
5. need to have
6. tell them to remember
7. would like our children to think
8. forget to insist

3.

3. The father warned (*or* is warning) his daughter (*or* her) to be home by 10:00 P.M.
4. The mother would like to celebrate her son's birthday (*or* his birthday) at home.

5. The daughter promises (*or* promised) to call as soon as she gets home.
6. The mother needs to use the car tonight.
7. The daughter reminds (*or* reminded) her mother to bring her lunch to school.
8. The father advises (*or* advised) his daughter (*or* her) to finish school.

4.

2. b
3. b
4. b
5. a
6. a

5.-7.

Answers will vary.

U N I T 24 Infinitive of Purpose

1.

to get
to take advantage of
to help
to store
to balance

2.

2. To withdraw $100.
3. To invite Rika and Taro to dinner.
4. To buy milk and eggs.
5. To buy batteries.
6. To get gas.

3.

2. c
3. f
4. a
5. b
6. d
7. e

3. She went to Lacy's Department Store (in order) to buy some dishes.
4. We disconnected our phone in order not to get any phone calls.
5. They started jogging (in order) to get more exercise.
6. He turned on the radio (in order) to listen to the news.
7. He didn't tell me he was sick in order not to worry me.

4.

2. 5
3. 2
4. 4
5. 4
6. 1
7. 6

5.-8.

Answers will vary.

UNIT 25 Infinitives with *Too* and *Enough*

1.

2. a
3. b
4. a
5. b
6. b
7. a
8. b

In Favor	Against
2	3
4	6
5	7
	8

2.

2. c
3. g
4. a
5. b
6. h
7. d
8. f

3.

2. fast enough for us to get
3. light enough for us to carry
4. too young to be
5. too noisy for me to sleep
6. too far for us to reach
7. good enough to eat
8. too hot to drink

4.

2

5.-7.

Answers will vary.

UNIT 26 Contrast: Gerunds and Infinitives

1.

2. T
3. F
4. T
5. F
6. T
7. T
8. T

2.

2. to trust
3. to forget, to learn
4. going
5. to remember
6. to turn off
7. Playing, improving

3.

2. meeting Alicia and Roger (last year)
3. spilling the grape juice
4. listening to music
5. going dancing, to go dancing
6. to go home
7. to give Sonia a ride home, to stay a little longer
8. to drive carefully

4.

avoid to go ➔ avoid going
stopped to worry ➔ stopped worrying
planning going ➔ planning to go *or* planning on going
consider to visit ➔consider visiting
enjoy to hear ➔ enjoy hearing

5.

3. Making new friends is difficult.
4. Relaxing is important.
5. It's fun to dance.
6. Telling the truth is important.
7. Getting to know someone like you is nice.
8. It's wonderful to be with you.

6.

Things Sonia Does: 2, 5, 7
Things Sonia Doesn't Do: 3, 4, 6

7.-9.

Answers will vary.

P A R T Review or SelfTest
VI

I.

2. to hit 3. having 4. winning 5. playing 6. to become 7. to make 8. becoming 9. doing 10. to go 11. to accept 12. to study 13. studying

II.

2. a 3. b 4. b 5. a 6. a 7. a 8. b

III.

2. not to make ➔ not making
3. want to making ➔ want to make
4. against wear ➔ against wearing
5. get used to live ➔ get used to living
6. realize ➔ to realize

IV.

2. to planning 3. for watching
4. about speaking 5. without worrying 6. in learning

V.

2. too messy 3. not cool enough
4. too tough 5. aggressively enough 6. loud enough

VI.

2. to 3. stopping 4. follow 5. It's
6. following 7. Stop 8. smoking 9. eating 10. eat

VII.

2. are flexible enough for them
3. advise them to think about
4. It's important to know about
5. don't have enough time
6. encourage you to start

PART VII Modals and Related Verbs and Expressions

U N I T Ability: Can, Could, Be able to
27

1.

haven't been able to (park the car), can't back up, could (start the car), could (steer it), couldn't (even make right turns), can (drive), can (even make difficult left turns), Can (I learn), (Sure you) can, (I want) to be able to (drive), can (take the test), was able to (schedule), won't be able to (park)

LANE Driving School
Student Progress Report
Skills: Check (✔) the week

Student's Name	Rita Pratt		Date of Road Test	May 20
	Week of			
Student can	May 2	May 9		
• start car	✔			
• steer car	✔			
• use signals		✔		
• make right turn		✔		
• make left turn		✔		
• drive in traffic		✔		
• park				
• back up				

2.

1. b. can 2. a. couldn't b. can't c. can d. could e. can
3. a. could b. can't c. couldn't d. can 4. a. couldn't b. can

3.

1. b. isn't able to skate 2 a. Were, able to speak b. was able to speak c. Are, able to speak 3. a. haven't been able to finish b. will, be able to do 4. were able to get 5. a. haven't been able to practice b. Will, be able to practice c. 'll be able to get together

4.

couldn't played ➔ couldn't play
couldn't to stand up ➔ couldn't stand up
could win ➔ was able to win
was able continue ➔ was able to continue
can't afford ➔ couldn't afford

5.

2. F 3. F 4. T 5. F 6. T 7. T

6.-7.

Answers will vary.

Permission: May, Could, Can, Do you mind if...?

1.

2. f 3. e 4. c 5. a 6. b

2.

b. Can he c. he can't 2. a. you may not b. May I c. you may
3. a. Could I b. could I 4. a. Can we b. you can't

3.

2. (B) 3. (D) 4. (B) 5. (B) 6. (D) 7. (C) 8. (A)

4.

2. Could I use your phone?
3. Can we park in front of the stadium?
4. May I please see your tickets? *or* May I see your tickets, please?
5. Can I smoke in the lobby?
6. Could we please move up a few rows? *or* Could we move up a few rows, please?
7. Can they tape the concert?
8. Do you mind if I leave?

5.

a. 2 (refused) b. 5 (refused) c. 1 (given) d. 4 (refused)
e. 3 (given)

6.-7.

Answers will vary.

UNIT 29 **Requests:** *Will, Would, Could, Can, Would you mind...?*

1.

2. Would you explain
3. Can you get, Will you answer
4. would you mind making
5. Could you give

2.

2. a 3. a 4. b 5. a 6. b

3.

b. Shut the door. c. Buy some cereal. d. Close the window.
e. Wait for a few minutes. f. Call back later. 2. Will you file
these reports, please? 3. Would you mind waiting for a few
minutes? 4. Can you buy some cereal? 5. Could you please
call back? 6. Would you shut the door, please?

4.

a, b, e, f, h

5.

Answers will vary.

UNIT 30 **Advice:** *Should, Ought to, Had better*

1.

2. shouldn't, 5 3. ought to, 1 4. 'd better not, 3
5. should, 2 6. 'd better, 4

2.

2. 'd better not 3. shouldn't 4. ought to 5. shouldn't
6. 'd better

3.

2. You should *or* ought to look neat 3. What time should I
arrive? 4. You'd better not *or* shouldn't arrive after 7:15.
5. Should I bring a gift? 6. You shouldn't buy an expensive
gift. 7. What should I buy? 8. I think you should *or* ought to
get some flowers.

4.

2. I think you ought to have a sandwich.
3. Perhaps you'd better not take any more. 4. Maybe he should watch more TV. 5. I think you should learn some new skills. 6. Maybe you shouldn't drive to work.

5.

1, 4, and 6

6.-7.

Answers will vary.

UNIT 31 Suggestions: Let's, How about...?, Why don't...?, Could, Why not...?

1.

Then let's go to Old Town.
Maybe we could go to the zoo tomorrow.
Why not go there for dinner tonight?
We could take the trolley from Old Town.
But let's not go to an expensive restaurant.

Places checked in guidebook:

Old Town
San Diego Harbor
Grand Cafe

2.

2. How about
3. Why doesn't
4. Why don't we
5. Maybe we could
6. Let's not

3.

2. How about going to the beach? 3. Let's not buy another one. 4. Maybe we could take a trip together. 5. Let's try that new pizza place. 6. Why not share a cab?

4.

Things to do in New York

have lunch in a Mexican restaurant

relax and read a guidebook

stay in San Diego

✔ stay in the youth hostel

✔ go roller blading in Central Park on Sunday morning

✔ go to a Crash concert in Madison Square Garden

✔ go to South Street Seaport for a jazz concert

✔ walk through Soho

meet Jane's sister at an art gallery

✔ eat in Chinatown

✔ eat in Little Italy

5.-6.

Answers will vary.

UNIT 32 Preferences: Prefer, Would prefer, Would rather

1.

Underlined phrases: 'd rather not spend, 'd prefer to live, 'd rather have, prefer walking to driving, would prefer not to rent, 'd rather not

Renter Preferences

Name: _____Arlene and Jim Lewis_____

Area: (North Side)   South Side   East End   West End

Type: (House)   Apartment

Size: __2__ Bedrooms   Maximum rent: __$600__

Transcription: _____ Car __X__ Bus __X__ Walk

Keep pets: __X__ Yes _____ No

2.

2. I'd rather not cook
3. I'd rather not.
4. I'd rather have
5. I'd rather not.
6. I'd rather see

3.

2. Does, prefer
3. Would, prefer
4. Do, prefer
5. Would, rather
6. Would, prefer

4.

would rather watching ➔ would rather watch
would rather see game shows to sports events ➔ would rather see game shows than sports events
prefer to reading ➔ prefer to read
they prefer read ➔ they prefer to read *or* they prefer reading
will prefer novels ➔ prefer novels

5.

Fish Dinner
soup, onion
rice
soda, diet
apple pie

6.-10.

Answers will vary.

UNIT 33 Necessity: Must, Have (got) to, Must not, Don't have to, Can't

1.

Underlined phrases: will have to get, you will, must have, will I have to get, can't use, Do I have to take, won't have to take, will have to take, has got to take

2. Prohibited   4. Necessary
3. Not Necessary   5. Necessary

2.

2. must not 3. must 4. must not 5. must 6. must 7. must
8. must not 9. must 10. must

3.

(The wording of some answers may vary slightly.)
Ann has to buy a road map.
She has to get the kids' school records.
She doesn't have to call the moving company, and she doesn't have to buy film.
Jim and Sue don't have to pack clothes and toys for the trip.
They have to say goodbye to friends. They also have to buy gifts for their teachers.

4.

1. b. can't start c. We have to check in
2. a. Do, have to stop b. we have to
3. a. 've b. had to wait
4. a. do, have to drive b. I have to
5. a. 's got to b. can't shout c. I've got to pay attention
6. a. 've got to buy
7. a. had to call

5.

2. don't have to   5. must not
3. must not   6. don't have to
4. don't have to

6.

a. 6 b. 3 c. 2 d. 1 e. 5 f. 4

7.-9.

Answers will vary.

UNIT 34 Expectations: Be supposed to

1.

Underlined Phrases:
was supposed to be
weren't supposed to have
was supposed to leave
are supposed to stay

True False Statements:

2. F 3. F 4. T 5. T

2.

2. a. Were, supposed to do b. were supposed to deliver
3. a. is supposed to start b. are, supposed to stand
4. a. 're not supposed to be b. isn't supposed to see
5. a. 'm supposed to wear b. 's supposed to rain

3.

I will be supposed to give ➔ I am supposed to give
I be also supposed to help ➔ I am also supposed to help
I supposed to leave ➔ I was supposed to leave

4.

2. isn't 3. are 4. is, are 6. are

5.

Answers will vary.

UNIT 35 Future Possibility: May, Might, Could

1.

may snow, might take, Maybe I'll take, could have, couldn't do, might not catch

Bill's schedule

certain:	9:00 meeting, call Alice
possible:	shovel snow, take 7:30 train, work until 8:00
impossible:	meet Alice for lunch

Alice's schedule

certain:	go to library—work on paper, go to class, take 6:30 train home
possible:	ride train with Bill, 6:00—meet Bill at station
impossible:	lunch with Bill

2.

2. could 3. might 4. may not 5. will 6. 'll 7. may

3.

Alice is going to call Bill at 9:00. She may *or* might buy some notebooks before class. She's going to go to a meeting with Mrs. Humphrey at 11:00. She may *or* might have coffee with Sue after class. She's going to go to work at 1:00. She may *or* might go shopping after work. She may *or* might take the 7:00 train.

4.

2. They couldn't. 3. It could be. 4. It could
5. It could be. 6. It could be.

5.

Friday
possible: sunny, low fifties

Saturday
certain: sunny, windy
possible: 60

Sunday
possible: cold, windy, snow

6.-7.

Answers will vary.

UNIT 36 Assumptions: May, Might, Could, Must, Have to, Have got to, Can't

1.

Underlined Phrases

could be serious, couldn't be dishonest, might be the key, has to have a very special reason, may want to be alone, must spend his time, must not be here

Statements

2. Possibility 3. Conclusion 4. Possibility 5. Conclusion
6. Conclusion

2.

2. might 3. must 4. could 5. might not 6. may 7. might
8. may

3.

2. Vincent must not be the clerk's real name.
3. He must be very clever.
4. Number 27 Carlisle Street must be City Bank.
5. Vincent's tunnel must not lead to those shops.
6. Vincent's tunnel must lead to the bank.

4.

2. That's got to be wrong. 3. It's got to cost less than $50.
4. It can't be after 11:00. 5. It has to be nearby. 6. You can't be sick.

5.

2. might 3. must be 4. might 5. might 6. must

6.

c. couldn't be 2. a. can't be b. Can, be c. can't be
3. a. could, be b. could be

7.

2. Possibility 3. Possibility 4. Conclusion 5. Conclusion
6. Conclusion 7. Possibility 8. Possibility 9. Possibility
10. Conclusion

8.-9.

Answers will vary.

10.

A close-up picture of the head of a housefly.

P A R T VII Review or SelfTest

I.

2. b 3. b 4. b 5. b 6. a 7. b 8. a 9. b

II.

2. should 3. could 4. 'd better 5. Let's 6. 've got to 7. How about 8. have to 9. might 10. don't have to

III.

can had ➔ can have
couples able to learn ➔ couples are able to learn
She'd not rather ➔ She'd rather not
mights ➔ might
would rather to fix up ➔ would rather fix up
will can ➔ will be able to
must not to try ➔ must not try
ought to appreciating ➔ ought to appreciate

IV.

2. must 3. won't be able to 4. Why don't you 5. has got to 6. have to 7. might 8. 'll be able to 9. is supposed to 10. won't have to

V.

2. 'd better not 3. 'd better not 4. don't have to 5. 'd better not 6. don't have to

VI.

2. It must be expensive. 3. He must not be at work today. 4. She might not like curry. 5. It couldn't be Carl's roommate. 6. She may not remember to come. 7. It could be very valuable. 8. He might be at the other airport.

VII.

2. Do, have to have 3. 'll be able to send 4. has got to finish 5. Will, be able to come 6. May, talk 7. can't wait 8. May, help 9. must send 10. Can, call

PART VIII Nouns and Articles

U N I T 37 Nouns and Quantifiers

1.

Proper Nouns
Katya, New York, May, Panama, Typhoon, Thanksgiving
Count Nouns
journey, world, goal, boat, birthday, years, miles, things, stars, ports, markets, cat, family, part, trip, sight, harbor
Non-count Nouns
courage, education, money, equipment, food, cooking, water, time, news, music, reading, loneliness

2.

2. work 3. 's 4. advice 5. beans 6. rice 7. potatoes 8. are 9. vegetables 10. are 11. Is 12. equipment 13. batteries 14. news 15. stops 16. clothing 17. cold 18. bothers 19. bags

3.

1. b. A few c. A little
2. a. a great deal of b. many c. a great deal of
3. a. a b. much c. some d. many
4. a. How many b. How much c. How much d. How many
5. a. little b. a lot of c. a few d. a little e. a few

4.

weathers are ➔ weather is
mails ➔ mail
Birthday ➔ birthday
october ➔ October
thunders ➔ thunder
many rain ➔ much rain
brave ➔ Brave
columbus ➔ Columbus
little coffee ➔ a little coffee
jewelries ➔ jewelry
electricities ➔ electricity
I'd better save them ➔ I'd better save it
a few waters ➔ a little water

5.

Ingredients they have enough of: brown sugar, cornflakes, raisins
Shopping list: butter, oatmeal, flour, eggs, chocolate chips

6.-7.

Answers will vary.

UNIT 38 Articles: Definite and Indefinite

1.

2. a 3. b 4. b 5. b 6. a

2.

2. the 3. the 4. a 5. a 6. the 7. The 8. an, the 9. the
10. a, an 11. The

3.

2. the 3. the 4. the 5. (no article) 6. (no article) 7. (no article) 8. (no article) 9. (no article) 10. The 11. the
12. the

4.

1. b. a c. the d. a e. (no article)
   He's Tarzan.
2. a. the b. An c. (no article)
   It's the Great Wall of China.
3. a. the b. (no article) c. (no article)
   It's Australia.
4. a. an b. (no article) c. The
   It's a roller coaster.
5. a. an b. the c. the
   She was Cleopatra.
6. a. the b. (no article) c. (no article) d. (no article)
   They're whales.

5.

beautiful girlfriend ➔ a beautiful girlfriend
a ape ➔ an ape
chased ape ➔ chased the ape
a first video game ➔ the first video game
a artist ➔ an artist
loved the video games ➔ loved video games
invented story ➔ invented a story
Story ➔ The story

6.

Part 1:
2. a 3. the 4. the 5. a 6. the

Part 2:
2. b 3. b 4. a 5. a 6. b

7.-8.

Answers will vary.

P A R T VIII Review or SelfTest

I.

1. b. How many letters
2. a. It doesn't
3. a. There's some new equipment b. several, computers
4. a. It's
5. a. too much salt b. It tastes
6. a. it
7. a. a lot of b. How many bags
8. a. few b. much
9. a. it

II.

2. a, a 3. the 4. The 5. the 6. the 7. a 8. a 9. the

III.

2. an Asia ➔ Asia
3. in world ➔ in the world
4. cookings ➔ cooking
5. A chocolate ➔ Chocolate
6. the medicine ➔ medicine
7. Vanilla ➔ vanilla
8. an cup ➔ cup
9. People ➔ people

IV.

2. enough 3. a lot of 4. How much 5. a little 6. a few
7. some 8. How many 9. any 10. much 11. a lot of 12. a few

V.

3. the 4. (no article) Money 5. (no article) Travel 6. (no article) Staying 7. The 8. (no article) Vegetables 9. (no article) Bicycles 10. The

VI.

2. an 3. The 4. a 5. the 6. The 7. The

VII.

1. b. some c. a d. an e. The f. The
2. a. some b. some c. some d. The e. the
3. a. a b. some c. the d. The e. a f. some g. the